SCOTTISH CLASSICAL STUDIES
FOUR

# THE CHARACTERISATION
# OF AENEAS

# SCOTTISH CLASSICAL STUDIES

SCOTTISH CLASSICAL STUDIES

# THE CHARACTERISATION
# OF AENEAS

*by*

## C. J. MACKIE

SCOTTISH ACADEMIC PRESS
EDINBURGH

First published in Great Britain, 1988
by Scottish Academic Press Limited
33 Montgomery Street, Edinburgh EH7 5JX

ISBN 0 7073 0490 3

**British Library Cataloguing in Publication Data**
Mackie, C. J.
    The characterisation of Aeneas.—
    (Scottish classical studies; v. 4)
    1. Aeneas
    I. Title    II. Series
    202'.13    BL820.A34
    ISBN 0-7073-0490-3

Printed in Great Britain
at the University Printing House, Oxford
by David Stanford, Printer to the University

# TABLE OF CONTENTS

To my mother and father

# PREFACE

The thesis from which this book arose was begun in October 1980 and was submitted for the degree of Doctor of Philosophy in the University of Glasgow in September 1984. I had intended to work solely on the subject of Turnus in the *Aeneid*, but as the study progressed it became clear that a book-by-book analysis of Aeneas in the poem might also be profitable if not essential. The Aeneas chapters as it turned out became the core of the thesis, and, happily, of a suitable length to be included in the current series of Scottish Classical Studies. I have to this purpose revised all the material, but the basic thoughts and arguments presented here differ very little from those in the thesis.

I have no doubts that this stage of publication would not have been reached without much valuable assistance from colleagues and friends. I owe a special debt of gratitude to Professor P. G. Walsh, who supervised my thesis with great thought and attention, and who stressed constantly the importance of looking at the *Aeneid* in the context of its Roman values and against its Homeric background. My debt to the work of other Vergil scholars, especially Austin, Knauer and R. D. Williams will become abundantly clear from the first pages. Professor D. M. MacDowell kindly read through the proofs and saved me from many errors (those that remain are, of course, my own). I would also like to thank the following for their assistance and encouragement: Dr K. J. McKay, Dr B. F. Curran, Professor David West, Professor R. G. Tanner, Professor W. R. Nethercut, Dr. R. Beare, Miss Suzanne Dorahy and Miss Alison Smith. Finally, I am grateful to the University of Glasgow who awarded me a research scholarship thereby allowing me to thrive in a city which I have come to regard as my second home.

Glasgow, February 1986                                        C. J. M.

# INTRODUCTION

The appearance of yet another work on the *Aeneid* calls for some justification. The already large critical corpus devoted to the poem requires us to question the need for each new work. There is a view that 'everything has been said on Vergil' (not, in my opinion, a rare view amongst Latinists) which may not be mere defeatism but a recognition of the achievements of critics in this field. It reflects a suspicion amongst some scholars that recent works on Vergil are less likely to alter established views than perhaps they ought to be.[1] There seems to be a feeling in some quarters that we are now getting further away from what Vergil meant by the *Aeneid* rather than closer to it.[2] The plethora of critical discussion on the *Aeneid* may not extend to every aspect of the poem, but it certainly extends to the major character who is the subject of this book. It is not always easy, after all, to write something of substance on the poem without making some kind of statement about Aeneas. The *Aeneid* is about people — Trojans, Greeks, Carthaginians and Italians: to discuss the issues of the poem is to discuss the major figures who feature in it. All the more surprising, perhaps, that there exists, to my knowledge, no systematic and comprehensive analysis of the characterisation of Aeneas in the *Aeneid*. Exactly what is meant by 'systematic' and 'comprehensive' will become apparent as the discussion proceeds. What we find in its place in the available secondary literature is what might be called 'selective analysis', in which the critic selects a passage or passages of the text to exemplify or support a particular view of a character. Thus, in his important contribution to the study of the characters, Viktor

[1] See, for example, Jasper Griffin's review of five new works on the *Georgics* in *Classical Review* 31 (1981) 23ff.

[2] See K. Quinn, *Virgil's 'Aeneid', A Critical Description* (London, 1968) 1f.: 'Understanding and appreciation of the poem, however, have seriously deteriorated. We are near the point where the poem is read for its past reputation. The next stage is oblivion'.

1

Pöschl[1] selects passages which help him to demonstrate his major points. In his study of Aeneas, for example, he cites the following passages: 1,94ff.; 1,119; 12,438ff.; 1,204ff.; 1,208f.; 4,331f.; 2,726ff.; 4,393ff.; 4,441ff.; 2,626ff.; 10,464f.; 5,1ff.; 5,868f.; 11,1ff.; 11,94ff.; 10,758f.; 11,108f.; 6,475f.; 6,719ff.; 1,94ff.; 1,437f.; 3,493ff.; 12,435ff.; 6,103ff.; 8,131ff.; 4,361; 6,460f.; 5,709f.; 12,435f.; 8,362ff. Pöschl could, no doubt, have expanded his analysis of Aeneas to include further references, but as it is he limits the selection to these thirty. This procedure I call 'selective' because, although the scholar clearly has a comprehensive knowledge of the poem, he presents his analysis of the characters by discussing or citing only certain references to them. Pöschl's approach to the characters is not unique but could be described as the standard critical method.[2] Inevitably in this method more references to the character are excluded than included. One wonders if Pöschl might have presented a different view of Aeneas had he discussed, for example, 10,510–605, 11,81f. and 12,945ff. In short, a fully comprehensive analysis is worth attempting to obtain a fully rounded view. The natural temptation in selective analysis of character, whether intentional or not, is to highlight some issues at the expense of others, on occasions suggesting or appearing to justify a point of view which may not be completely accurate, because it tells only *part* of the story. At the risk of being selective ourselves, let us look briefly at an episode of the poem and three critical reactions to it, which tell us something about selective analysis of character. In Book 12 oaths are sworn by Aeneas (176ff.) and Latinus (197ff.) and a treaty formed in anticipation

---

[1] V. Pöschl, *The Art of Vergil: Image and Symbol in the 'Aeneid'* (tr. G. Seligson, Ann Arbor, 1962) 34ff.

[2] I can think of no appraisal of Aeneas which does not follow similar lines, although a variation in this method is provided by G. Binder, *Aeneas und Augustus: Interpretationen zum 8.Buch der Aeneis* (Meisenheim am Glan, 1971), who provides a detailed analysis of Aeneas' entire role in Book 8 (but Book 8 only).

of single combat between Aeneas and Turnus. The Rutuli, however, renew the fighting, and then the Trojans too take up arms. Aeneas reacts as follows:

> at pius Aeneas dextram tendebat inermem
> nudato capite atque suos clamore vocabat:
> "quo ruitis? quaeve ista repens discordia surgit?
> o cohibete iras! ictum iam foedus et omnes
> compositae leges. mihi ius concurrere soli;                315
> me sinite atque auferte metus. ego foedera faxo
> firma manu; Turnum debent haec iam mihi sacra."

(12,311–7)

In the subsequent turmoil Aeneas is wounded (318ff.) and healed, with divine assistance (383–440), before rejoining the battle in great rage. Three of the responses to this episode are as follows:

1. 'And not only is the hero heroic and humane, but he is a just man and keeps faith; when in the twelfth book, the Rutulians break the treaty, and his own men have joined in the unjust combat ...' (he quotes 12,311–5) 'he claims for himself alone ... the right to deal with Turnus, the enemy of humanity and righteousness'.[1]

2. 'At this moment Aeneas's wrath breaks forth without restraint (*adsurgunt irae*, line 494), and he who shortly before had urged calm ('o cohibete iras') now reacts (498–9) with a display of violence rarely paralleled elsewhere in the epic because it is utterly purposeless'.[2]

3. 'Battle is joined: a "love" of war possesses all. Messapus is described as "greedy" (*avidus*) for the confounding of the truce. Vergil's Stoic sense that all passionate emotions are allied and all destructive and pernicious is evident here in his choice of

---

[1] W. Warde Fowler, *Religious Experience of the Roman People* (London, 1911) 423.

[2] M.C.J. Putnam, *The Poetry of the 'Aeneid'* (Cambridge, Mass., 1965) 173; see too his discussion, 167f.

vocabulary and imagery. How does Aeneas respond to all this? Impeccably. He identifies the cause (or a cause) — passion — and seeks to stem it, 313ff.

> "quo ruitis? quaeve ista repens discordia surgit?
> o cohibete iras!..."

But then ill-luck takes a hand...'[1]

It should not be imagined that these three responses to Aeneas' behaviour reflect the entire critical work on the speech.[2] Nevertheless, they do adequately exemplify the approach of Vergilian scholars to aspects of character. All three critical discussions are selective in the sense that the scholars have chosen to emphasise certain words of Aeneas in order to support their individual points of view about his character. In each case Aeneas' speech is quoted only in *part*, and different parts at that. Warde Fowler cites 311–15, Putnam 314(a) and Lyne 313f. All of them, for different reasons, stress Aeneas' restraint and rectitude as he urges his men to contain their anger (*o cohibete iras*! 314). Therefore, the student of Vergil who reads these critical views would (rightly, it seems to me) gain the impression that it is in Aeneas' nature to abide at all costs by a sworn treaty and that this fact is conveyed by the speech. The student would be wrong, however, to think that this is the only thing conveyed by the speech. Aeneas communicates two ideas as opposed to the one referred to in these critical discussions. The first part of the speech (313–315a) conveys Aeneas' moral sentiment that it is wrong to break a treaty which has been solemnly agreed with sworn oaths. As *pius* (311) suggests, Vergil here underlines Aeneas' *pietas*, and his restraint in the face of provocation. The second part of the speech (315b–317) communicates Aeneas' pragmatic sentiment that, if the treaty is broken completely, then he himself will lose his

---

[1] R.O.A.M. Lyne, 'Vergil and the Politics of War', *C.Q.* 33 (1983) 197.

[2] This speech is more fully discussed below, p. 195f.

opportunity to fight and kill Turnus. His joy in response to the initial offering of the treaty (12,107–12) was due partly to the fact that he saw an opportunity to sate his desire for vengeance. Now before his eyes he sees his opportunity slipping away. Moreover, the words that Vergil puts into Aeneas' mouth (*mihi ... soli* 315; *Turnum debent haec iam mihi sacra* 317) clearly echo those of Turnus as he approaches Pallas (*solus ego in Pallanta feror, soli mihi Pallas debetur* 10,442f.). Vergil evokes in our minds the death of Pallas and, by means of verbal repetition,[1] invites a comparison between Aeneas and Turnus. Aeneas desperately wishes to ensure that the Rutulian's action in killing Pallas will soon have its consequences.

Because all three critics concentrate on the first part of the speech, rather than both parts, they stress Aeneas' moral sentiment at the expense of the pragmatic. They appear to do so because the latter part is largely irrelevant to the point of view that they wish to project. Thus, whilst they succeed in demonstrating their own points of view, they fail to convey the full sense of Aeneas' motivation. At best this can give us an adequate, partial picture of Aeneas, and at worst it can provide a false picture. The fact is that selective analysis of character offers no opportunity for an overall perspective. Moreover, particular lines of Vergil's text can be to scholars what economic statistics are to politicians: certain parts can be taken from the whole to support an argument which is not always an accurate reflection of the entire material available. It is possible by this method even for eccentric interpretations of Aeneas to be given a semblance of validity

---

[1] Cf. 11,220–1; 12,466–7.

by the quotation of isolated lines in their support.[1] The progress made this century on the main character shows that this is not generally the case, yet at the same time it is clear that a more comprehensive approach is justified and necessary. In this book an attempt is made to analyse comprehensively rather than selectively the role of Aeneas throughout the poem. Inevitably, not every reference to him is given the full possible attention, but it is hoped that by this new, systematic approach to the character further progress on this subject may be made.

Before proceeding with an introductory look at some of the speeches of Aeneas, let us propose that Vergil was 'in control' of his material, rather than controlled by it, and that he devised methods of characterising the hero which were deliberate and designed to convey a particular effect. Given Vergil's status as an epic poet this is not a bold assumption and, in any case, the truth of it will, I think, become apparent as we proceed through the text. Clearly a method of crucial importance to the epic poet is the way in which he employs the speeches to present the desired picture of the relevant character. In recent years the importance of the speeches has been more widely recognised. In the introduction to his work on the subject, Gilbert Highet notes that a gap has been left by scholars who allot no separate treatment to the speeches.[2] Highet attempts to fill the gap by treating the speeches separately. He places emphasis on the direct speeches with particular reference to the rhetorical aspects. To this purpose he classifies them under curious headings — 'Formal and

---

[1] B. Otis, *Virgil: A Study in Civilized Poetry* (Oxford, 1963), is a prime offender. He discusses (357) the brutal *aristeia* of Aeneas (10, 510–605) and cites only those lines which help to explain his *furor* (515–7). He discusses (381f.) the death of Turnus without reference to Aeneas' *furor*, although Vergil gives emphasis to it (12,945ff.). Others highlight Aeneas' *furor* in an attempt to blacken his character: Putnam, 151ff.; A. Boyle, *Ramus* 1 (1972) 63ff. and 113ff.; S. Farron, *Acta Classica* 20 (1977) 204ff., etc. We are unlikely to make progress in analyses of character when critics select those passages that suit them, and discard those that do not.

[2] G. Highet, *The Speeches in Vergil's 'Aeneid'* (Princeton, 1972) 8.

Informal Speeches' — with the latter being sub-divided into 'Factual and Emotional Speeches'. Further division follows with comment on Prophecies, Descriptions ... Greetings, Farewells, Threats, Challenges, Prayers and so forth. The work is particularly useful for reference, and has detailed numerical classifications contained in the appendices. Highet largely rebuts the suggestion made by Roman critics that Vergil was more an orator than a poet.[1] As the headings and divisions might suggest, however, Highet does not try to assess Vergil's more subtle literary techniques. Although he recognises the importance of the speeches for characterisation,[2] Highet's treatment of this aspect is descriptive rather than analytical.[3] This is largely inevitable given his interest in rhetorical aspects and the fact that the speeches are treated separately; yet the reader is entitled to feel that important questions about characterisation remain unanswered. The aim of this work is to answer these questions: Does Vergil have criteria for allocating or not allocating speeches to Aeneas at given moments or situations? If so what are they? Why on occasions does Vergil use indirect speech (*oratio obliqua*) or free indirect speech (*style indirect libre*[4]) in preference to the direct speech? Are there reasons for the long periods throughout which Aeneas utters no direct speech, but is a protagonist in the narrative? In what ways do Vergil's methods of characterisation

---

[1] *ibid.* 3ff. and 277ff. P. Annius Florus wrote a dialogue in the second century A.D. entitled *Vergilius orator an poeta?*, after which the controversy survived until late in the fourth century. Highet directs much of his attention to this question.

[2] 15ff. ('The Speeches and Their Speakers'), and 185ff. ('The Speeches and Their Models').

[3] On occasions he is so insensitive as to be a lesson in how not to assess characters: 'Turnus is a man of action. In combat he talks little. Also, he is subject to fits of depression when he scarcely speaks (e.g. *Aen.* 12, 219–221)' (210). But Vergil has just stressed the inequality of the match and implies that Turnus too is aware of it.

[4] Such as in Book 4, 283f. and 9, 67f. The French term *Style Indirect Libre* is more associated with the modern novel than with ancient epic, though it seems applicable for the latter. See R. Pascal, *The Dual Voice* (Manchester, 1977) with a full bibliography in the notes; and S. Ullmann, *Style in the French Novel* (Cambridge, 1957). See also below, p. 79ff.

differ from those of Homer and how do they affect the reader's perception of the characters in the *Aeneid*?

Most scholars are aware of the importance of Knauer's fundamental work[1] which has provided detailed comparison of the works of Homer and Vergil. Apart from Knauer's own inferences about the modelling of the *Aeneid* on the Homeric works, the exhaustive indices encourage further investigations and comparisons. It is an important method of this work to exploit Knauer's indices to compare the speeches of Aeneas in the poem, and some narrative references, with their Homeric models. On some occasions there is little to be gained by such comparison, for some alleged parallels, at least in their situations, are far from close. On other occasions there is no Homeric parallel at all which, paradoxically, can in itself be a significant fact. Departure from Homeric detail can tell us as much about Vergil's aims and methods as imitation of it. In further cases there is a clear parallel between two speeches or episodes, but in these too there are usually differences which tell us something about Vergil's own design. The testing of the speeches against the Homeric background shows, amongst other things, that Vergil employed different, more considered methods of characterisation and made no attempt to create the same vivid, three-dimensional figures as Homer.[2] The failure of critics to recognise this, particularly in the case of Aeneas, has brought much criticism on Vergil, who has been accused of failing to create a hero the equal of Homer's Achilles.[3] As we shall see, the comparison of Aeneas' role with those of the Homeric models shows that he never made the

---

[1] G. N. Knauer, *Die Aeneis und Homer* (Göttingen, 1964).

[2] See below, p. 216ff.

[3] T. E. Page, *The Aeneid of Virgil I–VI* (London, 1894) XVII, spoke for many scholars of his time when he wrote that 'moreover, Virgil is unhappy in his hero. Compared with Achilles his Aeneas is but the shadow of a man'. Cf. W. Y. Sellar, *The Roman Poets of the Augustan Age: Virgil* (Oxford, 1877) 389f.; T. R. Glover, *Virgil* (London, 1930) 211; and more recently, M. R. Ridley, *Studies in Three Literatures* (London, 1962) 63f. See also R. D. Williams, *Virgil* (Oxford, 1967) 30ff.

attempt. It has now been long established that Aeneas is a new kind of hero with different motivation and priorities from the Homeric heroes,[1] yet little attention has been paid to the different techniques that Vergil employs to present him. There is a case for studying the poet's craft in depicting his characters.

Let us look briefly at Vergil's alteration of one Homeric episode in the *Aeneid* to see the difference in the presentation of character. In *Aeneid* 10 and 11, Aeneas is shown preparing to commit human sacrifice in response to the death of Pallas.[2] Vergil modelled the episode on the sacrifice by Achilles in the *Iliad* of twelve Trojan youths after Patroclus' death.[3] This is where the similarity ends, for the poets' methods of presentation differ considerably — a fact strangely ignored by critics who discuss this passage. Homer refers to Achilles' sacrifice on four separate occasions totalling 27 lines. In these Achilles utters three direct speeches, once promising to perform the sacrifice and twice when he actually does so.[4] Moreover, the Homeric episode is described clearly in a logical sequence — (a) the promise of sacrifice, (b) the capture of the youths, (c) the sacrifice itself. Homer's detail makes the act vivid and dramatic, with a gruesome touch as well.[5] The reader has not the slightest doubt of what Achilles has done or why he has done it. Vergil's presentation is different. Reference is made on two occasions to the sacrifice in six lines of obscure narrative.[6] Unlike Achilles, Aeneas utters no speech referring to any aspect of human sacrifice. In fact the obscure nature of Vergil's narrative at this point leaves it unclear whether

[1] See R.D. Williams' summary of the changing views on Aeneas in *Virgil* (Oxford, 1967) 30ff.

[2] For a full analysis of this episode, see below, p. 183ff.

[3] See *Il.* 18,333–7; 21,26–33; 23,19–23; 23,175–83.

[4] *Il.* 18,333ff.; 23,19ff. and 23,179ff.

[5] χαλκῷ δηϊόων, *Il.* 23,176. Vergil's lines too have gruesome touches (note 10, 520; 11, 82), but these describe probable sacrifice in the future, not specific contemporaneous happenings.

[6] 10, 517–20 and 11, 81–2.

or not sacrifice even takes place. It is possible for any but the
most careful reader to miss the reference or to forget that the act is
ever considered.[1]

We need not question Vergil's familiarity with the *Iliad* nor
his ability to manage his own material. There is no doubt that he
could easily have written the episode along Homeric lines with a
vivid and dramatic presentation of the act. The fact that he chose
not to do so must be accorded the same significance as the fact
that he links Aeneas with sacrifice at all.[2] Comparison with
Homer shows us that Vergil employed more intricate methods of
characterisation according to the requirements of the story. In
this case, for his own good reasons, Vergil, unlike Homer,
chooses not to underline the brutal reality of the hero's act. His
technique is rather to use the indirect (or narrative) method of
characterisation where Homer on the whole uses the direct (or
direct speech) method. We shall see that a great difference
between the two poets is the importance attached by Vergil to *indirect* techniques of characterisation, which in some cases alter the
reader's perception of a character from that of the Greek model.
In many cases, as here, this is done by using simple narrative
description instead of direct speech and narrative; but Vergil also
exploits more subtle techniques which are foreign to Homeric
epic.

One such technique is the poet's use of *oratio obliqua* to describe
the words or thoughts of a character. On some occasions this is
used because Vergil wishes to keep the tempo of the narrative.
This is the case in 12,758ff. when Aeneas threatens awesome

[1] A fact which perhaps explains the comparative lack of discussion about it. See Boyle's
discussion, *Ramus* 1 (1972) 68f. and 86, n. 22. T. Crane, 'A note on Aeneas' "human
sacrifice', *Aeneid* 10,517–20", *C.W.* 67 (1973) 176–7, argues, somewhat implausibly,
that Aeneas has little to do with the sacrifice, but merely sends the youths to Evander.

[2] R. D. Williams, *The Aeneid of Virgil: Books 7–12* (London, 1973) ad 10,519: 'Nothing would have been easier than for Virgil to omit this ghastly act of Achilles in his re-
working of the story; therefore the fact that he has included it must be accorded its full
significance'.

consequences if any of the Rutulians gives Turnus his sword:

> ille simul fugiens Rutulos simul increpat omnis
> nomine quemque vocans notumque efflagitat ensem.
> Aeneas mortem contra praesensque minatur                    760
> exitium, si quisquam adeat, terretque trementis
> excisurum urbem minitans et saucius instat.

(12, 758–62)

By presenting the speech indirectly Vergil retains the fluency in his description of Aeneas' relentless drive to victory. There are other occasions, however, when Vergil seems to use *oratio obliqua* as a means of presenting a character's sentiments or behaviour in a less prominent way than the direct speech. If an epic poet wishes to project a character into the limelight he will do so by means of long or repeated direct speeches. The most dramatic figure in the *Aeneid* is Dido, for she utters, in Book 4 alone, nine speeches totalling 189 lines — more than Aeneas does in the entire 'Iliadic' *Aeneid*.[1] Vergil has gone to great lengths to present her vividly in her tragic predicament by intensive application of his direct method of characterisation. The queen is thus a realistic, three-dimensional figure — an 'open book' as Austin calls her.[2]

Conversely, Vergil was aware that should he desire, for whatever reason, to withdraw a character from the dramatic limelight, yet still present that character's words or thoughts, then *oratio obliqua* is an ideal means of doing so. There are many examples of this indirect method of characterisation, perhaps the clearest being the depiction of Aeneas in Book 5. In this book Aeneas utters 12 speeches all of which, to some extent,

[1] Aeneas utters 345 lines in the first half of the poem and 182 lines in the second. Dido's 'dramatic' role is even more significant given the fact that Book 4 is the shortest book in the poem – 705 lines.

[2] R. G. Austin, *Aeneidos Liber Quartus* (Oxford, 1955) ad 393: 'One of the difficulties in understanding Aeneas is Virgil's very reticence. Dido is an open book: Aeneas we see only in half-glances, half-revelations ...'

represent his *pietas*.[1] Following the burning of the ships, however, Aeneas lapses into despondency about his mission and even considers remaining in Sicily:

> at pater Aeneas casu concussus acerbo
> nunc huc ingentis, nunc illuc pectore curas
> mutabat versans, Siculisne resideret arvis
> oblitus fatorum, Italasne capesseret oras.

(5, 700–3)

Just as Aeneas' general concern to follow the fates is the cornerstone of his *pietas*, so here his forgetfulness of them (*oblitus fatorum*) indicates his *impietas*. The hero is deeply concerned about the Trojans' possibility of succeeding in their fated mission.[2] Given the extent of their *labores* on land and sea this must be seen as a natural, human reaction to added misfortune. Yet despite this, Vergil does not seek to present vividly the despair of Aeneas. Had he wished to do so, he could easily have depicted these sentiments by a direct speech. Rather than do so Vergil presents them indirectly, thereby depicting Aeneas as a man who broods on his misfortune. If, as we have assumed, Vergil is a careful and deliberate poet, then his style of presentation here is in itself significant and tells us something about his own approach to character-presentation. Vergil chooses not to present these thoughts as a direct speech partly because it would highlight a temporary feature of Aeneas' character which he does not want to emphasise. It is not the work of chance that the only indirect presentation of Aeneas in Book 5 conveys his single moment of *impietas*. Just as Vergil obscures Aeneas' human sacrifice in two

---

[1] See the full discussion, below, p. 94ff.

[2] R. Heinze, *Virgils epische Technik* (Leipzig, 1903) 269f., saw this episode as a turning point in the character and fortunes of Aeneas; C. M. Bowra, *From Virgil to Milton* (London, 1945) 62, expressed disbelief that the hero should consider abandoning the mission. Neither these nor any other critic, to my knowledge, questions Vergil's use of *oratio obliqua* at this point.

terse narrative references,[1] so here he obscures the reality of
Aeneas' *impietas* by means of *oratio obliqua*. That this effect is deliberate and calculated is shown by similar instances throughout
the poem.

Because there are two methods of characterisation at work —
direct and indirect — we shall see that characterisation in the
narrative of the poem does not always reflect that in the direct
speeches. Vergil seems to have felt no obligation to conform to a
strict, uniform picture of the main character. The same is true of
Turnus: if we were to treat separately only the *narrative* references
to Turnus in Book 9 we would inevitably conclude that he is like
a wild animal who, with irrational rage, deals out death and
destruction to anyone who stands in his path. But it is *pietas* and
*virtus* that come through in the direct speeches.[2] Similarly,
Aeneas in Book 4 is consumed with doubts and regret about
leaving Carthage but we would never know it from his direct
speeches alone, because it is his *pietas* that is stressed in these.
Throughout the romance and in his great dilemma of how to
approach Dido with the news of his imminent departure, Aeneas
is a character of the narrative with no dramatic role to play. Only
when he has conquered his doubts and thus regained his *pietas*,
does Vergil present him directly.[3]

We shall see that by his two methods of characterisation —
direct and indirect — which may convey different things with
different force, Vergil is able to ensure that the reader's perspective of a character conforms to his (the poet's) wishes. He can thus
give prominence to one dimension of character and relegate other
dimensions to the narrative. The two techniques are complemen-
tary. By presenting directly only some of Aeneas' sentiments in

[1] See above, p. 9.

[2] For the full discussion, see my thesis, *Speech and Narrative: Characterisation Techniques in the 'Aeneid'* (University of Glasgow, 1984) 33ff.

[3] See below, p. 77ff.

Book 4 (and elsewhere) Vergil is not creating a false picture, for there is no conflict between speech and narrative. Given that Aeneas' doubts and natural passions at Carthage are obscured in the narrative, the view that he is a cold, non three-dimensional figure[1] is an understandable one. Nevertheless, close reference to the narrative tells us that he was in love with Dido and found it difficult to leave Carthage.[2] Thus Vergil projects an image of his hero in the direct speeches which is not utterly true, for it does not tell the entire story. Moreover, we shall see from the comparative numerical analysis of the speeches[3] that Vergil places less reliance on the direct method of characterisation than does Homer. The direct speeches make up a considerably smaller proportion of the *Aeneid* than they do in the *Iliad* or *Odyssey*. Accordingly, Aeneas has a smaller dramatic role than his Homeric counterparts, which further limits his rapport with the reader — a fact which Vergil knew and actively exploited.

Yet not only are Vergil's characters depicted in a different way from Homer's but, inevitably, they also act in accordance with a specifically Roman set of values. It could be said that such values as *pietas*, *fides*, *virtus*, *ratio*, *humanitas* and their antonyms form the basic infrastructure of the poem. Certainly, it is impossible to analyse comprehensively any character in the poem without detailed reference to them. Accordingly, the speeches of the hero and many narrative references to him are appraised in terms of these Roman ideas. The importance of this approach was seen in the preceding discussion, in which it was suggested that Aeneas' *pietas* or *impietas* was Vergil's criterion for the allocation or non-allocation of direct speeches. This idea will be extended and exemplified in the detailed analysis of the poem. The value of comprehensive analysis of character in the work of a master poet is

[1] See above, p. 8, n. 3.
[2] See 4, 221; 332; 395; 448.
[3] See Appendix, p. 219f.

that patterns begin to emerge which indicate his aims and methods of characterisation. We shall see that such patterns emerge in the presentation of Aeneas.[1]

It is anticipated that this work will fill a gap in the corpus of critical works on Vergil by providing a systematic and comprehensive analysis of the characterisation of Aeneas in the *Aeneid*. It is 'comprehensive' in that it follows his entire role in the poem; and 'systematic' in its application of a consistent method throughout. This method falls, broadly speaking, into three sections: first, an analysis of the speeches (direct and indirect) including comparisons with Homeric models; second, an appraisal of the poet's use of speech and narrative to depict character; and third, detailed consideration of the Roman values which pervade the work. The validity of this new method will, I hope, become apparent as we proceed through the text.

---

[1] On occasions Vergil deliberately breaks his own pattern, and this too helps us to ascertain and understand his techniques of characterisation.

# BOOK 1

It is no accident that in the *Odyssey* Homer delays the first appearance of Odysseus until almost one-fifth of the poem has elapsed.[1] There are many reasons for this delay, not least of which is that it allows Homer to stress the personal qualities of the man by indirect techniques of characterisation. The so-called *Telemacheia* demonstrates the κλέος and ἀρετή of Odysseus — that he is a great and respected man who is sorely missed by his household. His glorious personal history, which is narrated to Telemachus by Nestor, Menelaus and Helen,[2] is contrasted with the present sorry state of his house. Odysseus is needed desperately back in Ithaca. The dreadful behaviour of the suitors necessitates their eviction and punishment. The *Telemacheia* induces us to anticipate the appearance of Odysseus himself (Book 5) and the vengeance that he will eventually exact (Book 22ff.). Thus, although he does not actually appear in the first four books, Odysseus is always at the forefront of our attention. When he does appear (5, 149ff.), we are well acquainted with his character, his exploits at Troy and the cost to Ithaca of his absence.

The first appearance of Aeneas in the *Aeneid* could scarcely be more different; the hero utters his first speech after only 93 lines, with his name being first mentioned at line 92.[3] The first mention of his name thus coincides with his initial dramatic appearance, which is itself noticeably early. Whereas Aeneas is anonymous until line 92, Odysseus is named 9 times in the first 103 lines of the *Odyssey*.[4]

It would be absurd to suggest that there is ever any doubt as to

[1] The *Odyssey* is composed of 12,110 lines. Odysseus' first appearance in Book 5, 149ff. is after 2,370 lines.

[2] See *Od.* 3, 103ff.; 4, 78ff. and (esp.) 4, 235ff.

[3] See R. G. Austin, *Aeneidos Liber Primus* (Oxford, 1971) ad 92.

[4] Odysseus is named 79 times prior to his opening speech (5, 173ff.).

the identity of the *virum* in the first line. The naming of Aeneas
(92) merely confirms the understanding of the reader. The
prooemium introduces the hero in the context of his *labores* and
*magna facta*: 'the hero, his purpose, its significance, are succinctly
clear'.[1] Aeneas has left Troy to come to Italy by fate's decree (1–3)
and suffers greatly from the enmity of Juno even though he fulfils
the will of fate (4ff.). He is a <u>man distinguished by his *pietas*</u>,[2] yet
this quality does not save him from affliction at the gods' hands
(8ff.). Juno proceeds to display considerable malevolence towards
Aeneas from the outset. She desires the supremacy of Carthage,
yet the fates decree that such power will fall to Rome. Undeterred
by such decrees, and in direct opposition to them, Juno asks the
willing Aeolus (65ff.) to create a great storm which will over-
whelm the Trojan fleet as it approaches Italy. Aeolus quickly
obeys[3] and, as a result, day becomes night and the winds clash
together. The storm is described vividly by Vergil (81ff.). Aeneas
reacts with considerable trepidation:

> extemplo Aeneae solvuntur frigore membra;
> ingemit et duplicis tendens ad sidera palmas
> talia voce refert: "o terque quaterque beati,
> quis ante ora patrum Troiae sub moenibus altis          95
> contigit oppetere! o Danaum fortissime gentis
> Tydide! mene Iliacis occumbere campis
> non potuisse tuaque animam hanc effundere dextra,
> saevus ubi Aeacidae telo iacet Hector, ubi ingens
> Sarpedon, ubi tot Simois correpta sub undis              100
> scuta virum galeasque et fortia corpora volvit!"

(92–101)

[1] Austin, ad 1–7.

[2] *insignem pietate virum* 10.

[3] The storm parallels that created by Poseidon to punish Odysseus (*Od.* 5, 291ff.). See Pöschl's important discussion, 24ff.

The speech is modelled[1] on that of Odysseus in reaction to the
great storm created by Poseidon:

> καὶ τότ' Ὀδυσσῆος λύτο γούνατα καὶ φίλον ἦτορ,
> ὀχθήσας δ' ἄρα εἶπε πρὸς ὃν μεγαλήτορα θυμόν·
> "ὤ μοι ἐγὼ δειλός, τί νύ μοι μήκιστα γένηται;
> δείδω μὴ δὴ πάντα θεὰ νημερτέα εἶπεν,                    300
> ἥ μ' ἔφατ' ἐν πόντῳ, πρὶν πατρίδα γαῖαν ἱκέσθαι,
> ἄλγε' ἀναπλήσειν· τὰ δὲ δὴ νῦν πάντα τελεῖται,
> οἷοισιν νεφέεσσι περιστέφει οὐρανὸν εὐρὺν
> Ζεύς, ἐτάραξε δὲ πόντον, ἐπισπέρχουσι δ' ἄελλαι
> παντοίων ἀνέμων· νῦν μοι σῶς αἰπὺς ὄλεθρος.              305
> τρισμάκαρες Δαναοὶ καὶ τετράκις οἳ τότ' ὄλοντο
> Τροίῃ ἐν εὐρείῃ, χάριν Ἀτρεΐδῃσι φέροντες.
> ὡς δὴ ἐγώ γ' ὄφελον θανέειν καὶ πότμον ἐπισπεῖν
> ἤματι τῷ ὅτε μοι πλεῖστοι χαλκήρεα δοῦρα
> Τρῶες ἐπέρριψαν περὶ Πηλείωνι θανόντι.                   310
> τῷ κ' ἔλαχον κτερέων, καί μευ κλέος ἦγον Ἀχαιοί·
> νῦν δέ με λευγαλέῳ θανάτῳ εἵμαρτο ἁλῶναι."

(Od. 5, 297–312)

When Odysseus utters his speech of despair in response to the
storm the reader is aware of his great battle exploits, his family
and the troubles that afflict his household. We know of his close
relationship with the gods and also of the malevolence of Poseidon.[2] We have followed the voyage of Odysseus on the raft from
the outset at Calypso's island. Thus, when the storm breaks over
Odysseus and he laments his ill-fortune, the hero is a familiar,
dramatic figure.[3] The prooemium of the Aeneid, by contrast, has

[1] See Knauer, indices ad loc. Highet, 187ff., discusses Aeneas' speech and its Homeric
parallels. His conclusion (191), however, is not altogether satisfactory: 'It is clear, therefore, that Vergil when introducing Aeneas wished to present him in a situation compar-
able to that of Homer's Odysseus, but with a character somewhat more chivalrous and
Achillean'.

[2] For Pallas Athena's love for Odysseus, see Od. 3, 221ff. For the gods' love for him, but
Poseidon's hatred, see Od. 1, 19ff. and 5, 282ff.

[3] See Odysseus' earlier speeches Od. 5, 173ff. and 215ff.

informed the reader merely that the hero is a Trojan who has fled the city, who has a unique destiny and who is ill-treated by the gods despite his *pietas*. The reader's first view of Aeneas is his reaction to the storm. Odysseus wishes that he had fallen at Troy for a specific reason: that he would have received funeral-rites and fame (κτερέα and κλέος 311), but as it is he faces the prospect of a miserable death at sea (λευγαλέῳ θανάτῳ 312). Death at Troy brings honour and fame; death at sea does not. Similarly, in *Il.* 21,273ff.,[1] Achilles fears that he is about to drown in the Scamander. He prays to Zeus (273ff.) in a state of utter pessimism, believing that his mother has deceived him in the manner of his death (275ff.), and wishes for a more heroic end (279ff.). The prospect of a λευγαλέος θάνατος (281) brings the same despair to Achilles as it does to Odysseus (*Od.* 5,297ff.): the manner of death is as important as death itself. Death by drowning is not an end worthy of a man of Achilles' ἀρετή; such a death is better suited to a swineherd boy (282). Death at the hands of Hector would have been a worthy end: the stature of the slayer reflects on the slain.

In response to the storm that overcomes him and his men, Aeneas is filled with both terror and despair.[2] His limbs are loosened[3] and he stretches out his hands to the stars.[4] Such is

---

[1] Knauer, indices ad *Aen.* 1,94b–101.

[2] In his discussion T. R. Glover, 210, argues that never again do we see Aeneas in such despair. Comparison with his reaction to the burning of the ships (5,700ff.) would suggest otherwise. The view of Heinze (266ff., and *passim*) and that of Pöschl (36ff.) is that Aeneas' character develops throughout the first half of the poem: they see 5,700ff. as a final hesitation, a turning point in his character. See my discussion below, p. 109ff.

[3] *solvuntur frigore membra* 92. Vergil uses the same formula to describe the limbs of the dead Turnus (12,951). Aeneas moves from a position of vulnerability at the beginning to one of dominance at the end.

[4] The motif of stretching out arms often denotes *pietas*: cf. 2,688; 5,686; 6,685 and 9,16.

his despair that dying *ante ora patrum* (95) seems like good fortune. He thinks automatically of other Trojans (*pietas*)[1] — Hector and Sarpedon both dead at Troy — and, although a survivor, believes that he now suffers a worse fate. Aeneas cries out with a sense of melancholy and nostalgia. As he faces death he thinks not of glory but of his Trojan homeland and its former inhabitants. Thus Troy has a special significance for Aeneas that it does not have for Odysseus. We can say in short that 'Aeneas' supreme value is not *kudos* but *pietas*'.[2]

Vergil has been criticised for showing Aeneas in a moment of great weakness at the very outset of the poem.[3] Yet the poet has good reasons for conveying from the first the depths of despair into which his hero has sunk. Vergil shows that the *labores* have taken their toll of his hero's morale. Aeneas displays qualities of melancholy and nostalgia, both of which help to depict his *pietas* in the face of adversity. Moreover, the storm and Aeneas' reaction to it represent the dramatic preparation to the Dido episode. The despondency of Aeneas is reinforced throughout the first book. Vergil wishes us to understand that Aeneas' state of mind makes the prospect of respite at Carthage all the more enticing. Thus, even in the first scene in which Aeneas appears, Vergil has one eye on the Dido episode.

Having survived the storm Aeneas climbs onto a high peak to

---

[1] Pöschl, 35, also makes this point.

[2] M.O. Lee, *Fathers and sons in the Aeneid: tum genitor natum* (Albany, 1979) 182.

[3] Servius, ad 92, criticises Vergil's use of the Homeric model. See the comments of Austin, ad 92, and A.J. Gossage, 'Aeneas at Sea', *Phoenix* 17 (1963) 131ff. G. Carlsson, 'The Hero and Fate in Virgil's *Aeneid*', *Eranos* 43 (1945) 129n.2, suggests that, as at 5,700ff., Aeneas here is *oblitus fatorum*. The difference is that at no point in the earlier speech (1,94ff.) does Aeneas actually consider abandoning his mission. Vergil stresses Aeneas' *pietas* in the earlier episode and his *impietas* in the latter.

search for his missing men (180ff.).[1] He sees no ship but spies a herd of stags and proceeds to shoot seven of them — one for each of his ships (184–93). The episode is modelled[2] on *Od.* 9,152ff. and *Od.* 10,153ff. In the former Odysseus and his men shoot a large number of goats. All his comrades join him in the hunt but Odysseus himself receives the largest portion; his own ship receives ten goats whereas the others take nine (159f.). Although all of the men take part in the hunt, Odysseus, by virtue of his rank as an ἀγαθός, receives special treatment ("ἐμοὶ δὲ δέκ' ἔξελον οἴῳ" 160). In *Od.* 10,153ff. Odysseus happens upon a stag and kills it, thereby staving off hunger. Homer describes vividly the shooting of the stag and Odysseus' struggle with the carcass. Aeneas shoots seven stags providing food for his seven ships but he is not described as having any problem lifting them. Vergil does not concern himself with the details of the hunt. His priority is to present Aeneas (and Achates[3]) providing for the physical needs of his men, who seem to remain passive spectators throughout. The poet thus stresses Aeneas' concern for his men, his *pietas*.

Yet for all his success in the hunt, Aeneas cannot have peace of mind.[4] He uses the newly acquired source of food as a means of raising the spirits of his men:

> "o socii (neque enim ignari sumus ante malorum),
> o passi graviora, dabit deus his quoque finem.
> vos et Scyllaeam rabiem penitusque sonantis                    200
> accestis scopulos, vos et Cyclopia saxa
> experti: revocate animos maestumque timorem
> mittite; forsan et haec olim meminisse iuvabit.

---

[1] A fact which exhibits his *pietas*.

[2] Knauer, indices ad loc.

[3] For Achates' role in the poem, see Austin, ad 188.

[4] See B. Otis' discussion of Vergil's techniques here in 'The Originality of the *Aeneid*' in *Virgil*, ed. D. R. Dudley (London, 1969) 52ff.

per varios casus, per tot discrimina rerum
tendimus in Latium, sedes ubi fata quietas                205
ostendunt; illic fas regna resurgere Troiae.
durate, et vosmet rebus servate secundis."
talia voce refert curisque ingentibus aeger
spem vultu simulat, premit altum corde dolorem.

(198–209)

Knauer[1] cites *Od.* 10, 174–7 and 189–97, and 12, 208ff. as the
closest Homeric models for Aeneas' speech. In the former Odysseus utters two speeches urging his men to join him in eating the
beast he has just killed and in so doing stave off hunger (174–7).
He invites his men to think of the options open to them in this
strange land (i.e. Aeaea — Circe's island). Odysseus himself can
see no option and tells his men so (193); for he has observed the
island from the peak and seen only thick bush with smoke rising
from the middle (193–7). In the latter model (*Od.* 12, 208ff.)
Odysseus speaks to the ἑταῖροι as their ship approaches Scylla
and Charybdis:

"ὦ φίλοι, οὐ γάρ πώ τι κακῶν ἀδαήμονές εἰμεν·
οὐ μὲν δὴ τόδε μεῖζον ἔπι κακὸν ἢ ὅτε Κύκλωψ
εἴλει ἐνὶ σπῆϊ γλαφυρῷ κρατερῆφι βίηφιν·              210
ἀλλὰ καὶ ἔνθεν ἐμῇ ἀρετῇ βουλῇ τε νόῳ τε
ἐκφύγομεν, καί που τῶνδε μνήσεσθαι ὀίω.
νῦν δ' ἄγεθ', ὡς ἂν ἐγὼ εἴπω, πειθώμεθα πάντες.
ὑμεῖς μὲν κώπῃσιν ἁλὸς ῥηγμῖνα βαθεῖαν
τύπτετε κληῖδεσσιν ἐφήμενοι, αἴ κέ ποθι Ζεὺς          215
δώῃ τόνδε γ' ὄλεθρον ὑπεκφυγέειν καὶ ἀλύξαι·
σοὶ δέ, κυβερνῆθ', ὧδ' ἐπιτέλλομαι· ἀλλ' ἐνὶ θυμῷ
βάλλευ, ἐπεὶ νηὸς γλαφυρῆς οἰήϊα νωμᾷς.
τούτου μὲν καπνοῦ καὶ κύματος ἐκτὸς ἔεργε
νῆα, σὺ δὲ σκοπέλου ἐπιμαίεο, μή σε λάθῃσι            220
κεῖσ' ἐξορμήσασα καὶ ἐς κακὸν ἄμμε βάλῃσθα."
ὣς ἐφάμην, οἱ δ' ὦκα ἐμοῖς ἐπέεσσι πίθοντο.

[1] Knauer, indices ad loc.; see too Austin's note, ad 198ff.

Σκύλλην δ' οὐκέτ' ἐμυθεόμην, ἄπρηκτον ἀνίην,
μή πώς μοι δείσαντες ἀπολλήξειαν ἑταῖροι
εἰρεσίης, ἐντὸς δὲ πυκάζοιεν σφέας αὐτούς.                      225
                                                  (Od. 12, 208–25)

In the earlier model (Od. 10, 174–7 and 189–97) Odysseus is
characterised by his basic instincts for survival and his forthright
pessimism. He states bluntly that he can think of no device that
will ease their plight. In the second case Odysseus is more
reticent as to the dangers ahead. He urges his men to have
confidence in his own natural abilities (ἐμῇ ἀρετῇ βουλῇ τε νόῳ
τε 12, 211). His men will survive if they do as he says. He does
not elaborate on Scylla (223ff.) in case his men should panic, yet
he is still quietly confident that his ability as leader can overcome
the dangers. It is his instinct for survival that necessitates
reticence on the subject of Scylla.

Aeneas tells his men that they have suffered greater misfortune
than this; some god will assist them now as before.[1] The Trojans
have survived Scylla and the rocks of the Cyclopes and they must
now put away their fear and press ahead with their journey. The
fates are pointing to Italy as their new home (205f.).[2] Odysseus
hopes for deliverance by Zeus (215) from the dangers they are
about to face, and Aeneas too hopes that some deus (199) will end
their ordeal. Nothing in the Homeric models, however, corres-
ponds to Aeneas' fata and fas (205f.). Vergil's hero sees labours
which must be borne both in the short and the long terms. Mere
survival is not enough; they must complete their fated mission.

Despite his exhortation Aeneas' heart is full of despondency
(208f.). He stoically feigns hope in order to lift the spirits of his
men. Both men and mission are foremost in his mind, and at this
stage he sees that the prospects are bleak. Aeneas' despondency

---

[1] Cf. deus (Aen. 1, 199) and Ζεύς (Od. 12, 215).

[2] On Aeneas' knowledge of the name Latium (205), see Conington and Nettleship, The
Works of Virgil vol. 2 (London, 1883) ad loc.

arises from his *pietas*: so strong is his commitment for the Trojans to follow the fated way that obstacles are intolerable. Moreover, he has a genuine concern for the safety of his missing men and groans (*gemit* 221) as he thinks about them. Vergil describes him as *pius Aeneas* (220) for this reason, because he, more than anyone (*praecipue* 220), is preoccupied with their safety.[1] This is the first use of the epithet in the poem, and again here we see the link between *pietas* and despondency. Not until his men are safely with him again does Aeneas become content.[2]

The encounter between Venus and Jupiter (223ff.) is prompted by the goddess' fear for her son and his mission. She expands upon the Roman theme first intimated in the prooemium. She expresses concern that Jupiter has somehow changed the course of destiny (*quae te, genitor, sententia vertit?* 237). Is this treatment the reward for piety? (*hic pietatis honos?* 253). Jupiter replies (257ff.) that nothing has changed, for the fates are firm that Aeneas will found Rome. He proceeds to spell out the glorious future of Rome — the Italian wars, Alba Longa, and the Iulii descended from Iulus himself. There will be no bounds to Roman greatness (*imperium sine fine dedi* 279). The glory of Rome will continue with the rule of Augustus. The gates of war will be closed and *Furor impius* (294) will have its hands bound behind its back.[3] Jupiter demonstrates his good faith by sending Mercury

---

[1] For *pius* and *pietas* to describe Aeneas, see Austin, ad 10; A.S. Pease, *Aeneidos Liber Quartus* (Harvard, 1935) ad 393; P. Boyancé, *La Religion de Virgile* (Paris, 1963) 58ff.; and J.P. Brisson, 'Le "pieux Énée"!', *Latomus* 31 (1972) 379–412.

[2] See especially 1,595ff.

[3] The reference here to *Furor impius* is significant for the theme of the *Aeneid* in general and for the deaths of Dido and Turnus in particular. In my view, however, the reference has misled many scholars to the view that *furor* is, by definition, *impius*. We shall see, on the contrary, that *furor* and *pietas* are, in Aeneas' case, perfectly compatible. For the concept of *pius furor* and its victory over *impius furor*, see below, p. 170ff.

to ensure that Dido (*fati nescia* 299) should not mistreat the stranded Trojans.[1]

At 305ff. we return to the action on the human level. *Pius Aeneas* (305)[2] attempts to explore the surrounding countryside. After hiding his remaining ships he proceeds with the shadowy Achates along a path and suddenly encounters his mother dressed like a Spartan maiden or Thracian Harpalyce. Her utterance to Aeneas (321–4) furthers this pretence as she asks them whether they have seen her sister chasing a wild boar. Aeneas replies as follows:

> "nulla tuarum audita mihi neque visa sororum,
> o quam te memorem, virgo? namque haud tibi vultus
> mortalis, nec vox hominem sonat; o, dea certe
> (an Phoebi soror? an Nympharum sanguinis una?),
> sis felix nostrumque leves, quaecumque, laborem          330
> et quo sub caelo tandem, quibus orbis in oris
> iactemur doceas: ignari hominumque locorumque
> erramus vento huc vastis et fluctibus acti.
> multa tibi ante aras nostra cadet hostia dextra."

(326–34)

The speech is modelled on Odysseus' supplication to Nausicaa after his awakening on the beach:

> αὐτίκα μειλίχιον καὶ κερδαλέον φάτο μῦθον·
> "γουνοῦμαί σε, ἄνασσα· θεός νύ τις ἦ βροτός ἐσσι;
> εἰ μέν τις θεός ἐσσι, τοὶ οὐρανὸν εὐρὺν ἔχουσιν,          150
> Ἀρτέμιδί σε ἐγώ γε, Διὸς κούρῃ μεγάλοιο,
> εἶδός τε μέγεθός τε φυήν τ' ἄγχιστα ἐΐσκω·
> εἰ δέ τίς ἐσσι βροτῶν, τοὶ ἐπὶ χθονὶ ναιετάουσι,

---

[1] This on the whole appears a superfluous gesture, although Dido after her flight from Tyre (340ff.) is somewhat xenophobic (562ff.). See R.C. Monti, *The Dido Episode and the 'Aeneid'* (Leiden, 1981) 77, for the view that the gesture of Jupiter reflects a prejudicial attitude against the Carthaginians on Vergil's part.

[2] For his *pietas* here, see Austin, ad loc.

τρισμάκαρες μὲν σοί γε πατὴρ καὶ πότνια μήτηρ,
τρισμάκαρες δὲ κασίγνητοι. "                    155
(Od. 6, 148–55)

The Homeric speech in its entirety (149–85) is by far the longer[1] (37 lines as opposed to 9), consisting of a verbose appeal to the princess. Odysseus' personality comes to the fore as he questions Nausicaa's very mortality. He is prepared to use the amount of flattery that the situation demands. There is no doubt in Odysseus' own mind that Nausicaa is mortal:[2] Homer makes it clear that he utters a μειλίχιον καὶ κερδαλέον ... μῦθον (148). He is characterised by his strong instinct for survival: 'Odysseus's first encounter with Nausicaa was perhaps the severest test of tact and resourcefulness in his whole career'.[3]

Whereas Odysseus confronts a mortal, Aeneas is confronted by a goddess. Aeneas quickly realises Venus' immortality but he cannot identify her and address her as he would like. He is not in the mood for flattery but is eager for assistance. Unlike the naked Odysseus, who frightens the Phaeacian women except for Nausicaa, whom he attempts to put at ease with a gentle speech, Aeneas is himself addressed before he has the opportunity to speak. Aeneas does not fear for his own survival in a strange land as Odysseus does (Od. 6, 119f.). Aeneas answers Venus (326) with haste in order to supplicate her as a goddess.[4] His *pietas* is shown both in his supplication and in the urgency with which it

[1] Odysseus' speech is also the model for that of Aeneas to Dido (1, 595ff.). See below, p. 40ff.

[2] Odysseus addresses Nausicaa as ἄνασσα (149) and γύναι (168) whereas Aeneas addresses Venus in disguise as *virgo* (327) and *dea* (328). Once Aeneas is over the shock of encountering the 'maiden', he has no doubts about her immortality.

[3] W. B. Stanford, *The Ulysses Theme* (Oxford, 1954) 52. Stanford seems to go too far, however, in suggesting (52) that Odysseus has 'gentle sensibility towards a young unmarried girl's feelings' whilst thinking perhaps of his own sister Ctimene or his son Telemachus (who could have been born a girl).

[4] Cf. Aeneas' speech to the vision of Hector at 2, 281ff. and Austin's notes (*Aen.* 2) ad 281 and 282.

takes place. One line only (326) is devoted to answering her question, three lines (327–9) show his reverence towards her, and four lines concern the plight of him and his men (330–3). We are reminded that the basic difference in situation between Odysseus and Aeneas is that the former is utterly alone attempting to survive, whereas the latter feels personal responsibility for the welfare of his men. The final line of Aeneas' speech (334) also stresses his *pietas*: many a victim will fall for her at the altars. With the assistance of the goddess Aeneas hopes to lead his men out of their predicament.

Venus denies her immortality by implying (335ff.) that she is a Tyrian maiden. She explains some facts about the country into which Aeneas has come. She tells him of Dido's suffering at Tyre, her husband cruelly murdered by her own brother, and her subsequent flight to Africa where she founded the city of Carthage. The speech is long by Vergilian standards (36 lines), partially doing the work of the narrative, and displays a sympathetic view of Dido. It is a poignant irony that such a narration should come from the deity most responsible for Dido's death. The speech itself functions as a dramatic preparation for Dido herself.[1] At this point we begin to anticipate the entrance of the queen. At the end of her speech (369f.), Venus questions the Trojans: who are they, where have they come from, and where do they go? Aeneas responds as follows:

> quaerenti talibus ille                                            370
> suspirans imoque trahens a pectore vocem:
> "o dea, si prima repetens ab origine pergam
> et vacet annalis nostrorum audire laborum,
> ante diem clauso componet Vesper Olympo.
> nos Troia antiqua, si vestras forte per auris        375
> Troiae nomen iit, diversa per aequora vectos

---

[1] We might contrast the lack of a similar detailed dramatic preparation in Aeneas' case; see above, p. 16ff.

> forte sua Libycis tempestas appulit oris.
> sum pius Aeneas, raptos qui ex hoste penatis
> classe veho mecum, fama super aethera notus;
> Italiam quaero patriam, et genus ab Iove summo.          380
> bis denis Phrygium conscendi navibus aequor,
> matre dea monstrante viam data fata secutus;
> vix septem convulsae undis Euroque supersunt.
> ipse ignotus, egens, Libyae deserta peragro,
> Europa atque Asia pulsus."          385
>
> (370–85)

Aeneas' speech is made *imo ... a pectore* (371) — a formula which reflects the strong emotion with which he speaks.[1] In addressing her as *o dea* (372), he refuses to accept her claim to mortality (335ff.). He is all too aware of his own suffering and is at pains to stress his *labores*: the day would end before he could narrate to her the extent of them (372ff.). In *Od.* 3,113–7[2] Nestor tells Telemachus that he could not describe the woes of the Achaeans at Troy had he five or six years. In *Od.* 11,328–30 Odysseus narrates to the Phaeacians the story of his νέκυια ; he could not describe the shades of women that he saw 'before the immortal night would pass away' ( πρὶν γάρ κεν καὶ νὺξ φθῖτ' ἄμβροτος 330). In *Od.* 14,196–8 Odysseus tells Eumaeus that it would take a full year to tell of the suffering he endured. In each of the Homeric parallels the hero reflects upon past occurrences. The great difference in Aeneas' case is that misfortune is still real and still being experienced: his despondency is all the more intense because his suffering is real both in the past and present.

In the second part of the speech (375ff.) Aeneas elaborates on the wanderings of the Trojans, and his narrative is interspersed with complaints that he has suffered unjustly. He contrasts his self-acknowledged *pietas* with the hardship and misfortune that

---

[1] Cf. 1,485; 2,288; 6,55; 11,377; 11,840.

[2] Knauer, indices ad loc., cites these three Homeric parallels.

he has had to endure. He particularly stresses his own *pietas*: *sum pius Aeneas* (378),[1] *penatis classe veho mecum* (378–9), *fama super aethera notus* (379), *genus ab Iove summo* (380), *matre dea monstrante viam data fata secutus* (382) We might agree that *querentem* (385) 'summarises the content of his speech'.[2] Aeneas believes that he acts in a right and dutiful manner (378–9) and that his fame stretches to the heavens, yet he must still wander unknown and destitute (384). There is a striking contrast between *notus* (379) and *ignotus* (384) showing Aeneas' sense of his own worth and the unjust treatment he feels that he receives at the gods' hands. In the Homeric parallel to Aeneas' speech,[3] Odysseus laments the troubles that the gods have placed upon him, yet he evinces a resilient acceptance of such woes. He never implies that he deserves better:

> *"εἴμ' Ὀδυσεὺς Λαερτιάδης, ὃς πᾶσι δόλοισιν*
> *ἀνθρώποισι μέλω, καί μευ κλέος οὐρανὸν ἵκει."*
>
> (*Od.* 9, 19–20)

Odysseus is addressing Alcinous about whose mortality he has no doubts. He expects nothing of the king other than to be treated with hospitality. He does not complain about his lot to Alcinous for this would achieve nothing. Aeneas complains to the 'maiden' before him out of hope that she, as a goddess (372), might actively assist him in his predicament. He feels that he has done all that could have been asked of him (*pietas*), and expects to be spared the wrath of the gods.

Venus replies by ignoring Aeneas' self-introduction (*quisquis es* 387). She directs him to Carthage where he will be reunited with his men (389ff.). She points to an omen (393ff.)— twelve swans scattered by an eagle are seen either to reach the land, or peer down on the land already reached.[4] On their return the swans

---

[1] James Henry, *Aeneidea* (London, 1873) ad 381, gives an elaborate and passionate reply to the criticisms of C. J. Fox who found Aeneas' self-introduction too much to bear. See also W. B. Anderson, '*Sum pius Aeneas*', *C.R.* 44 (1930) 3f.

[2] R. D. Williams *The Aeneid of Virgil: Books 1–6* (London, 1972) ad 384–5.

[3] Knauer, indices ad 378f.

[4] *Sic* Austin, ad 396.

sport with flapping wings and circle the sky uttering musical cries. Aeneas' ships too[1] are either in the harbour or approach it under full sail. It is implied that his men are joyful to be safely beside land. Aeneas should merely proceed where the way leads him (401).

As she turns to go away there is a bright flash from her neck, a divine fragrance from her ambrosial hair, and her dress flows down to her feet (402ff.).[2] Aeneas recognises his immortal mother:

> ille ubi matrem                                              405
> agnovit tali fugientem est voce secutus:
> "quid natum totiens, crudelis tu quoque, falsis
> ludis imaginibus? cur dextrae iungere dextram
> non datur ac veras audire et reddere voces?"
> talibus incusat gressumque ad moenia tendit.             410
> at Venus obscuro gradientis aëre saepsit,
> et multo nebulae circum dea fudit amictu,
> cernere ne quis eos neu quis contingere posset
> molirive moram aut veniendi poscere causas.
>
> (405–14)

Venus acts in two different ways: first, for her own reasons, she betrays her own identity on the point of departure, thus showing playful cruelty towards her son. In so doing she makes all the worse Aeneas' despondency: he is resentful and confused as to why they cannot join hands and hold converse. Venus' second act is to cover Aeneas and Achates in a protective mist (411f.) so that no one is able to see or delay them (413f.). In the reader's eyes (but not Aeneas') Venus' second action negates the first: *at Venus* (411) signifies the contrast in her two actions. She has deceived him and made him feel utterly deserted but her genuine concern is not seriously in question. The mist symbolises the love and

---

[1] Cf. *reduces* 390 and 397. Page, ad loc., has an excellent note on the omen.
[2] Cf. the Iris/Turnus episode in Book 9, 1ff. There appears to be a parallel between Aeneas' recognition of Venus (1, 405–6) and Turnus' recognition of Iris (9, 16–17).

protection of mother for son.[1] Vergil does not allow the reader to feel deep pathos for the hero whose real welfare is so clearly ensured. Jupiter too has prophesied Aeneas' eventual foundation of his line in Italy (1, 257ff.) so that the reader knows that all will be well for the despondent hero. It has been noted[2] that 'we are reminded that after the death of Anchises Aeneas has no family comfort; he cannot even embrace his goddess mother, and his son is too young to help. In *crudelis tu quoque* he summarises his despair'. The death of Anchises causes Aeneas considerable grief as does that of Creusa at Troy.[3] The structure of the early books of the poem, however, does not allow the reader a glimpse of Aeneas' close personal experiences. At this stage of the poem we know nothing of Anchises or of Creusa, and scarcely anything of Ascanius.[4] Although recognising the frustration and anger of Aeneas as he cries out to his departing mother, the reader is unable to sympathise with him for the loss of a wife and father who heretofore are unmentioned. Yet whereas our empathy and sympathy for Aeneas are strictly limited by a wealth of detail about his glorious future and a lack of detail about his past, we recognise instantly his *pietas* as he fruitlessly appeals to his mother. Vergil stresses the bond which the son feels for his mother.[5]

Aeneas moves on to observe the city (418f.) and marvels at the fine achievements of the builders (421ff.). They are like bees in the young summer (430ff.). The sight of this flourishing new city brings Aeneas to exclaim:

[1] This, it seems to me, is its primary function. Austin, ad 411, stresses the dramatic purpose of the mist for lines 498–578; and Otis, 65, argues that 'the mist is also a symbol of his (Aeneas') spiritual removal from the scene'.

[2] Williams, ad 407f.

[3] For the effect of the death of Anchises on Aeneas, see 3, 707ff. and Book 5, *passim*. For the death of Creusa, see 2, 730ff.

[4] See 1, 267ff. and 288.

[5] There is no close Homeric parallel for this speech (407ff.) of Aeneas.

"o fortunati, quorum iam moenia surgunt!"[1]

(437)

Conington[2] notes that 'the want of a city is the keynote of the *Aeneid*'. In a state of homelessness[3] Aeneas can only look with envy upon those who have a city. This speech too stresses his *pietas* — his urgent desire to follow fate by building his own city. His despondency here reflects his inability to achieve this fated end. In his position of insecurity Aeneas sees Dido as a fortunate woman, yet if we look forward we may sense an element of irony in his words. Fortune smiles on Dido for only a brief part of the poem: her material prosperity is unable to help her psychological ruin as Aeneas departs.

Aeneas and Achates proceed amongst the townspeople shrouded in the mist (439–40). We are reminded again that, although Aeneas is dejected about his state of homelessness (437), his goddess mother is ensuring his protection and welfare. There is a contrast between mood and reality — the dispirited hero (437) and the very harmlessness of his plight as symbolised by the mist (439–40).

Aeneas' spirits rise when he sees the temple wall being built in reverence to Juno. He anticipates the arrival of the queen (454) but suddenly sees a frieze on the temple walls (456ff.) showing with graphic detail the war at Troy.[4] Aeneas reacts as follows:

> constitit et lacrimans "quis iam locus," inquit, "Achate,
> quae regio in terris nostri non plena laboris?        460
> en Priamus. sunt hic etiam sua praemia laudi,
> sunt lacrimae rerum et mentem mortalia tangunt.
> solve metus; feret haec aliquam tibi fama salutem."

[1] Knauer, indices ad loc., cites no Homeric parallel.

[2] Conington, ad loc.

[3] Some scholars have referred to Aeneas as a 'D.P.' — a Displaced Person; see, for example, M. Di Cesare, *The Altar and the City: A Reading of Vergil's 'Aeneid'* (New York, 1974) 1ff.

[4] For a detailed discussion of this passage, see R. D. Williams, 'The Pictures on Dido's Temple (*Aeneid* 1. 450–93)', *C.Q.* 10 (1960) 145ff.

sic ait atque animum pictura pascit inani
multa gemens, largoque umectat flumine vultum.     465
(459–65)

In *Od.* 6,324ff.[1] Odysseus prays to Athena that he may go to
the city of the Phaeacians and be made welcome there. Athena
hears his prayer but does not help him immediately out of fear of
Poseidon (328ff.). Odysseus proceeds into the city and is met by
Athena in disguise (7,14ff.). Athena sheds a mist (ἀχλύς)
around him (7,41ff.) because Odysseus is dear to her (φίλα
φρονέουσ' ἐνὶ θυμῷ 7,42). The mist in the Homeric case has
little symbolic value but is simply a means devised by Athena of
disguising Odysseus from the xenophobic Phaeacians. Unlike the
Vergilian case there is no contrast between the mood of the hero
and the reality of the situation. Odysseus is characterised by his
cautiousness (7,81ff.) rather than his gloom, and appears
unaware that he is concealed at all. Homer is unspecific on this
point:

καὶ τότε δή ῥ' αὐτοῖο πάλιν χύτο θέσφατος ἀήρ.

(7,143)

The mist merely disperses (χέω): it is never implied that Odysseus is actually aware of it. The difference is that in Vergil Aeneas
and Achates clearly have some control over when to appear into
the light of day.[2] It is significant that Aeneas remains despondent out of fear for his lost men (*pietas*).

The description of Dido's temple (446ff.) parallels that of
Alcinous' palace in the *Odyssey*.[3] Homer describes the physical
features of the building and the gardens (7,81ff.). Odysseus is
amazed at the sight (7,133ff.) before proceeding with his appeal
to Arete (7,146ff.). In so doing he gains the goodwill and hospi-

[1] Knauer, indices ad 459–65, cites *Od.* 8,85–92 as the closest model — Odysseus' tears
in response to Demodocus' song.
[2] See 514ff. and 579–89.
[3] Knauer, indices ad loc.

tality of the Phaeacians and begins the story of his adventures (7,241ff.). He tells the Phaeacians about his seven years on the island of Ogygia with the goddess Calypso. He does not, however, mention his name, his destination, or that he fought at Troy. On the next day Demodocus, the minstrel, sings of the Trojan war, of Odysseus, Achilles and Agamemnon (8,72ff.). Odysseus weeps (8,83ff.), seen only by Alcinous who, with a good sense of the moment, suggests that the games commence. Odysseus performs admirably in the games and earns the respect of the Phaeacians. Demodocus sings again (8,266ff.), this time of the adulterous love of Aphrodite and Ares. There follow dancing, an exchange of gifts and a feast. Demodocus is asked by Odysseus (8,487ff.) to sing of the wooden horse. This he does and the story gives great glory to Odysseus. Again the hero weeps (8,521ff.), seen only by Alcinous, who now asks him (8,550ff.) for details of himself; did one of his relations die at Troy?

Odysseus' fame is so great that it has penetrated the mythical world of the Phaeacians. Book 8 reasserts the greatness of the hero which was first emphasised in the *Telemacheia* (Books 1–4). The games show that his physical stature and abilities are still great. He is equal to or better than the best of men, and we already anticipate vengeance against the suitors. Odysseus' fame is such that the Phaeacians will make an avid audience for the narration of his adventures (Books 9–12).

In a similar way the Carthaginians are aware of Aeneas and his exploits. Aeneas' recognition of this fact allows him to think with confidence for the first time (450ff.). The pictures signify to Aeneas that the inhabitants possess *humanitas*, and that his own *fama* has extended to the shores of Africa (488). That the frieze appears on a *temple* wall signifies the *pietas* of the inhabitants. Where he expected to find barbarians,[1] he discovers a people who care for humanity and its suffering.

[1] Austin, ad 461f.

Aeneas is, therefore, in a position of advantage. Unlike
Odysseus (7,133ff.) he has foreknowledge that his own fame has
reached such distant shores. Moreover, in the Homeric case the
tears of Odysseus (8,83ff, and 521ff.) have a dramatic function.[1] Alcinous sees the weeping hero and feels compelled to ask
the reason for such a response to the tales of Troy (8,577ff.).
Odysseus answers by narrating his adventures; the tears effect the
story. Aeneas too sheds tears[2] in response to the frieze — a clear
parallel to those of Odysseus. The difference is that in Aeneas'
case the tears do not have a dramatic function. Instead they serve
to underline the hero's essential quality, his *pietas*, as he laments
the deaths of his compatriots. No reaction like that of Alcinous is
possible from Dido because she is still unaware of his presence.

Aeneas' speech in reaction to the frieze also reflects his *pietas*.
As he casts his eyes over the temple wall he laments the lot of
Priam (461) and regrets the ill-fortune suffered by his country-
men (460) and notes that Carthaginians too show sympathy for
the lot of mankind (461f.).[3] Aeneas then demonstrates his
concern for Achates — *solve metus ... aliquam tibi ... salutem*
(463): 'it is characteristic of Aeneas that he tries to comfort his
companion'.[4] Thus, as it is presented both in the narrative and
the direct speech, Aeneas' reaction can be seen to underline his
*pietas*.

Whilst Aeneas is still in a state of wonder at the frieze on the

[1] See W. R. Johnson's discussion, *Darkness Visible* (Berkeley, 1976) 99ff.

[2] *lacrimans* 459; *largoque umectat flumine vultum* 465; *lacrimans* 470 (see also 485). Page,
ad 459, criticises the three references to tears as 'feeble': see Austin's comment, ad loc. In
the underworld Aeneas sees the shade of Dido and is described three times as shedding
tears (6,455, 468 [see below, p.133 n.1] and 476). The significant difference is that his
tears at Carthage help to underline his *pietas*, whereas those in the underworld do not; see
below, p.129f.

[3] Lines 461f. have been the subject of endless debate; see Austin's note, ad loc.;
A. Parry, 'The Two Voices of Virgil's *Aeneid*', *Arion* 2 (1963) 66–80; and A. Boyle, *Ramus*
1 (1972) 74ff.

[4] Austin, ad loc.

temple wall Dido suddenly appears in his view (494ff.). We have
been expecting her appearance for a considerable time. Venus
(335ff.) narrated Dido's misfortunes at Tyre and her subsequent
flight to Africa. As he looked around Carthage Aeneas himself
anticipated the queen's arrival (*reginam opperiens* 454). Moreover,
by placing Penthesilea *furens* at the very climax of the frieze
(490ff.), the poet further develops the reader's anticipation of
Dido's arrival.[1]

Dido is described on her arrival as especially beautiful (*forma
pulcherrima Dido* 496). She is surrounded by a throng of youths
(497) and is likened to Diana on the banks of the Eurotas or along
the ridges of Cynthus (498ff.). The simile is modelled on
Nausicaa's likeness to Artemis in *Od.* 6,102ff.[2] where the
princess is singing whilst playing ball-games. Probus[3] criticised
the appropriateness of Vergil's simile claiming that it was better
suited to Nausicaa's singing and playing than Dido's directions
to her people. Vergil's borrowing from Homer, however, is
different for deliberate reasons: the likening of Dido to Diana
creates more complex verbal echoes and associations which reach
throughout the work.[4] Nausicaa's beauty is encompassed within
the simile (6,108f.) whereas Dido's beauty is stated in the
narrative beforehand (496). The physical beauty of Dido,
however, is only one of her features.[5] She possesses great joy as
she presses on with her work (502f.). Nausicaa takes simple
pleasure in a ball-game whereas Dido is enthralled at the building
of her city. Dido's happiness is contrasted with Aeneas' melancholia: she has succeeded in the very thing in which he has failed.

[1] See Pöschl's discussion, 147 and G. Williams, *Technique and Ideas in the 'Aeneid'* (New
Haven and London, 1983) 68ff.

[2] Knauer, indices ad loc., also compares *Od.* 4,122 in which Helen is like Artemis with
a bow of gold (χρυσηλάκατος).

[3] Aulus Gellius, 9,9,12ff.; cf. Austin's comment, ad 498ff.; Pöschl, 60ff.; and D.
West, 'Multiple-Correspondence Similes in the *Aeneid*', *J.R.S.* 59 (1969) 43f.

[4] See Williams, ad 498f.

[5] Although not necessarily a secondary one; so Austin, ad 498ff.

Dido is joyful in her success. She is surrounded by a throng (497) as Diana is followed by a thousand Oreads (499f.). As Diana guides her dancers (499) so Dido guides the construction of her city (503ff.). Her *pietas* is given further emphasis[1] in this description of her guiding the welfare of her people (503ff.). Furthermore, she possesses *dignitas* and *maiestas* (506),[2] and *iustitia* (507f.).[3]

As Aeneas is observing the appearance of the queen he catches sight of his men — Antheus, Sergestus and Cloanthus, and all the others whom he once thought were lost:

> iura dabat legesque viris, operumque laborem
> partibus aequabat iustis aut sorte trahebat:
> cum subito Aeneas...
>
> (507–9)

The hero's head suddenly turns from Dido to his men. Aeneas is amazed (*obstipuit* 513)[4] at the sight: both he and Achates desire avidly to join hands with their comrades, but they remain hidden in the divine cloud (514ff.). Instead they wait in order to see what is to happen to their friends, where the fleet is, and why they have appeared at the temple (516ff.). The reaction of Aeneas (and Achates) to the sight of his men exemplifies his *pietas*: he shows love and concern for their safety just as he did at their loss (1, 217ff.).

We are now in a position to reflect upon Vergil's presentation of his hero so far. All of Aeneas' seven speeches up to this point forcefully underline his *pietas*. Moreover, we have seen that the poet alters the Homeric presentation of events to stress this

---

[1] Cf. 446f.

[2] See Pöschl, 69.

[3] The nature of the frieze and her generosity to the Trojans (562ff.) also stress her *humanitas*. Unlike the case of Turnus we see all of these noble characteristics in Dido well before her infection at the gods' hands (657ff.). For the concept of *humanitas* in the *Aeneid*, see below, p. 217, n. 1.

[4] Cf. Dido's amazement at the sudden appearance of Aeneas (613ff.).

fundamental quality of Aeneas. Because of the emphasis given to
Aeneas' piety Vergil's hero is a different, less three-dimensional
figure than is Homer's Odysseus in Phaeacia. On reflection we
could say that Aeneas, to this point in Book 1, has on the whole a
passive role and responds or reacts to six different happenings.
These can be listed as follows: (1) the storm and misfortune
(81–222); (2) the appearance of his mother (305–417); (3) the
view of the city (418–440); (4) the view of the temple and its
pictures (441–493); (5) the sight of Dido (494–508); (6) the sight
of his men (509–519). We can say without any doubt that Aeneas
reacts unequivocally to *five* of these occurrences and that in each
case the poet stresses his piety. We might list these reactions as
follows: (1) 94–101, 198–207 and *passim*; (2) 326–334,
372–385 and 407–9; (3) 437 and *passim*; (4) 459–63 and *passim*;
and (6) 513ff. We could reasonably have expected a clear response
from Aeneas to (5) — the sight of Dido — but his reaction is in
fact more difficult to discern. Vergil describes Dido in the
narrative as *pulcherrima*, and we might reasonably infer, given
Aeneas' subsequent love for the queen, that this is also the hero's
reaction to her. The poet in fact seems to be implying that the
choice of the word *pulcherrima* is that of Aeneas himself.[1] In the
simile of Dido as Diana, Latona is described as watching her
daughter silently and being filled with joy at the sight:

> Latonae tacitum pertemptant gaudia pectus
>
> (502)

It has been plausibly suggested[2] that this line 'conveys the effect
which Dido has upon those watching her, particularly Aeneas'.
A mother's joy at the sight of her daughter would, on the face of
it, seem inappropriate for Aeneas' emotional reaction to a woman
of great beauty; yet Aeneas observes Dido silently as Latona does

---

[1] See Otis' chapter 'The Subjective Style', 41ff.

[2] Williams, ad loc. See Sainte-Beuve's difficulty with this passage, *Étude Sur Virgile*
(Paris, 1857) 293.

Diana: the parallel is a close one. The fundamental point is that the substance of Aeneas' reaction to Dido is never made clear.[1] There is instead an implicit response: the thoughts of the hero are obscured. Vergil uses indirect rather than direct techniques at this point because an utterance or a vivid response to the beauty of a woman would not exemplify Aeneas' *pietas*. We begin to see that the hero's *pietas*, or the lack of it, is Vergil's criterion for using direct or indirect techniques of characterisation.

Ilioneus speaks to Dido on behalf of the Trojans already in the city (522–58). He narrates the story of their journey from Troy to Italy and of the storms which struck them *en route*, leaving them shipwrecked on Dido's shore (522ff.). He complains of the rough treatment that they have received (539ff.) and pleads for her hospitality. He stresses the piety of the Trojans (526) and urges Dido to be mindful of the gods (542f.). In questioning her *pietas* Ilioneus mentions his own leader:

> "rex erat Aeneas nobis, quo iustior alter
> nec pietate fuit, nec bello maior et armis.                    545
> quem si fata virum servant, si vescitur aura
> aetheria neque adhuc crudelibus occubat umbris,
> non metus, officio nec te certasse priorem
> paeniteat."
>
> (544–9)

> "sin absumpta salus, et te, pater optime Teucrum,
> pontus habet Libyae nec spes iam restat Iuli..."
>
> (555–6)

Ilioneus hopes that the fates will save such a *pius* man, for if they do the Trojans will fulfil their mission. If, however, Aeneas is lost at sea the Trojans will go to Sicily where they are assured a home. The success or failure of the mission depends on Aeneas.

---

[1] The reader does not miss the lack of a reaction from Aeneas for two reasons: first, because one is implied anyway in the narrative, and second, because the reader's focus, like Aeneas', shifts suddenly to the lost Trojans: *cum subito Aeneas* ... 509ff.

Ilioneus describes him emotionally — he was[1] as just, as *pius* and as great in arms as anyone; so great that his very survival would assuage all the speaker's fears. Thus he addresses him as *pater optime Teucrum* (555). The speech characterises Aeneas indirectly as the *Telemacheia* does Odysseus.[2] We have seen already (220ff. etc.) Aeneas' love and concern for his men: now we see that it is reciprocated. The speech reinforces Aeneas' *pietas* from a different angle as well as bringing before Dido the name and fame of the Trojan king.

Dido's response seems largely to suggest that Ilioneus' pleas are superfluous. She acts with spontaneous generosity: the Trojans may do as they wish by leaving for Italy (569) or for Sicily (570), or even remain on equal terms in Carthage (572ff.). What Dido possesses is the Trojans' also and they will be treated as equals: *urbem quam statuo, vestra est* (573). Dido's only wish is that Aeneas himself were present (575f.). She will send people forth to look for him (576ff.).

Aeneas and Achates had for a long time been burning (*ardebant* 581) to burst from the cloud. The shadowy Achates is the first to speak and urges Aeneas (582–5) to reappear into the daylight for all is safe (*omnia tuta vides* 583). Aeneas needs little inducement and bursts forward in sensational style:

> vix ea fatus erat cum circumfusa repente
> scindit se nubes et in aethera purgat apertum.
> restitit Aeneas claraque in luce refulsit
> os umerosque deo similis; namque ipsa decoram
> caesariem nato genetrix lumenque iuventae                    590
> purpureum et laetos oculis adflarat honores:
> quale manus addunt ebori decus, aut ubi flavo
> argentum Pariusve lapis circumdatur auro.
> tum sic reginam adloquitur cunctisque repente

---

[1] Ilioneus' use of the imperfect *erat* signifies that he fears the worst.
[2] See discussion above, p. 16ff.

improvisus ait: "coram, quem quaeritis, adsum,                595
Troius Aeneas, Libycis ereptus ab undis.
o sola infandos Troiae miserata labores,
quae nos, reliquias Danaum, terraeque marisque
omnibus exhaustos iam casibus, omnium egenos,
urbe, domo socias, grates persolvere dignas               600
non opis est nostrae, Dido, nec quidquid ubique est
gentis Dardaniae, magnum quae sparsa per orbem.
di tibi, si qua pios respectant numina, si quid
usquam iustitiae est et mens sibi conscia recti,
praemia digna ferant. quae te tam laeta tulerunt          605
saecula? qui tanti talem genuere parentes?
in freta dum fluvii current, dum montibus umbrae
lustrabunt convexa, polus dum sidera pascet,
semper honos nomenque tuum laudesque manebunt,
quae me cumque vocant terrae." sic fatus amicum           610
Ilionea petit dextra laevaque Serestum,
post alios, fortemque Gyan fortemque Cloanthum.

                                                    (586–612)

The beautification of Aeneas (589ff.) and the simile used to
describe it (592ff.) are modelled on two Odyssean episodes
(6,229ff. and 23,156ff.).[1] In the former Athena adds beauty
to Odysseus in order to impress Nausicaa, who had previously
thought of him as shabby (ἀεικέλιος 6,242). The trans-
formation succeeds in its purpose and she thinks of him as
god-like. In the latter case Athena sheds beauty upon Odysseus
prior to his self-revelation to Penelope (23,156ff.). This aids
Penelope's recognition of her husband — she sees him more as she
remembers him.

Vergil has been criticised for his presentation of the beautification of Aeneas: '(the episode is) a piece of imitation, dull and
unconvincing, as nearly all the purely Homeric touches are in the

---

[1] See Knauer's indices, ad loc.

character and story of Aeneas'.[1] R.G. Austin[2] has gone a long way towards correcting this view: 'Aeneas has long been an idealized hero to Dido (cf. 617), and the Goddess of Love shows him to her on his first appearance as beautiful and god-like, fulfilling her highest hope'. In short, the shedding of beauty on to Aeneas should be seen as the beginning of Venus' psychological manipulation of Dido. Athena's purpose in the Odyssean cases is immediate and benign, whereas Venus' is elaborate and sinister.

Aeneas' self-introduction (595f.)[3] is dramatic indeed, but he does not dwell on himself but rather proceeds immediately (597ff.) to give thanks to Dido. She is the only one who has pitied the lot[4] of those Trojans who survived the slaughter by the Greeks and have subsequently suffered great hardship on land and sea, lacking everything. So great is her generosity that Aeneas feels unable to give due thanks (*grates ... dignas* 600), but prays at least that the gods will give *praemia digna* (605). He regards her as one of the *pios* (603)[5] who is most worthy of honour and good reward. This part of the speech is modelled on Odysseus' supplications to Nausicaa and Arete:

> "σοὶ δὲ θεοὶ τόσα δοῖεν ὅσα φρεσὶ σῇσι μενοινᾷς,
> ἄνδρα τε καὶ οἶκον καὶ ὁμοφροσύνην ὀπάσειαν
> ἐσθλήν· οὐ μὲν γὰρ τοῦ γε κρεῖσσον καὶ ἄρειον,
> ἢ ὅθ' ὁμοφρονέοντε νοήμασιν οἶκον ἔχητον
> ἀνὴρ ἠδὲ γυνή."

(*Od.* 6, 180–184)

[1] Glover, 215f.; cf. Conington, ad loc.

[2] Austin, ad 589ff.

[3] The Homeric parallels for 595f. (Knauer's indices, ad loc.) are *Od.* 21,207f. and *Od.* 24,321f. — Odysseus' self-introductions to Eumaeus and Laertes.

[4] Helenus (3, 294ff.) and Acestes (1, 195ff.) are both Trojans; see Austin, ad 597.

[5] Which, of course, she is, for the following reasons: (1) because she is shown building a temple to Juno (446ff.), (2) because she directs the welfare of her people (507f.), and (3) because, in giving hospitality to the Trojans, she acts in accordance with the laws of *Iuppiter hospitalis* (731ff.). I see little in Aeneas' speech, or elsewhere, to support the view that *pius* means 'compassionate'; so W.R. Johnson 'Aeneas and the Ironies of *Pietas*', *C.J.* 60 (1965) 360ff.

τούσδε τε δαιτυμόνας, τοῖσιν θεοὶ ὄλβια δοῖεν
ζωέμεναι, καὶ παισὶν ἐπιτρέψειεν ἕκαστος
κτήματ᾽ ἐνὶ μεγάροισι γέρας θ᾽ ὅ τι δῆμος ἔδωκεν. "

(Od. 7, 148–50)

Odysseus is specific in his hopes for the Phaeacians and for
Nausicaa: he wishes for the princess a husband, a home and
oneness of heart (ὁμοφροσύνην 6, 181). These things, Odysseus says, will bring happiness to Nausicaa. For the Phaeacians he
wishes prosperity (ὄλβια 7, 148) in general and, more specifically, the capacity to hand down acquisitions (κτήματα 150) and
honour (γέρας 150). The prayers of Odysseus for good fortune to
smile both on Nausicaa and the Phaeacians are made from a
position of insecurity; the survival-motive dominates his thinking. Aeneas, by contrast, has been granted hospitality by Dido
and is desperately grateful to her. Aeneas' hopes for Dido are less
specific than those of Odysseus, yet he speaks with the deepest
sincerity. His words, however, resound with tragic irony, for
within fifty lines Venus begins to apply her *novas artis* (657) to
Dido.[1] The eventual 'rewards' of the queen's hospitality to the
Trojans are her decline and death. Her tragedy in Book 4 is all the
more powerful because of her noble spirit. Odysseus' words, by
contrast, lack these deeper implications: there is nothing to
suggest that Nausicaa and the Phaeacians ever lack the prosperity
that Odysseus prays for.[2]

Aeneas' flattery to Dido (605f.) is modelled on that of Odysseus to Nausicaa at *Od.* 6, 149ff.[3] The significant difference is
that whereas Odysseus utters a μειλίχιον καὶ κερδαλέον ...
μῦθον (148), Aeneas is utterly sincere. Aeneas ends his speech

[1] Boyle, *Ramus* 1 (1972) 77, argues that lines 603–5 direct 'the reader's attention to the
moral injustice of Dido's plight'. They certainly point out that Dido's *humanitas* and *pietas*
are cruelly repaid by Venus.

[2] On the fate of the Phaeacians, see *Od.* 13, 128–87.

[3] Knauer, indices ad 603–5.

by promising to Dido the only thing that he can — that her honour, name and praises will endure, whatever lands call him (607ff.). These lines, which have no clear Homeric model,[1] are also spoken with deep sincerity, yet here too there is a strong element of tragic irony; for within a short time, in a bitter response to her tragic dilemma, Dido evokes an avenger to rise up.[2] Aeneas' city and that of Dido will be implacable enemies until the eventual destruction of the latter.

After saying these words Aeneas grasps the hands of his comrades (*pietas*). Aeneas' speech to Dido is his last utterance of Book 1. The final section of the book concentrates on the queen — her amazement that the goddess-born Aeneas stands before her, her hospitality towards the Trojans and the manipulation of her person by Venus and Cupid. Aeneas' love for his son compels him to send Achates to the ships to bring Ascanius to the city (643ff.). Venus plays upon his *pietas*, disguises Cupid as Ascanius, and steals Aeneas' son away (657ff.). The task laid upon Cupid is to infect Dido with a deep and powerful love. This he proceeds to do, and the end of the book sees Dido becoming more and more consumed with love, asking Aeneas again and again to tell the stories of Troy and of his own wanderings.

[1] Knauer, indices ad loc.
[2] See 4,624ff.

# BOOK 2

The second book of the *Aeneid* may be divided into three sections:

1. 1–249: The narration begins; the deception of the Trojans by Sinon; the Wooden Horse and death of Laocoon.
2. 250–558: The destruction of Troy; the death of Priam; the 'heroic impulse'[1] of Aeneas.
3. 559–804: The Helen episode; Aeneas and his family; flight from Troy.

Aeneas does not appear as a character in the first section of his own narrative, although at the outset of the book he stresses that the memory of Troy is painful to him:

> "infandum, regina, iubes renovare dolorem,
> Troianas ut opes et lamentabile regnum
> eruerint Danai, quaeque ipse miserrima vidi          5
> et quorum pars magna fui. quis talia fando
> Myrmidonum Dolopumve aut duri miles Ulixi
> temperet a lacrimis? et iam nox umida caelo
> praecipitat suadentque cadentia sidera somnos.
> sed si tantus amor casus cognoscere nostros          10
> et breviter Troiae supremum audire laborem,
> quamquam animus meminisse horret luctuque refugit,
> incipiam."                                          (3–13)[2]

The reader, who has seen Aeneas' lachrymose reaction to the pictures on Dido's temple, appreciates the hero's reluctance to tell of Troy's destruction. The queen herself, who did not see his reaction to the frieze, is forced to persevere with her request.[3] The pain and grief of telling the story stress the *pietas* of the narrator.[4]

---

[1] See Quinn, 1ff.

[2] As well as *Od.* 9, 1–15 (see below, p. 46, n. 1) Knauer in his indices (ad 3f.) compares *Od.* 7, 241f. in which Odysseus says to Arete that it is difficult to tell of all the troubles the gods have given him.

[3] See 1, 750ff. and 2, 10f.

[4] As did his tears in response to the frieze (1, 456ff.); see above, p. 32ff.

45

He himself had no small part in the events of that night and remembers them all too vividly. Yet so painful is the memory of them that he is reluctant to tell the tale.[1]

With one exception[2] these opening lines are the only ones in the first section in which Aeneas refers to his own thoughts or actions. The first person plural is used throughout this section:[3] Aeneas is merely one of the Trojans. He too is deceived by Sinon's lies[4] and is equally aghast at the death of Laocoon. The comparative anonymity of Aeneas amongst the Trojans allows the reader to concentrate on Sinon's deceit, Priam's generosity, and the horrific deaths of Laocoon and his sons.

In the second section of the book (250–558) Aeneas relates his own actions and experiences during the destruction of the city. The sleeping Aeneas sees a vision of Hector, who looks nothing like the great hero that defeated Patroclus but is befouled with blood from his many wounds. Aeneas weeps as he greets him (*flens* 279)[5] and is the first to speak:

> "o lux Dardaniae, spes o fidissima Teucrum,
> quae tantae tenuere morae? quibus Hector ab oris
> exspectate venis? ut te post multa tuorum
> funera, post varios hominumque urbisque labores

[1] Cf. *Od.* 9,12ff. in which Odysseus, in response to Alcinous (8,536ff.), laments the woes of his past. Dido is specific in her requests to Aeneas (1,750ff.) whereas Alcinous, who is still unsure of his guest's identity, merely seeks to know more about the stranger and why he responds with tears to tales of Troy. Aeneas shows greater reluctance to tell the story than does Odysseus, who concentrates on his *own* suffering: κήδε' ἐπεί μοι πολλὰ δόσαν θεοὶ οὐρανίωνες. (*Od.* 9,15).

[2] *horresco referens* (204) is used parenthetically, referring to Aeneas as narrator (i.e. in Carthage).

[3] See 25, 74, 105, 145, 212, 234, 244 and 245; cf. G. Sanderlin, 'Vergil's Protection of Aeneas in *Aeneid* II', *C.W.* 66 (1972–3) 82ff.

[4] R.G. Austin, *Aeneidos Liber Secundus* (Oxford, 1964) XIV: 'we have to infer that he was deceived like the rest about the Horse'.

[5] His emotional response to the vision of Hector underlines his *pietas*. The mood of sorrow is further intensified by the reference to the tears (271) of *maestissimus Hector* (270) and *maestas voces* (280).

defessi aspicimus! quae causa indigna serenos    285
foedavit vultus? aut cur haec vulnera cerno?"

(281–6)

Aeneas is clearly puzzled by the vision before him; his words 'have
the inconsequential nature of a dream'.[1] His great love for
Hector (*pietas*) is stressed immediately — he is, to Aeneas, the
light of the Dardan land and the surest hope of the Trojans.[2] The
repeated 'o' stresses the emotion of the speaker.[3] In his dream
Aeneas is unaware that Hector is dead: what delay has kept him
and why does he bear such terrible wounds?

Hector is unconcerned with trivialities (287). Aeneas, he says
(289ff.), must flee from the flames because the enemy now hold
the walls. Enough has been done to defend Troy; if it could have
been saved, Hector himself would have saved it (291ff.). Aeneas
must take the *sacra* and Penates, and for these seek the great city
which he will finally establish after long wanderings at sea
(293ff.). Hector's speech is 'terse':[4] his concern is to prompt
Aeneas into fleeing Troy rather than to answer the questions of his
old friend.[5]

In chronological terms Aeneas' utterance to Hector (281ff.) is
his first in the poem. The episode is in some ways like the first
appearance of Turnus (7,413f.) who in his sleep is confronted by
the demon Allecto disguised as Calybe. In each case the hero is
vague and somnolent. The vision that confronts Turnus attempts
unsuccessfully to lead him into war; the episode is characterised
by the conflict of wills and the force that Allecto must use to have

[1] Williams, ad loc.

[2] Knauer, indices ad loc., cites *Il.* 23,94–8 as a Homeric parallel for Aeneas' speech. In
this episode the ghost of Patroclus appears before Achilles telling the latter to bury him
(69–92). Achilles (unlike Aeneas) proceeds to follow the injunction of his former friend
(95f. and 103ff.).

[3] Austin, ad loc. We might compare Aeneas here with his speech to the disguised
Venus at 1,326ff.

[4] Williams, ad 268f.

[5] *nate dea* (289) is the only personal reference.

her way. Aeneas too is confronted in his sleep (*in somnis* 270) by a vision,[1] but in this episode there is not the same conflict of wills. In stressing the need to flee Troy Hector commends to Aeneas a course of action foreign to his mentality, yet the latter's will (unlike Turnus') always remains his own.[2] Moreover, as Vergil presents the episodes, Turnus' natural inclination is to peace whereas that of Aeneas[3] is to war.

The sound of Troy's destruction reaches Aeneas in his father's house (298ff.). The hero wakes from his sleep and proceeds to investigate: Hector was right (290), for the enemy hold the walls. Aeneas immediately rushes into arms:

> "arma amens capio; nec sat rationis in armis,
> sed glomerare manum bello et concurrere in arcem
> cum sociis ardent animi; furor iraque mentem
> praecipitat, pulchrumque mori succurrit in armis."
>
> (314–7)[4]

Aeneas' behaviour here demonstrates his 'heroic impulse',[5] his natural irrational urge to defend his city, and, if necessary, to die in so doing. It is significant that Aeneas, in a natural response to the situation (*arma amens capio* 314), is pictured acting like Turnus after his infection by the demon Allecto (*arma amens fremit* 7, 460).[6] Aeneas utterly loses his *ratio* (314)[7] and is dominated completely by fury and anger (*furor iraque ... * 316f.). In this state of mind he leaves the house of Anchises in which his father, wife and son sleep unprotected. In so doing he neglects to follow

[1] On the subject of dreams and visions in the poem, see H. R. Steiner, *Der Traum in der Aeneis* (Berne, 1952) esp. 29ff. and 62ff.

[2] On this see W. A. Camps, *An Introduction to Virgil's 'Aeneid'* (Oxford, 1969) 23.

[3] 2, 314ff.

[4] Knauer, indices ad 315–317, compares *Il.* 15, 496–499 which is not, however, a close parallel.

[5] See Quinn, 1ff.

[6] Heinze, 32 n. 1, also draws this comparison.

[7] Aeneas' statement, *nec sat rationis in armis* (314), has significant implications for the hero's nature in war and for the meaning of the poem. See below, p. 171ff. and p. 211ff.

Hector's injunction that he should flee Troy taking with him the *sacra* and Penates. Hector's words to him have no effect; the hero still does not fulfil his duty of leaving Troy to found a new city.

As Aeneas prepares to rush into the fray Panthus arrives bearing the *sacra* and Penates. He is the priest of Apollo (319) and brings with him his *parvus nepos* (320). Panthus is in short the epitome of piety[1] and bears the sacred objects of which Hector had just spoken. Aeneas, however, still fails to recognise his responsibilities:

> "quo res summa loco, Panthu? quam prendimus arcem?"[2]
>
> (322)

Regardless of the state of battle Aeneas is determined to act with the sword. Panthus, however, replies dolefully (324ff.) that their city has fallen (*fuit Ilium* 325) and that Jupiter has changed sides. He elaborates on the hopeless task of warding off the attackers. Aeneas hears the tale of woe, but far from being deterred, rushes into battle:

> "in flammas et in arma feror, quo tristis Erinys,
> quo fremitus vocat et sublatus ad aethera clamor."
>
> (337–8)

Aeneas' instincts drive him into a battle in which he can expect to be killed.[3] Again he acts bravely but contrary to the commands

---

[1] On this episode see Heinze, 33ff.; R. Allain, 'Une "nuit spirituelle" d'Énée', *R.E.L.* 24 (1946) 189ff.; B. Fenik, 'Theme and Imagery in *Aeneid* 2 and 4', *A.J.P.* 80 (1959) 6ff.; K. Quinn, *Latin Explorations* (London, 1963) 208ff.; E. L. Harrison, 'Divine Action in *Aeneid* 2', *Phoenix* 24 (1970) 324f. and Austin, ad 320. As Harrison (*ibid.* 324) points out, Aeneas' responsibilities are intimated on two levels – the divine, by Hector (289ff.), and the human by Panthus' appearance (318ff.).

[2] See Austin's note, ad loc., on this difficult line. Knauer, indices ad loc., cites no Homeric parallel for this speech.

[3] Panthus (324–35) makes the state of battle quite clear. See too Aeneas' sentiments at 353ff.

of Hector.[1] He now assumes the position of *dux* and exhorts his men to follow the path of fortune:

> "quos ubi confertos ardere in proelia vidi,
> incipio super his: 'iuvenes, fortissima frustra
> pectora, si vobis audentem extrema cupido
> certa sequi, quae sit rebus fortuna videtis:                    350
> excessere omnes adytis arisque relictis
> di quibus imperium hoc steterat: succurritis urbi
> incensae. moriamur et in media arma ruamus.
> una salus victis nullam sperare salutem.'
> sic animis iuvenum furor additus. inde, lupi ceu              355
> raptores atra in nebula, quos improba ventris
> exegit caecos rabies catulique relicti
> faucibus exspectant siccis, per tela, per hostis
> vadimus haud dubiam in mortem mediaeque tenemus
> urbis iter."
>
> (347–60)[2]

Aeneas recognises the futility of the charge he is about to lead into the city; for the gods have departed leaving behind their shrines and altars (351ff.). Yet he urges his men to die in battle, for this is better than defeat and slavery (353f.).[3] Aeneas adds *furor* to their courage (355) and they become like wolves driven by a rabid hunger and by their own cubs left behind which are thirsty for blood (355ff.).[4] In the later books this kind of simile

[1] Cf. *teque his ... eripe flammis* (Hector, 289) and *in flammas et in arma feror* (Aeneas, 337).

[2] Knauer, indices ad loc., cites no Homeric model for Aeneas' speech (348ff.) but cites *Il.* 12, 299–306 as a parallel to the simile of the wolves.

[3] Cf. Aeneas' sentiments at 2, 317 and those of Turnus at 11, 416ff.; see too Heinze, 32, n. 2.

[4] In his excellent article on the imagery in Book 2, 'The Serpent and the Flame', *A.J.P.* 71 (1950) 379–400, Bernard Knox writes (392): 'But the suggestion, implicit in the simile and its immediate sequel, that Aeneas has usurped the attributes of the serpent that has so far stood for violence and deceit deepens immeasurably the sense of his wrongness and folly, and reminds us how far Aeneas has strayed from his duty, which is not to fight, but to yield to a greater purpose, as he does yield in the end'.

is used to describe the enemies of Aeneas,[1] and hence it is significant that Vergil uses it to describe the Trojans themselves. There is a clear parallel in the early pictures of Aeneas and Turnus, although the latter is the victim of a demonic infection. Aeneas acts in accordance with his instincts. The *virtus* of the Trojans and their mad rage (*furor*) incite them into a battle that they will certainly lose. Aeneas' behaviour here is consistent with his initial response to the sight and sound of Troy's destruction (314ff.). Hector's injunction is still forgotten.

Aeneas now vividly describes the battle for the city (363ff.). The Trojans kill a party of Greeks and don their armour (385ff.). In their disguise they are able to mingle with the Greeks and kill many of them. They see Cassandra dragged from the temple (402ff.), at which sight Coroebus,[2] in a fit of fury (*furiata mente* 407),[3] rushes into the fray. Aeneas and the others follow and many are killed.[4] Aeneas describes the fighting in Priam's palace and the death of the king himself (438ff.). The Greeks burst into the scarcely defended building. They kill the wounded Polites, son of Priam, *ante ora patris* and then proceed to kill the king himself (526ff.). After Priam sees his own son killed, he prays (535ff.) that Pyrrhus may get his due rewards and reminds him that Achilles had respected the rights of the suppliant: 'Pyrrhus utters lies when he calls Achilles his father' (540–3). The speech, however, has no effect on Pyrrhus who ruthlessly kills the old man (547ff.). The death of Priam stirs Aeneas into thinking of his

---

[1] See Pöschl's list of the similes in the poem referring to Aeneas and Turnus, 98f. Austin, ad 356, compares the wolf-simile used to describe Turnus at 9,59ff. Williams, ad loc., also compares 9,565f. and 11,809ff.

[2] On the important role of Coroebus in the fighting, see Sanderlin, *C.W.* 66 (1972–3) 84.

[3] Cf. Aeneas — *furiata mente* (588).

[4] Amongst those killed is Panthus, on whom Aeneas reflects as follows: *nec te tua plurima, Panthu, labentem pietas nec Apollinis infula texit.* (429–30).

own father (559ff.).[1] He thinks also of his wife Creusa and small
son Ascanius (562f.). Aeneas looks around and sees that his
comrades have either deserted him or fallen into the flames. At
this point he sees Helen lurking silently, close to Vesta's shrine,
in fear of her life:

> "illa sibi infestos eversa ob Pergama Teucros
> et Danaum poenam et deserti coniugis iras
> praemetuens, Troiae et patriae communis Erinys,
> abdiderat sese atque aris invisa sedebat.
> exarsere ignes animo; subit ira cadentem                    575
> ulcisci patriam et sceleratas sumere poenas.
> 'scilicet haec Spartam incolumis patriasque Mycenas
> aspiciet, partoque ibit regina triumpho?
> coniugiumque domumque patris natosque videbit
> Iliadum turba et Phrygiis comitata ministris?             580
> occiderit ferro Priamus? Troia arserit igni?
> Dardanium totiens sudarit sanguine litus?
> non ita. namque etsi nullum memorabile nomen
> feminea in poena est, habet haec victoria laudem;
> exstinxisse nefas tamen et sumpsisse merentis              585
> laudabor poenas, animumque explesse iuvabit
> ultricis famam et cineres satiasse meorum.'
> talia iactabam et furiata mente ferebar..."

$$(571-88)[2]$$

One of the objections of Servius[3] to this passage is that it is
shameful (*turpe*) for Aeneas or any brave man to rage against a
woman in this manner. Aeneas admits to the same view (583ff.)

[1] Aeneas' first recognition of his responsibilities, in this case for his family, marks the
beginning of the third section of the book (559–804).

[2] Knauer, indices ad loc., cites no Homeric model for this passage.

[3] Servius, ad 592. For the main arguments for and against the authenticity of this passage, see R. G. Austin, 'Virgil *Aeneid* 2. 567–88', *C.Q.* 11 (1961) 185–98 (for) and G. P.
Goold, 'Servius and the Helen Episode', *H.S.C.P.* 74 (1970) 101–68 (against). K.
Büchner, *P. Vergilius Maro*, *R.E.* 8A (Stuttgart, 1955) 331ff., following Servius, argues
that Vergil would have replaced these lines, and stresses their inconsistency with the picture of Helen in Book 6, 511ff. For my argument that this inconsistency is deliberate, see
below, p. 134ff.

and we may infer that this was also the view of the poet himself. It is, therefore, all the more significant that Vergil includes the reference at all. The point is that so great is the loathsomeness of Helen to the sight of Aeneas that he feels he must kill her; for she may return in triumph to see her home and family, whilst Troy is destroyed with the king and people killed. In such circumstances it is a pleasure to kill such a nefarious creature, even though it brings him no honour to do so.

Thus Aeneas' *pietas* in response to the death of Priam which begins the third section of Book 2 proves to be notably short-lived. It is evident, on reflection, that Aeneas is in a state of *furor* throughout almost the entire second section of the book.[1] At the first sight of the flames he erupts into a fury (314ff.) even though the vision had counselled him to act prudently by leaving the city (289ff.). In so doing he leaves Anchises, Creusa and Ascanius, as well as the *sacra* and Penates, unguarded in his house (322ff.). He leads his men into a battle knowing full well that they cannot win (348ff.). As the third section begins, Aeneas' desire for vengeance obliterates his concern for his family (*furiata mente ferebar* 588).

On the face of it Vergil draws a simple distinction between two states of mind — *pietas*, being loving concern for family as well as for the *sacra* and Penates; and *furor*, being a mad irrational rage which, from time to time, controls Aeneas' actions. Up to line 589 it would seem that the conflict between *furor* and *pietas* in Aeneas is well-defined and that *furor* has easily the upper hand. At this point, however, begins one of the most important and far-reaching episodes in the poem. For just as Aeneas is about to kill Helen, Venus intervenes and stops him from doing so. We shall see that from this point *pietas* begins to take on a more complex meaning and the dichotomy between *pietas* and *furor* in

---

[1] 250–558. Aeneas is, however, characterised by his initial calmness at 279ff.

the character of Aeneas ceases to be so exact. Venus speaks as follows:

> 'nate, quis indomitas tantus dolor excitat iras?
> quid furis? aut quonam nostri tibi cura recessit?     595
> non prius aspicies ubi fessum aetate parentem
> liqueris Anchisen, superet coniunxne Creusa
> Ascaniusque puer? quos omnis undique Graiae
> circum errant acies et, ni mea cura resistat,
> iam flammae tulerint inimicus et hauserit ensis.     600
> non tibi Tyndaridis facies invisa Lacaenae
> culpatusve Paris, divum inclementia, divum
> has evertit opes sternitque a culmine Troiam.
> aspice (namque omnem, quae nunc obducta tuenti
> mortalis hebetat visus tibi et umida circum     605
> caligat, nubem eripiam; tu ne qua parentis
> iussa time neu praeceptis parere recusa).'

(594–607)

Venus shows to Aeneas the gods themselves, Neptune, Juno, Minerva and Jupiter assisting the Greeks in the destruction of the city (608–18). He must flee and put an end to this toil;[1] she herself will guard him on his return to Anchises' threshold.

The tenor of Venus' speech is encompassed in her question to him — *quid furis?*, 'why (for what reason, to what purpose) do you rage?' There are more important things to be done: Anchises, Creusa and Ascanius are still alive, though only through Venus' intervention (596ff.). It is not the hated face of Helen, nor Paris, but the gods who destroy the city; and yet Aeneas strives to defend it. It profits nothing to kill Helen when other things need urgently to be done. Aeneas must divert his energies in the face of omnipotent opposition. He must cease one *labor* (the killing of Helen and the fight for Troy) that, by fleeing the city, he may undertake another (*eripe, nate, fugam finemque impone labori* 619).

---

[1] *eripe, nate, fugam finemque impone labori* (619). Cf. Hector's words to Aeneas: *'heu fuge, nate dea, teque his' ait 'eripe flammis'* (289).

Venus does not stress the immorality of killing a defenceless woman at an altar because morality is not her chief concern.[1] It is the *futility* of Aeneas' actions, their lack of direction, that bothers her. Venus' speech is often interpreted as a lesson for Aeneas in the moral value of restraining the passions.[2] In fact she implies no such thing: with his *furor* there is nothing fundamentally wrong *per se*, only that on this occasion it is hopelessly misdirected. Nor does Aeneas interpret the speech as a moral lesson. Whilst at Carthage with Dido he reflects upon his furious reaction that night to the sights and sounds of Troy's destruction:

"arma amens capio; nec sat rationis in armis."

(314)

This is uttered not so much in a spirit of moral superiority as it is a statement of man's nature in the war situation — a statement which, in the rest of the poem, proves as true for Aeneas as for less significant heroes. A part of the critical tradition has tended to link Aeneas' *pietas* in the later books with the gradual overcoming of his *furor* in Book 2.[3] Yet Aeneas is *impius* throughout much of the second book, not because he is overcome with irrational rage, but for two more basic reasons: first, because he is forgetful of

---

[1] See G. P. Goold, *H.S.C.P.* 74 (1970) 157 and A. Körte, 'Zum zweiten Buch von Vergils *Aeneis*', *Hermes* 51 (1916) 145ff.

[2] See, for example, R. P. Bond, 'Aeneas and the Cardinal Virtues', *Prudentia* 6 (1974) 76, who suggests that 'despite arguments against the authenticity of this passage (i.e. 2, 567–88), it is crucial to the development of Aeneas' awareness of his responsibilities; the episode is an integral part of the trials which lead ultimately to Aeneas' acquisition of true rational courage'. The end of the poem can hardly signal the victory of *ratio*. C. M. Bowra, 'Aeneas and the Stoic Ideal', *G. &R.* 3 (1933–4) 8ff., has an interesting discussion on this subject; see too below, p. 134ff.

[3] See, for example, Williams, ad 567f.: the Helen episode 'should remind us that the efforts of Aeneas in the poem to control violence in himself and others meet with only very imperfect success. Aeneas is a man of violence who tries hard to learn a better way'. I see no evidence in the poem for this view of the hero. Aeneas' propensity for heroic violence *in the war situation* never changes; what does change is the direction in which this *furor* is applied.

family, *sacra* and Penates; and second, because his mad rage *conflicts with the course of destiny*.

On the conflict between heroism and piety Dryden wrote:[1] 'That quality, which signifies no more than intrepid courage, may be separated from many others which are good and accompanied with many which are ill. A man may be very valiant, and yet be impious and vicious. But the same cannot be said of piety which excludes all ill qualities and comprehends even valour itself with all other qualities which are good'. As we follow Aeneas through the poem we find that the opposite of Dryden's argument is the case.[2] Aeneas' *pietas* comes more and more to signify the relationship of his actions to the course of fate. This is the case particularly in the later books and at the very end of the poem where the hero's *pietas* rests on this relationship.[3] But his *pietas* never 'excludes all ill qualities'. The Helen episode shows us that Aeneas is capable of contemplating barbarous action. In later episodes, as in 10,510–605, he actually carries such actions through, yet Vergil still describes him as *pius* (10,591). No god interferes in this case because Aeneas' cruelty aligns itself with the course of fate.[4] Similarly, in the death of Turnus, the role of the *Dira* as Jupiter's agent signifies that Aeneas' furious act (12,945ff.) furthers the progress of fate. For this reason, there is

[1] J. Dryden, *The Works of Virgil Translated into English Verse*, ed. John Carey, Vol. 1 (1819) 266; see Quinn, 21f.

[2] On the English Augustan Age and Vergil, see R. D. Williams, 'Changing Attitudes to Virgil: a study in the history of taste from Dryden to Tennyson', in *Virgil*, ed. D. R. Dudley, (London, 1969) 119ff.

[3] The reference to Jupiter's role in the destruction of Troy (617–8) is thus a crucial one. See discussions below, p. 165ff. and p. 210ff.

[4] R. Coleman, 'The Gods in the *Aeneid*', *G. &R.* 29 (1982) 154, makes the point that 'no divine guidance is at hand to save (Aeneas) from himself on these occasions (10,521ff., 537ff., 786ff. and 12,945ff.)'. Coleman offers no reason for the lack of divine intervention. E. Kraggerud, *Aeneisstudien*, *Symb. Osl.* Supplement 22 (Oslo, 1968) 22f., comes to a similar conclusion to my own, that Aeneas in the later books, but not in 2,567ff., acts in accordance with *fatum*.

no need to question, as some do,[1] the hero's piety at the end of the poem. The *pietas* of Aeneas is at no point in the poem nullified simply by the brutality of his actions.

Aeneas returns to his father's house (632ff.)[2] but finds Anchises reluctant to leave the city; instead he will seek his own death and forgo the loss of burial (645f.).[3] Despite all the pleas of Aeneas, Creusa and Ascanius, the old man remains unmoved. In a burst of frustration[4] Aeneas reacts as follows:

> "rursus in arma feror mortemque miserrimus opto.                655
> nam quod consilium aut quae iam fortuna dabatur?
> 'mene efferre pedem, genitor, te posse relicto
> sperasti tantumque nefas patrio excidit ore?
> si nihil ex tanta superis placet urbe relinqui,
> et sedet hoc animo perituraeque addere Troiae          660
> teque tuosque iuvat, patet isti ianua leto,
> iamque aderit multo Priami de sanguine Pyrrhus,
> natum ante ora patris, patrem qui obtruncat ad aras.
> hoc erat, alma parens, quod me per tela, per ignis
> eripis, ut mediis hostem in penetralibus utque          665
> Ascanium patremque meum iuxtaque Creusam
> alterum in alterius mactatos sanguine cernam?
> arma, viri, ferte arma; vocat lux ultima victos.
> reddite me Danais; sinite instaurata revisam
> proelia. numquam omnes hodie moriemur inulti.' "          670
>                                                    (655–70)

Aeneas 'has not yet recognised that his destiny imposes on him

---

[1] So Putnam 193ff.

[2] On the problem of *ducente deo* (632), see Austin, ad loc. There is also an interesting discussion by E. L. Harrison, *Phoenix* 24 (1970) 322f., who argues that the *deus* referred to is Jupiter.

[3] Otis, 244, has a good discussion on the significance of Anchises' role in this section of the book.

[4] R. B. Lloyd, 'Anchises in the *Aeneid* ', *T.A.Ph.A.* 88 (1957) 47, points out that 'with Anchises' refusal to depart *pietas in patrem* comes into direct conflict with *pietas in deos*'.

the obligation of survival'.[1] Again he rushes into arms and seeks death (655). Aeneas cannot bear to leave his father behind having just witnessed the slaughter of Priam by Pyrrhus. If Anchises wants to die, Pyrrhus will soon arrive and no mercy will be shown, for the son of Achilles kills men at the altars. He invokes his mother — *alma parens* (664); why did she rip him from the flames only to encounter an obstinate father and see his family murdered? Aeneas would prefer to kill Greeks and in so doing exact vengeance in defeat. Aeneas is confused and unable to conceive of a future beyond Troy. The advice of his mother seems to him to conflict with the behaviour of his father.[2]

Creusa reminds him (675ff.) that she and Ascanius, as well as Anchises, are in need of defence. She clings to the feet of Aeneas and holds up Ascanius before him (673f.). With the family in despair at the situation which they face, a light appears on top of Ascanius' head with harmless flames lapping at his hair and temples (680ff.).[3] Anchises, calls for a further sign (689ff.) which appears (692ff.) leading them to Ida's forest. These omens are convincing enough for Anchises, who decides to leave the city with his son (701ff.). Aeneas replies to his father as follows:

> "ergo age, care pater, cervici imponere nostrae;
> ipse subibo umeris nec me labor iste gravabit;
> quo res cumque cadent, unum et commune periclum,
> una salus ambobus erit. mihi parvus Iulus          710
> sit comes, et longe servet vestigia coniunx.
> vos, famuli, quae dicam animis advertite vestris.
> est urbe egressis tumulus templumque vetustum
> desertae Cereris, iuxtaque antiqua cupressus
> religione patrum multos servata per annos;          715
> hanc ex diverso sedem veniemus in unam.

[1] Williams, ad 634f.

[2] Knauer, indices ad loc., cites no Homeric parallel for this speech.

[3] Cf. the omen of Lavinia's hair 7,71ff. B.M.W. Knox, *A.J.P.* 71 (1950) 398, discusses the omen at 2,680ff. and (*ibid.* n. 42) compares it to that of Lavinia's hair.

tu, genitor, cape sacra manu patriosque penatis;
me bello e tanto digressum et caede recenti
attrectare nefas, donec me flumine vivo
abluero."                                                           (707–20)

In every respect the speech underlines the *pietas* of Aeneas as he prepares his family for their departure from the city. He will carry Anchises on his own shoulders and will bear the task.[1] Ascanius will accompany his father, and Creusa will follow in their path. Aeneas also takes thought for the servants and instructs them to meet at the temple of Ceres at the edge of the city (712ff.). The hero's *pietas* is also shown in his scrupulous avoidance of touching with blood on his hands the *sacra* and Penates which Anchises will carry. In fleeing the city with *sacra* and Penates Aeneas acts fully in accordance with the injunctions of Hector (289ff.) and Venus (594ff.). He thus makes the first step on the journey that will end with the establishment of his fated city. Whilst the speech, therefore, gives emphasis to Aeneas' final and important acceptance that his duty lies elsewhere, it also acts as a prelude to the tragic disappearance of his wife Creusa.[2] Aeneas' narration of the loss of his wife and his own frantic search for her form the bulk of the final episode in the book. The reader might well infer that Dido, who has already been pictured 'drinking deep draughts of love',[3] would have shown a particular interest in this part of Aeneas' story.

As they approach the gates they hear the noise of a crowd of men and, in fear of Greeks, rush forward with haste (730ff.). As they dash towards a safe exit Creusa disappears from the group (736ff.). Aeneas in a frantic state (*amens* 745), lamenting his lot, reproaches gods and men. He puts Ascanius, Anchises and the Penates[4] into the charge of his allies and returns to search for

[1] There is no close Homeric parallel for this speech (Knauer's indices, ad loc.).

[2] Of course this is especially true of 711.

[3] *infelix Dido longumque bibebat amorem* (1, 749).

[4] *Ascanium Anchisenque patrem Teucrosque penatis* (747). This line succinctly conveys Aeneas' responsibilities as he prepares to leave the city.

Creusa. Back in the city he sees the extent of the Greek destruction, their plunder and some of the prisoners they have taken (750–67). He even dares to shout aloud for Creusa, without success, when suddenly her *imago* appears before his eyes (772ff.). He is amazed at the sight of her, his hair stood on end and his voice held fast in his throat (774). She tells him (776ff.) that she was not fated to join him on his journey. He will have a long and arduous voyage and will come to Hesperia where he will have joyful times, a kingdom and a royal wife.[1] He should not shed tears for Creusa who does not resent her lot. She tells him to show love towards their son and bids him a final farewell. Aeneas in tears and wanting to say many things attempts three times to embrace her image, failing each time (790ff.). At last when night has passed he rejoins his fellow Trojans whose numbers have grown, takes up his father, and heads for the mountains (796ff.).

---

[1] It is sometimes argued that this reference, and those in Book 3, to Aeneas' future in a new land help to make a strong case against Dido's viewpoint in Book 4. Aeneas explains quite clearly both his fate, as he understands it, and his intention to go to Italy: Dido should have listened more carefully and taken heed of his plans. Such a view misses the whole point of the Dido episode; for so powerful is the god that infects her (1,657ff.) and so intoxicated by Aeneas is the queen, that the realities of their situations do not, until too late, concern her.

# BOOK 3

Aeneas has an important dramatic role in Books 1 and 2 of the poem: in the first he utters 8 direct speeches totalling 64 lines and in the second, apart from the many autobiographical references in the last two sections,[1] he utters 6 direct speeches totalling 53 lines. It is significant that in the third book of the poem, which tells of Aeneas' adventures in between his departure from Troy (Book 2) and his arrival in Carthage (Book 1), he has a comparatively small dramatic role. The hero's narration of his adventures may be seen to parallel Odysseus' wanderings as told to the Phaeacians in *Od.* 9, 10 and 12.[2] In each case the storyteller reflects upon his experiences on land and sea; Odysseus and his men travel in a world of fantasy, whereas Aeneas and his men attempt to unravel the mysteries of prophecy and to fulfil the destiny allotted them by the fates. The roles of Odysseus and Aeneas, however, in their own narrations, differ considerably.[3] Vergil allots to Aeneas a less prominent role in the narration than does Homer to Odysseus. This can be seen in two different ways; first, Aeneas' dramatic (direct speech) role is considerably less significant than that of Odysseus;[4] and second, in the narrative itself he makes far fewer autobiographical references than does Odysseus.

Book 9 of the *Odyssey* is essentially a personal reminiscence of personal experiences and actions. There are (unlike *Aen.* 3) only two major characters – Odysseus himself and Polyphemus, one of

---

[1] 250–558 and 559–804; see above, p. 46ff.

[2] *Od.* 11, the *Nekuia* of Odysseus, although part of the wanderings, is more properly the model for the sixth book of the *Aeneid*; see below, p. 114ff.

[3] Otis, 251ff. makes some perceptive comments on the subject of Book 3: 'No book is more Odyssean, yet what gives the tone and sets the mood are precisely its non-Odyssean elements'.

[4] The speeches of Odysseus in *Od.* 9, 10 and 12 comprise approximately 27% of all the direct speeches, whereas those of Aeneas in *Aen.* 3 comprise only 12% of those in the book.

the Cyclopes. Between them, these two characters utter 101 of the 114 lines of direct speech in the book. The conflict of different wits and physical power is central to the drama of Book 9. The narrative never really strays from Odysseus — he is always personally involved.[1] At 9,331ff. he organises the drawing of the lots to see which of his men will lift the stake and push it into Polyphemus' eye. He himself is excluded from the lot because he is automatically involved.[2] Odysseus instigates the scheme to blind Polyphemus and leads the way in carrying the plan through.

In a similar fashion Odysseus is also the central character in Book 10 which tells the story of their arrival at Circe's island. Almost all of the 29 speeches in the book are spoken to Odysseus or uttered by him.[3] None of his men, with the possible exception of Eurylochus, ever attains the stature of a 'real' character. Homer focuses clearly on the hero and leaves the ἑταῖροι in the narrative background. In only one episode is Odysseus absent from the action:[4] in this some of his companions come upon the house of Circe and are changed into pigs. The episode is important in that it draws Odysseus into a situation where he must confront Circe and her spells. Thus Homer shifts his focus away from Odysseus for a moment, only to show that the hero is required elsewhere.

Book 12 of the *Odyssey* begins with Circe's narration of the places which Odysseus will visit and the labours which he must endure (37ff.). In this sense the book is most like *Aen.* 3, because of the part played by prophecy. Circe, however, is much more definite; there is no ambiguity in her prophecy and no doubt in the mind of the recipient. Although she does mention Ithaca

---

[1] There is one exception, at 9,399ff., where Polyphemus seeks help from the other Cyclopes: ' ὦ φίλοι, Οὖτίς με κτείνει δόλῳ οὐδὲ βίηφιν ' (9,408). 'Nobody' is, in any case, a reference to Odysseus.

[2] Note ἐμοὶ σὺν 332.

[3] There is one exception — Polites to the ἑταῖροι , 10,226–8.

[4] See 10,210–43.

(137ff.) it is the journey itself that most concerns her. Her prophecy is poetically vivid, concentrating on the obstacles to be encountered. We never relate Circe's prophecy to a wider theme. The sorceress foretells Odysseus' future having taken him apart from his men (33ff.), and gives to him a recipe for survival. In Book 12, as in the earlier books, the ἑταῖροι remain in the dramatic background. When (at 420ff.) Odysseus alone survives the dangerous obstacles we are neither disappointed nor surprised, for our attention has been on him throughout the story of the wanderings. Homer develops a uniqueness in Odysseus' character as a preparation for his return to Ithaca where he will be confronted again by great danger. The wanderings of Odysseus present one man's struggle for survival, in which context the ἑταῖροι are dispensable.

In *Aen.* 3 the list of *dramatis personae* is longer and the dramatic role of the hero less prominent than in these books of the *Odyssey*. Anchises utters 6 speeches, 32 lines;[1] Aeneas 4, 33; Andromache 3, 31; Helenus 2, 96; Achaemenides 2, 49. There are also speaking roles for Polydorus, Apollo, Penates and Celaeno. The longer list of speaking characters, however, does not in itself explain the smaller part played by Aeneas. In Book 3 and elsewhere Vergil is content to limit the dramatic prominence of his hero to an extent probably never contemplated by Homer.[2] Similarly, a disparity can be seen in the number of autobiographical references made in the respective narratives. In *Od.* 9 Odysseus refers to himself (in the first person singular) as the subject of a sentence once, on average, in every 8 lines; in *Od.* 10 once in every 6 lines; and in *Od.* 12 once in every 5. Aeneas, by contrast, makes

---

[1] For Anchises' important role in Book 3, see L. J. D. Richardson, '*Facilis iactura sepulcri*', *Proc. Roy. Irish Acad.* 46 (1940) 85ff.; R. B. Lloyd, *T.A.Ph.A.* 88 (1957) 44ff.; R. B. Lloyd, '*Aeneid* III: A new approach', *A.J.P.* 78 (1957) 133ff.; H. T. Rowell, 'The Scholium on Naevius in *Parisinus Latinus* 7930', *A.J.P.* 78 (1957) 1ff.; Otis, 251ff.; Highet, 34f. and G. Williams, 275ff.

[2] See Appendix, below, p. 219f.

far fewer autobiographical references — once in every 13.5 lines
of narrative in *Aen.* 3. Thus, in his own narrative, Odysseus is
twice as prominent a figure as is Aeneas in his.[1]

The third book of the *Aeneid* begins the story of the Trojans'
travels following the destruction of their city. They build a fleet
at Antandros during the winter following Troy's destruction
(5f.). Initially Aeneas narrates events from the viewpoint of all
the Trojans (*agimur* 5, *molimur* 6, *contrahimus* 8).[2] The first
autobiographical reference soon follows:

> "vix prima inceperat aestas
> et pater Anchises dare fatis vela iubebat,
> litora cum patriae lacrimans portusque relinquo          10
> et campos ubi Troia fuit. feror exsul in altum
> cum sociis natoque penatibus et magnis dis."

(8–12)

The personal reference to Aeneas stresses his *pietas* — his tearful
exit from his beloved homeland with his allies, his father, his son
and Penates. We may note that, in this early section of the book,
the first person plural (5, 6, 8) describes the stages of the voyage,
whereas the singular has particular reference to the *pietas* of the
hero. We shall see that this technique is largely typical of the
narrative style in Book 3.

Aeneas proceeds to Thrace (*feror* 16)[3] and begins to build a
city after his own name (*Aeneadasque ... fingo* 18). He sacrifices to
Venus and the other gods (*sacra ... ferebam* 19) and slays a bull on
the shore to Jupiter (*mactabam ... taurum* 21). Aeneas then draws

---

[1] This fact has, to my knowledge, been largely ignored in the critical works in which
the wanderings of Aeneas and Odysseus are discussed.

[2] The poet stresses the uncertainty (*incerti* 7) of the Trojans at the outset as to where their
destiny lies (4ff.). One function of the third book is to show how these doubts and uncer-
tainties are removed.

[3] On this ἔκφρασις , see R. D. Williams, *Aeneidos Liber Tertius* (Oxford, 1962) ad
13–16. The use of the singular (*feror* 16) here to describe the journey foreshadows Aeneas'
important role in the Polydorus episode (19ff.).

near to a mound and attempts to cover the altar with green growth when he sees blood flow from the broken stems — a horrible portent (*accessi* 24, *conatus* 25, *tegerem* 25, *video* 26). In sacrificing to the gods and in his attempt to build a city for his people Aeneas demonstrates his *pietas*; and thus again we may note that the autobiographical references emphasise this ideal. Aeneas proceeds to rip a second shoot (*insequor* 32) and this time black blood flows from the bark. Aeneas begins to pray (*venerabar* 34) to the nymphs and to Mars that they may make the omen more favourable. He attempts again to tear out a reed (*adgredior*, *obluctor* 38) and this time a groan sounds from the earth. The dead Polydorus speaks from beneath the ground (41–6) telling Aeneas not to tear at him but to leave the Thracian shores. Aeneas is stunned (*obstipui* 48): his hair stands on end and his voice catches in his throat. He refers these portents to the elders and seeks an explanation for them (*refero*, *posco* 59). He receives counsel from the elders that they should depart from the *scelerata terra* (60).[1] All the Trojans give funeral rites to the dead Polydorus, set up altars and offer warm milk and the blood of victims (62ff.). It is significant, and largely in keeping with the narrative method of this book, that the autobiographical references to Aeneas (16–59) describe a religious experience and the hero's own scrupulous behaviour in it (*pietas*).

The journey to Delos is described in the first person plural (*provehimur* 72).[2] Again the poet uses *huc feror* (78) to foreshadow a religious experience which the hero has (on Delos 84ff.).[3] On their arrival Aeneas prays at the temple of Phoebus:

---

[1] In referring these portents to the *proceres* and to his father in particular (58), Aeneas displays both his desire to follow the correct procedure (see Williams' note (*Aen.* 3), ad 59) and his dependence on others at this point.

[2] As well as the third person plural (70f.).

[3] Cf. 3, 16 and above, p. 64 n. 3.

"iungimus hospitio dextras et tecta subimus.
templa dei saxo venerabar structa vetusto:
'da propriam, Thymbraee, domum; da moenia fessis          85
et genus et mansuram urbem; serva altera Troiae
Pergama, reliquias Danaum atque immitis Achilli.
quem sequimur? quove ire iubes? ubi ponere sedes?
da, pater, augurium atque animis inlabere nostris.'
vix ea fatus eram..."                                        (83–90)

Knauer[1] cites a Homeric parallel for this speech in the *Iliad*:

"Ζεῦ πάτερ, Ἴδηθεν μεδέων, κύδιστε μέγιστε,
δός μ' ἐς Ἀχιλλῆος φίλον ἐλθεῖν ἠδ' ἐλεεινόν,
πέμψον δ' οἰωνόν, ταχὺν ἄγγελον, ὅς τε σοὶ αὐτῷ          310
φίλτατος οἰωνῶν, καί εὑ κράτος ἐστὶ μέγιστον,
δεξιόν, ὄφρα μιν αὐτὸς ἐν ὀφθαλμοῖσι νοήσας
τῷ πίσυνος ἐπὶ νῆας ἴω Δαναῶν ταχυπώλων."

(*Il.* 24, 308–13)

Zeus hears Priam and sends the omen — an eagle dashes across
the city bringing joy to those who see it (314–21). Priam's piety
is thus rewarded by a sign from heaven allowing the old man to
have confidence in his plan to meet Achilles and plead with him
for Hector's body. Vergil evidently exploits the piety-of-Priam
motif to underline the piety of Aeneas. The latter seeks a home for
his weary men and prays for an omen (*augurium*) which will
indicate the will of Apollo. The answer that Aeneas receives,
however, is less clear than Priam's. Phoebus replies (94–8) that
they must seek out their ancient mother, which is interpreted by
Anchises (103ff.) to signify Crete, from where Teucer had come
in ancient times. Anchises too is the epitome of *pietas* as he
interprets the omen and makes sacrifice to Neptune, Apollo, to
Storm and to the Zephyrs (118–20).

The journey between Delos and Crete (124ff.) is described
largely in the first person plural (*linquimus*, *volamus* 124, *legimus*

---

[1] Knauer, indices ad loc.

127, *adlabimur* 131). This is consistent with the narration of their initial journeys (5ff.) and of the voyage to Delos (69ff.). At 132ff., however, on their arrival in Crete, Vergil again focuses on Aeneas himself:

> "et tandem antiquis Curetum adlabimur oris.
> ergo avidus muros optatae molior urbis
> Pergameamque voco, et laetam cognomine gentem
> hortor amare focos arcemque attollere tectis....
> iura domosque dabam."                              (131–4 and 137)

Here again the autobiographical references underline the *pietas* of the hero[1] as he strives avidly for his longed-for city and exhorts his people both to love their hearths and to raise the citadel with buildings. Moreover, like Dido at Carthage,[2] he gives laws to his people and also provides homes for them. It is Aeneas' deep consciousness of his pastoral role that makes him such a different kind of hero from Homer's Odysseus. Yet it is worth noting that his piety is backward-facing as he attempts to re-create the old Troy (Pergamum) in a new land.

The contentment of the Trojans is short-lived for a pestilence begins to destroy everything, compelling them to seek again the omens of Apollo at Delos. A return to this island proves unnecessary, however, for the Penates and sacred images of the gods appear before Aeneas:

> "nox erat et terris animalia somnus habebat:
> effigies sacrae divum Phrygiique penates,
> quos mecum ab Troia mediisque ex ignibus urbis
> extuleram, visi ante oculos astare iacentis..."
>
> (147–50)

---

[1] The plural *adlabimur* (131) immediately followed by the singular *molior* (132) etc., which stresses Aeneas' *pietas*, shows clearly the poet's narrative technique in Book 3.

[2] Cf. the description of Dido: '*iura dabat legesque viris, operumque laborem partibus aequabat iustis aut sorte trahebat*' (1,507f.).

Here too the narrative autobiographical reference helps to convey Aeneas' *pietas*. The relative clause (149f.) is, strictly speaking, superfluous to the narrative, for we are aware of the Penates and their exit from Troy with Aeneas.[1] The hero thus reiterates his piety in taking them in the first place. The Penates state (154–71) that they have followed Aeneas[2] over the sea from Troy and will continue to do so. His true destiny lies not in Crete but in the lands of Italy — *mutandae sedes* (161). Jupiter denies to Aeneas the Dictaean fields (171). To these words Aeneas reacts immediately:

> "talibus attonitus visis et voce deorum
> ...
> corripio e stratis corpus tendoque supinas
> ad caelum cum voce manus et munera libo
> intemerata focis. perfecto laetus honore
> Anchisen facio certum remque ordine pando."

> (172 and 176–9)

Aeneas piously lifts his hands and voice to the heavens and offers sacrifice at the hearths. *Intemerata* (178) indicates[3] that Aeneas is careful to ensure that the ritual is properly performed (*pietas*). He is joyful that the mystery of his destined land appears to be over. He quickly consults his father Anchises who realises the significance of the vision (182ff.).[4]

Their next journey too, from Crete to the Strophades, is told in the first person plural.[5] When they lay out food it is snatched by

---

[1] See Book 2, 293, 320, 717ff. and 747.

[2] The Penates imply great praise of Aeneas (156–9 and *passim*) especially in the destiny of his descendants and city.

[3] See Servius' note, ad 178.

[4] Thus again we see that Aeneas' own part in these events reflects his *pietas*.

[5] *paremus* 189, *deserimus* 190, *damus, currimus* 191, *iactamur* 197, *excutimur, erramus* 200, *erramus* 204, *insurgimus* 207, *intravimus* 219, *videmus* 220, *inruimus, vocamus* 222, *exstruimus, epulamur* 224, *instruimus, reponimus* 231. The use of the plural here is in keeping with the description of the earlier voyages, 5ff., 69ff. and 124ff.

the Harpies (225ff.). Aeneas orders his men to take arms against them:

> "sociis tunc arma capessant
> edico, et dira bellum cum gente gerendum."
>
> (234–5)

Aeneas' command underlines his paternal role and is his only involvement in the episode of Celaeno and the Harpies. The next mention of Aeneas himself refers to his visit to Actium:

> "postibus adversis figo et rem carmine signo:
> AENEAS HAEC DE DANAIS VICTORIBVS ARMA;
> linquere tum portus iubeo et considere transtris."   (287–9)

The episode has clear Augustan echoes.[1] Aeneas places the sign on the entrance portals (*postibus adversis* 287) of Apollo's temple and, in so doing, follows the correct procedure. His consecrated gift and his commands to the Trojans to leave Actium (289) serve to demonstrate clearly his *pietas*.

The pattern of the narrative continues as Aeneas describes the subsequent journey (to Buthrotum) in the first person plural.[2] Here in Epirus they learn that Helenus and Andromache have established nearby a new Troy (294ff.). Aeneas reflects upon this news as follows:

> "obstipui, miroque incensum pectus amore
> compellare virum et casus cognoscere tantos.
> progredior portu classis et litora linquens."
>
> (298–300)

Aeneas longs to address Helenus and find out what has happened to them: his *amor* to do so reflects his piety.[3] Thus here again the poet focuses on Aeneas for a moment in order to present and further underline this essential quality of his hero.

---

[1] See Williams (*Aen.* 1–6) ad 278f. and 280.

[2] *abscondimus* 291, *legimus*, *subimus* 292, *accedimus* 293.

[3] Williams (*Aen.* 3) ad loc. describes *miroque incensum pectus amore* (298) as 'a strong phrase suggesting the overwhelming longing of the exile to meet his old friend'.

Andromache is making offerings in a grove in front of their
new city when Aeneas sees her (302ff.). She is taken aback with
surprise, scarcely able to believe that he is flesh and blood
(310ff.), and asks him if he is truly alive; if he is not, where is
Hector (311ff.)? Aeneas responds to her as follows:

> "vix pauca furenti
> subicio et raris turbatus vocibus hisco:
> 'vivo equidem vitamque extrema per omnia duco;          315
> ne dubita, nam vera vides.
> heu! quis te casus deiectam coniuge tanto
> excipit, aut quae digna satis fortuna revisit,
> Hectoris Andromache? Pyrrhin conubia servas?'"
>
> (313–9)[1]

Aeneas answers with brevity: indeed he does live although
through all extremes. Yet, although he is clearly unhappy with
his lot, he thinks chiefly of others.[2] He pities the lot of
Andromache (*pietas*); what has happened to her, bereft of
husband, since the fall of Troy?

Andromache narrates (321ff.) the story of her fortunes — her
enforced marriage to Pyrrhus, his death at Orestes' hands and her
subsequent marriage to Helenus. She asks of Ascanius — does he
think of his missing mother and does he emulate the *virtus* of
Aeneas and Hector? Aeneas meets Helenus before proceeding to
the town:

> "procedo et parvam Troiam simulataque magnis
> Pergama et arentem Xanthi cognomine rivum
> agnosco, Scaeaeque amplector limina portae."
>
> (349–51)

---

[1] Knauer, indices ad 317f., cites *Il.* 6,462b f. as a parallel — Hector's premonition that
the lack of a man to protect her will bring pain and enslavement to Andromache. It is an
interesting parallel, for in Vergil's version she has in fact earlier become a slave as Hector
had feared.

[2] Cf. Aeneas' speech to Venus at 1,326ff. in which he gives a perfunctory reply to the
goddess in order to pay her due worship.

Aeneas is so moved at the sight of this *parva Troia*, this imitation of Pergamum and the small river by the name of Xanthus, that he embraces and kisses[1] the posts of the new Scaean gate. We need not labour the point that the personal reference to Aeneas himself underlines his *pietas*. It is a fundamental part of Aeneas' character that he is profoundly moved by anything that reminds him of home.[2]

The time comes, however, for Aeneas and his men to leave for Italy. The hero asks Helenus[3] to use his prophetic powers to tell him what the future holds:

> "his vatem adgredior dictis ac talia quaeso:
> 'Troiugena, interpres divum, qui numina Phoebi,
> qui tripodas Clarii et laurus, qui sidera sentis          360
> et volucrum linguas et praepetis omina pennae,
> fare age (namque omnis cursum mihi prospera dixit
> religio, et cuncti suaserunt numine divi
> Italiam petere et terras temptare repostas;
> sola novum dictuque nefas Harpyia Celaeno               365
> prodigium canit et tristis denuntiat iras
> obscenamque famem), quae prima pericula vito?
> quidve sequens tantos possim superare labores?'"

(358–68)

Aeneas appeals to Helenus whom he believes to be privy to Apollo's will and capable of reading the omens by 'astrology, and then augury from the cries or flights of birds'.[4] Aeneas has followed heaven's will and makes for Italy and he wishes to continue his voyage but the Harpy Celaeno has made a menacing

---

[1] Williams (*Aen.* 3) ad loc. compares *Aen.* 2, 490.

[2] Otis' point, 260f., is that Buthrotum is the parting of the ways; this is the old Troy which Aeneas must renounce.

[3] The prophetic Helenus is modelled on Homer's Circe. His long prophetic speech (374ff.) parallels that of Circe (*Od.* 12, 37ff.).

[4] So Williams (*Aen.* 1–6) ad 360–1.

prophecy[1] which appears to threaten their whole mission. In this speech he again demonstrates his desire to succeed in the foundation of his destined city (*pietas*). The divine signals had promised him prosperity but how is he to avoid *pericula* and overcome *labores*?[2]

Helenus cannot reply in full, for much is hidden by the fates (379f.), and Juno forbids him to say more. He nevertheless tells Aeneas of his journey to Italy (381–462): he will pass Circe's island and must avoid the near Italian coast which is inhabited by Greeks; they will skirt Sicily and pass by Scylla and Charybdis before reaching Cumae. They must give prayer to Juno; and also, on arrival at Cumae, must consult the Sibyl, priestess of Apollo. This is of particular importance and he must not begrudge time spent with her. The Sibyl will tell him of the obstacles, including wars in Italy, which must be overcome, and she will also grant to him prosperous passage.

As the Trojans prepare to leave, Helenus says farewell to Anchises, giving some final advice — to disembark on the western side of Italy. He tells him to 'go fortunate in the piety of your son' ('*vade' ait 'o felix nati pietate*' 480). This conveys indirectly the essential quality of the Trojan hero,[3] who at this point utters his final speech in his long narration:

> "vivite felices, quibus est fortuna peracta
> iam sua: nos alia ex aliis in fata vocamur.
> vobis parta quies: nullum maris aequor arandum,        495
> arva neque Ausoniae semper cedentia retro
> quaerenda. effigiem Xanthi Troiamque videtis
> quam vestrae fecere manus, melioribus, opto,

---

[1] See 247ff. and also 7, 107ff. On the inconsistencies and contradictions in Book 3, see Williams (*Aen.* 3) 19ff.

[2] Knauer, indices ad loc., cites no close Homeric parallel for this speech.

[3] Although, of course, it should be remembered that Aeneas himself is narrating the tale. As at 1, 378 he shows no reticence in referring to his own *pietas*.

auspiciis, et quae fuerit minus obvia Grais.
si quando Thybrim vicinaque Thybridis arva          500
intraro gentique meae data moenia cernam,
cognatas urbes olim populosque propinquos,
Epiro Hesperiam (quibus idem Dardanus auctor
atque idem casus), unam faciemus utramque
Troiam animis: maneat nostros ea cura nepotes."          505
(493–505)

That he speaks with deep emotion,[1] with tears welling in his
eyes, conveys the love of Aeneas for his Trojan friends (*pietas*). He
deeply regrets the wearisome voyage to which he and his men are
subjected but reiterates his preparedness to follow fate.[2] He
laments the fact that the fields of Italy seem always to be receding
from them. They desire to plough their own fields but instead
must plough the seas.[3] Aeneas shows pleasure at the better
fortune of Helenus, Andromache and their people, and hopes
that such prosperity will continue. When Aeneas has finally
founded his own city, they will be one in spirit.[4] His *pietas* is
seen in his devotion to the Trojan people and determination to
found his fated city. As in Book 1[5] his despondency results from
his failure to establish the fated home for his people.

The next journey, to Italy (Castrum Minervae) and Sicily, is
described largely from the viewpoint of all the Trojans in the first
person plural (506–688). In this section of the book there is one

[1] On Vergil's use of *adfari* (*adfabar* 492) to convey affection, see R.G. Austin, *Aeneidos Liber Sextus* (Oxford, 1977) ad 455, and discussion below, p. 129ff.

[2] Knauer, indices ad loc., compares *Od.* 13, 38–46 in which Odysseus bids farewell to Alcinous. The great difference in the episodes is the mood of the two heroes — Odysseus is content and hopes for a happy return home, whereas Aeneas is despondent that they must continue with their efforts to find a home. Odysseus shows gratitude to Alcinous and the Phaeacians, whereas Aeneas is envious of his friends' good fortune.

[3] Williams (*Aen.* 3) ad 495 compares Creusa's words at Troy: *longa tibi exsilia et vastum maris aequor arandum* 2, 780.

[4] Cf. Dido's sentiments at 4, 624ff. calling her nation and Aeneas' into war. Note that Aeneas' speech ends with *nepotes* (3, 505) and Dido's ends with *nepotesque* (4, 629).

[5] See above, p. 21ff.

autobiographical reference (537f.), in which Aeneas, on their arrival in Italy, sees an omen — four white horses grazing in a vale. Thus here again the poet focuses on a religious experience of his hero. Anchises takes the omen to mean that they face war in their new land (539ff.).[1] The Trojans' journey takes them to Castrum Minervae, to Etna, where they confront Polyphemus, and along the southern coast of Sicily to Drepanum. As they approach the joyless shore of Drepanum (707), however, the narrative technique changes when Aeneas suddenly describes the voyage from his point of view (*praetervehor* 688). The alteration in narrative style is significant for prior to this, as we have seen, Vergil has been consistent in describing the wanderings in the plural of the verb. Yet as the story comes to its conclusion, the poet focuses more clearly on Aeneas himself:

> "iussi numina magna loci veneramur, et inde
> exsupero praepingue solum stagnantis Helori."

(697–8)

Williams notes[2] that 'the singular *exsupero* after the plural *veneramur* is a little harsh'. It is evident that Vergil could easily have avoided such harshness if, as before, he had narrated the voyage from the viewpoint of all the Trojans. Moreover, it is apparent that this autobiographical reference, unlike those preceding it, does not reflect his *pietas*. Thus in this way too the narrative style is altered. This is true too of the description of the voyage from Lilybaeum to Drepanum:

> "teque datis linquo ventis, palmosa Selinus,
> et vada dura lego saxis Lilybeia caecis.
> hinc Drepani me portus et inlaetabilis ora
> accipit."

(705–8)

[1] Vergil evidently desires at this point to increase Anchises' dramatic importance: note his speeches at 528–9, 539–43 and 558–60. This foreshadows Anchises' death and makes Aeneas' later sense of loss (708ff.) ring more true.

[2] Williams (*Aen.* 3) ad 698.

The sudden change to the singular (*praetervehor* 688, *exsupero* 698, *linquo* 705, *lego* 706 and *me* 707) foreshadows the loss of Anchises, which is told at the end of the book (708–15), and also reintroduces Aeneas directly into the narrative prior to Dido's reaction to the long story (4,9ff.). The reader focuses clearly on the hero prior to the news of his father's death. Vergil's intention is to convey the full effect that the loss of Anchises has on Aeneas.[1] Similarly, Dido's attention at the end of the story is on Aeneas himself, a fact which foreshadows her deep response to him and his story at the outset of the following book. Vergil decisively makes the last reference in the story reflect a personal loss to Aeneas so that Dido in response will empathise and sympathise all the more with his particular misfortune. It is fitting that the final autobiographical references in the story (708ff.) underline the narrator's *pietas* — his great love for and dependence on his father. Moreover, the loss of Anchises comes as a complete shock to Aeneas (712ff.). Such filial *pietas* is also seen later, in Book 5, in which the poet describes the games held in Sicily in honour of Anchises.

Let us briefly reassert some of the points made in this section about the presentation of Aeneas in *Aen.* 3 compared with that of Odysseus in *Od.* 9, 10 and 12. To begin with we saw that Aeneas' dramatic role is considerably smaller than that of Odysseus. Whereas Aeneas utters approximately 12% of the direct speech in Book 3, his Homeric counterpart utters 27% of the speeches in the equivalent books. Statistical comparisons in critical works of this nature do not always make convincing reading, but the difference here in the dramatic roles of Aeneas and Odysseus is

---

[1] It is interesting to see how the translators of Vergil have coped with this intermingling of singular and plural at this late stage of the book. C. Day Lewis (London, 1952) 72 resolves any difficulty by translating the singular (*praetervehor* 688, *exsupero* 698, *linquo* 705 and *lego* 706) into the English plural. W. F. Jackson Knight (Penguin, 1979) 96 does the same at 688 and 698 but translates 705–6 into the singular. Their translations, therefore, do not capture clearly the alteration in Vergil's narrative technique at the end of the book.

significant. Moreover, as in Book 1, all of Aeneas' direct speeches in the third book underline his *pietas*.[1] In the first (85–9) he supplicates Apollo; in the second (315–9) he laments his own fortune and more especially shows an interest in and pity for the life of Hector's Andromache. In the third speech (359–68), conscious of his responsibilities to fulfil his mission, he appeals to Helenus to clarify their future; and in the fourth (493–505) he earnestly wishes good fortune for Helenus and his people and also shows his own determination to follow fate. It is here that the portrayal of Aeneas in Book 3 differs most from that Odysseus in *Od.* 9,10 and 12: in his dramatic role Aeneas is presented as a man utterly committed to his family and his people, and determined to lead them to their fated home. Odysseus, by contrast, in his dramatic role is shown to possess a wide variety of qualities not all of which stress his rectitude. Vergil does not attempt to create the same kind of hero, a three-dimensional figure, as Homer does.

Similarly, Vergil follows this kind of technique in the narrative of Book 3 by having Aeneas make far fewer autobiographical references than Odysseus.[2] Thus he is a less prominent figure in the wanderings than is Odysseus. Moreover, the autobiographical references, like the four direct speeches, almost without exception help to underline his *pietas*. Odysseus' autobiographical references do not conform to such a pattern and thus, in the narrative too, he appears a more natural, individual figure than does Aeneas.

[1] For Aeneas' speeches in Book 1, see above, p. 37ff. The same link between Aeneas' speeches and his *pietas* is to be found in all the books of the poem in which he appears, except Book 2 and Book 6, 268–901 (on which, see below, p. 120ff.).

[2] Odysseus on average makes twice as many autobiographical references as does Aeneas.

# BOOK 4

The renown of the encounter between Aeneas and Dido has tended to disguise the fact that the hero's dramatic role in Book 4 is comparatively small.[1] Aeneas utters only 2 direct speeches totalling 35 lines, whereas Dido utters 9 speeches, 189 lines — more than a quarter of the book. From beginning[2] to end Vergil focuses most clearly on the tragic queen. The first section (1–295) describes Dido's growing passion for Aeneas which culminates in a 'marriage' contrived by Venus and Juno. Aeneas' role in this section is as the object of Dido's love. Vergil, notably, denies his hero an active, dramatic role in the book until his *pietas* has been regained and a decision made to continue the voyage to Italy. Throughout his romance with Dido and during his dilemma of how to tell her of his impending departure Aeneas is characterised in the narrative by Vergil's indirect methods. Thus Book 4 conforms to the pattern which we saw in Books 1 and 3: Aeneas is characterised directly in his moments of piety, and indirectly when his thoughts or conduct do not conform to this ideal.

The hero and the story of his adventures (Books 2 and 3) have a compelling effect on Dido (1ff.), who has been infected already by Cupid's darts (1,657ff.). Aeneas is the unwitting (*nescius* 72) catalyst of a love which proves disastrous to Dido.[3] Juno recognises Venus' victory in the infecting of Dido, but still hopes to outmanoeuvre her divine rival (93ff.). Events are arranged so that Aeneas and Dido, whilst on a hunting expedition, will shelter from a storm alone in the same cave. As he leaves for the hunt

[1] Although see K. Quinn, *Latin Explorations* (London, 1963) 29 and my discussion above, p. 11ff.
[2] The book begins *At regina* (1), thus foreshadowing Dido's important role. Cf. 12, 1 (*Turnus ut infractos adverso Marte Latinos*) which foreshadows the Rutulian's important role in the last book of the poem.
[3] For the implications of the hunting simile at 4, 69ff., see Pöschl, 80ff. and Otis, 72ff.

Aeneas is described as follows:

> ipse ante alios pulcherrimus omnis
> infert se socium Aeneas atque agmina iungit.
> qualis ubi hibernam Lyciam Xanthique fluenta
> deserit ac Delum maternam invisit Apollo
> instauratque choros, mixtique altaria circum                    145
> Cretesque Dryopesque fremunt pictique Agathyrsi:
> ipse iugis Cynthi graditur mollique fluentem
> fronde premit crinem fingens atque implicat auro,
> tela sonant umeris: haud illo segnior ibat
> Aeneas, tantum egregio decus enitet ore.                        150
>                                                          (141–150)[1]

We see Aeneas here through Dido's eyes just as we saw her for
the first time through his eyes (1,494ff.). In that case Dido was
likened to the beautiful and graceful Diana (1,498ff.). She was
described as *pulcherrima* (1,496) whereas Aeneas here is *pulcherrimus* (4,141). Dido is, in both episodes, followed by a vast throng
(*magna iuvenum stipante caterva* 1,497 and *magna stipante caterva*
4,136). Diana bears the *pharetra* at 1,500 as does Dido at
4,138.[2] It is clear that the picture of Dido at 4,136ff. reinforces
that of Dido/Diana at 1,494ff. and also balances the picture of
Aeneas/Apollo at 4,141ff. The beauty and grace of Aeneas as
Apollo, the sun-figure, correspond to that of Dido as Diana, the
moon.[3] Outwardly, all seems right that they be a perfect match.

In the midst of the hunting a storm breaks and the couple alone
enter into a cave for shelter. The 'marriage' of Dido and Aeneas is
described symbolically by Vergil (166–8). Although there has
been, from Book 1, inexorable movement towards such an act

---

[1] There is no close Homeric model for this picture of Aeneas, although it does resemble
that of Jason in the *Argonautica* (1,307–10), who is compared as he leaves his house to
Apollo about to set out for places sacred to him. Vergil's simile is more elaborate, paying
attention to the beauty and grace of Aeneas.

[2] Cf. Venus' reference to the *pharetra* at 1,323 and Pöschl's discussion, 68.

[3] Pöschl, 60ff. has a detailed discussion on this subject.

the poet does not elaborate on this scene but concentrates immediately on the consequences that will result (169–72). Dark
consequences take no time in appearing. *Fama* spreads the news
of Dido's *culpa* throughout Libya (173ff.).[1] King Iarbas hears the
story of their romance and, resentful and jealous, prays to Jupiter
(206ff.) complaining of the treatment he has received at Dido's
hands. Jupiter hears the king and sends Mercury to shake Aeneas
from his lethargy: his mother did not promise him for this, but so
that he would found the race from Teucer's blood and put the
whole world under laws (223–37). Jupiter reminds him of his
duty to heaven, to himself, to Ascanius and to his people. His
destiny lies in Italy, not in Africa. As in the case of Venus' intervention in Book 2 (594ff.) Jupiter's intention is to redirect the energies of Aeneas to the fated course.[2] The morality of Aeneas' relationship with Dido does not concern Jupiter any more than the
morality of killing Helen concerned Venus: he must follow fate
and not delay in Carthage. As commanded, Mercury journeys to
Carthage and reports to Aeneas the sentiments of Jupiter
(265–76). For the first time in the book the poet presents the sentiments of his hero:

> at vero Aeneas aspectu obmutuit amens,
> arrectaeque horrore comae et vox faucibus haesit.          280
> ardet abire fuga dulcisque relinquere terras,
> attonitus tanto monitu imperioque deorum.
> heu quid agat? quo nunc reginam ambire furentem
> audeat adfatu? quae prima exordia sumat?
> atque animum nunc huc celerem nunc dividit illuc          285
> in partisque rapit varias perque omnia versat.

[1] On the *dea foeda* (195) *Fama*, see N. Rudd, *Lines of Enquiry* (Cambridge, 1976) 36f.
Rudd's section entitled 'Dido's *Culpa*' (32–53) is the best to date on the subject of Dido's
role in the poem.

[2] Aeneas, as a result of his relationship with Dido, now spends his time dressed in Tyrian attire helping to build Carthage rather than his own fated city (259ff.).

haec alternanti potior sententia visa est:
Mnesthea Sergestumque vocat fortemque Serestum,
classem aptent taciti sociosque ad litora cogant,
arma parent et quae rebus sit causa novandis                    290
dissimulent; sese interea, quando optima Dido
nesciat et tantos rumpi non speret amores,
temptaturum aditus et quae mollissima fandi
tempora, quis rebus dexter modus. ocius omnes
imperio laeti parent et iussa facessunt.                        295
(279–95)

In the face of such *mandata* Aeneas burns to leave lands which
have become dear to him (281), yet he must prepare to do so in
such a way that *optima Dido* remains unaware (291ff.). Aeneas'
stunned response to the sudden appearance of Mercury is conveyed by the repetition of *a* at 279–85.[1] It is significant that in
response to Mercury's injunction Aeneas decides immediately
and firmly to leave Carthage; his dilemma is how to do so and how
to break the news of his imminent departure to Dido. Notably,
the poet presents this dilemma indirectly by using free indirect
speech (283ff.) rather than the direct. Thus the reader's involvement in the dilemma of Aeneas is with Vergil, the narrator,
rather than with the character himself. The poet removes Aeneas
in this moment of doubt from the dramatic limelight. Vergil's
technique and intention here can best be seen in a broader
context:

1. *Aeneas*:
heu *quid agat*? quo nunc reginam ambire furentem
audeat adfatu? quae prima exordia sumat?
atque animum nunc huc celerem nunc dividit illuc
in partisque rapit varias perque omnia versat.

(4,283–6)

---

[1] Williams, ad loc.

2. *Aeneas*:
heu, *quid agat?* vario nequiquam fluctuat aestu,
diversaeque vocant animum in contraria curae.

(12, 486–7)

3. *Dido*:
"en, *quid ago?* rursusne procos inrisa priores
experiar, Nomadumque petam conubia supplex?"

(4, 534–5)

4. *Turnus*:
                    "gemitumque cadentum
accipio? *quid ago?* aut quae iam satis ima dehiscat
terra mihi?"                                (10, 674–6)

5. *Turnus*:
"nam *quid ago?* aut quae iam spondet Fortuna salutem?"

(12, 637)

The dilemma of Dido (4, 534f.), like that of Turnus
(12, 637), is a tragic one: what are they going to do in situations
of some desperation? At 10, 674ff. Turnus, who has been tricked
into following a phantom Aeneas and thus leaving his men alone
on the battlefield, realises the full extent and implications of his
'desertion'. The important point is that the dilemmas of Dido
and Turnus here are presented by the direct method of characterisation; they utter their own cries of lamentation. The presentation of them at these moments is vivid and dramatic; the reader
focuses clearly on them and is prompted to react directly and
sympathetically. Vergil establishes a clear rapport between
reader and character. The narrator plays no direct role in these
dilemmas of Dido and Turnus.

Aeneas' dilemmas of how to break the news to Dido of his
imminent departure (4, 283ff.) and how to catch Turnus on the
battlefield (12, 486f.)[1] are conveyed by means of the indirect deli-
berative. The narrator asks the questions whilst Aeneas himself
acts out the dilemmas. Thus the reader's direct involvement

[1] On Aeneas' pursuit of Turnus on the battlefield, see below, p. 199f.

in these dilemmas is with the narrator rather than with the character. Unlike the cases of Dido and Turnus, Aeneas is placed in the dramatic background. The reader is left in some doubt about Aeneas' exact response to the sudden appearance of Mercury.[1] Do these questions (283f.) report Aeneas' own words or thoughts? Does he think of the lands of Carthage as *dulcis* (281) and of Dido herself as *optima* (291)? Vergil's implication is that these do reflect the thoughts of Aeneas himself. If this is the case, it is all the more significant that the poet does not allow us to hear these words from Aeneas himself.

There are basically two reasons for Vergil's indirect presentation of the dilemma of Aeneas (279ff.). In the first place the poet wishes to give dramatic emphasis in Book 4 to the tragic predicament of the suffering Dido. To stress with equal vividness the dilemma of Aeneas might detract from the reader's empathy and sympathy for the tragic queen. Vergil does not desire that the reader's sympathy be shared between the two characters: the vast imbalance in their dramatic roles is intended to focus our attention and sympathy on the decline and death of the queen. The second reason for presenting the dilemma indirectly is that the poet here, as throughout the poem, seeks to project Aeneas into the dramatic limelight only at moments where his *pietas* cannot be questioned.[2] The hero's dilemma is one of personal

[1] Contrast the view of Otis, 83: 'These (281ff.) are *Aeneas'* thoughts and sensations: we now stand as it were in his own quivering shoes and see how he is, finally, forced to act. The initiative has at last passed to him'. See also K. Quinn, *Latin Explorations* 40, who argues that 'when Aeneas tells his men the reasons for departure, we are not given his actual speech, but a reported summary (289–94). Again Virgil's purpose is not only to speed the narrative, but to reduce to a minimum the evidence put on record against Aeneas'.

[2] The best single example of this technique at work is at 5,700ff., Aeneas' reaction to the burning of the ships; see above, p. 11ff. and below, p. 109ff.

relations with a woman[1] — how is he, himself in love,[2] to approach the queen who is *furens* with *amor* (283)? His quandary does not exemplify his *pietas* and therefore Vergil presents it indirectly. It is for this reason that Aeneas utters no direct speech until almost half of the book has elapsed — because all the while, neglectful as he is of his duty to follow fate, he is in a state of *impietas*. Vergil could easily have expressed Aeneas' predicament directly as he does in the cases of Dido and Turnus; but rather than do so, he retains his own pattern by making the hero's *pietas* the essential criterion for the allocation of a direct speech.

As we have seen Vergil shows no such reticence in the case of Dido in Book 4. In the final 400 lines of the book she utters 8 speeches totalling 168 lines. The first two of these are addressed to Aeneas (305–30 and 365–87). In the first of these she confronts him on his plan to leave Carthage and addresses him as *perfide* (305). It is a deeply emotional speech; she quickly realises that he is fleeing from *her* (*mene fugis?* 314) and pleads *per conubia nostra, per inceptos hymenaeos* (316) for him not to do so. She relates her vulnerability to external forces if he leaves (320ff.). He is once more merely *hospes* when before he was *coniunx* (323f.). All would be worthwhile at least if she had borne a *parvulus* Aeneas (328f.).[3] The speech reflects her regal responsibility and her womanly aspirations — all about to crumble if Aeneas departs. On Vergil's part it is a sympathetic observation of the feminine psyche. Aeneas responds to her as follows:

---

[1] We might compare the way that Vergil avoids presenting a clear response by Aeneas to the beauty and grace of Dido at 1,494–509; see above, p. 37ff.

[2] For the love of Aeneas for Dido, see 221, 332, 395 and 448. I am unconvinced by the argument of S. Farron, 'The Aeneas-Dido Episode as an attack on Aeneas' mission and Rome', *G. &R.* 27 (1980) 34ff., who suggests that Aeneas has no regrets in leaving Dido because he feels scarcely any love for her. He argues (35): 'There is no indication of his (Aeneas') love in the first half of book 4'; but 221 would seem to be specific on this point.

[3] On Dido's longing for a child and heir, see Rudd's discussion, 47f.

               ille Iovis monitis immota tenebat
lumina et obnixus curam sub corde premebat.
tandem pauca refert: "ego te, quae plurima fando
enumerare vales, numquam, regina, negabo
promeritam, nec me meminisse pigebit Elissae       335
dum memor ipse mei, dum spiritus hos regit artus.
pro re pauca loquar. neque ego hanc abscondere furto
speravi (ne finge) fugam, nec coniugis umquam
praetendi taedas aut haec in foedera veni.
me si fata meis paterentur ducere vitam       340
auspiciis et sponte mea componere curas,
urbem Troianam primum dulcisque meorum
reliquias colerem, Priami tecta alta manerent,
et recidiva manu posuissem Pergama victis.
sed nunc Italiam magnam Gryneus Apollo,       345
Italiam Lyciae iussere capessere sortes;
hic amor, haec patria est. si te Karthaginis arces
Phoenissam Libycaeque aspectus detinet urbis,
quae tandem Ausonia Teucros considere terra
invidia est? et nos fas extera quaerere regna.       350
me patris Anchisae, quotiens umentibus umbris
nox operit terras, quotiens astra ignea surgunt,
admonet in somnis et turbida terret imago;
me puer Ascanius capitisque iniuria cari,
quem regno Hesperiae fraudo et fatalibus arvis.       355
nunc etiam interpres divum Iove missus ab ipso
(testor utrumque caput) celeris mandata per auras
detulit: ipse deum manifesto in lumine vidi
intrantem muros vocemque his auribus hausi.
desine meque tuis incendere teque querelis;       360
Italiam non sponte sequor."       (331–61)

The closest Homeric parallel[1] is Odysseus' address to Calypso as
he prepares to depart from her island:

---

[1] Knauer, indices ad loc.

τὴν δ᾽ ἀπαμειβόμενος προσέφη πολύμητις Ὀδυσσεύς·
"πότνα θεά, μή μοι τόδε χώεο· οἶδα καὶ αὐτὸς                          215
πάντα μάλ᾽, οὕνεκα σεῖο περίφρων Πηνελόπεια
εἶδος ἀκιδνοτέρη μέγεθός τ᾽ εἰσάντα ἰδέσθαι·
ἡ μὲν γὰρ βροτός ἐστι, σὺ δ᾽ ἀθάνατος καὶ ἀγήρως.
ἀλλὰ καὶ ὣς ἐθέλω καὶ ἐέλδομαι ἤματα πάντα
οἴκαδέ τ᾽ ἐλθέμεναι καὶ νόστιμον ἦμαρ ἰδέσθαι.                        220
εἰ δ᾽ αὖ τις ῥαίῃσι θεῶν ἐνὶ οἴνοπι πόντῳ,
τλήσομαι ἐν στήθεσσιν ἔχων ταλαπενθέα θυμόν·
ἤδη γὰρ μάλα πολλὰ πάθον καὶ πολλὰ μόγησα
κύμασι καὶ πολέμῳ· μετὰ καὶ τόδε τοῖσι γενέσθω."
                                                      (Od. 5, 214–24)

Odysseus is not torn by an obligation or desire to remain with
Calypso.[1] His aim is a simple one — to return home (219f.); and
even the beauty of Calypso cannot deflect him from this. The
goddess has kept him on her island against his will and the hero
has, for the most part, been unhappy away from his home.[2] Zeus'
decision to have Odysseus freed is therefore transmitted to
Calypso, whereas in the fourth *Aeneid* the will of Jupiter is told
via Mercury to the hero himself.[3] Aeneas, unlike Odysseus, has a
conflict of desires, for he has 'imprisoned' himself by his affair
with Dido. His problem is not the achievement of freedom in the
physical sense, but how to approach Dido with an explanation for
his imminent departure (279ff.). Thus, keeping his mind fixed
on the injunctions of Jupiter (331f.), he tells her that he is not
ungrateful for her generosity, nor does he in any way resent her;
he will always remember her, but he never entered into a
marriage (338f.).[4] Furthermore, if circumstances allowed, he

[1] Highet, who discusses Aeneas' speech to Dido in some detail (72ff.), also draws some comparisons with the Homeric parallel.

[2] See, for example, *Od.* 1, 11ff.

[3] Part of Dido's tragedy is her lack of understanding of what is happening around her. She, unlike Aeneas, is not privy to the words of Mercury or to the workings of fate. When these are told to her by Aeneas (345ff.) she reacts with sarcastic disbelief (376ff.).

[4] On the *'coniugium'* and Dido's breaking of her vow to Sychaeus, see Rudd, 39ff.

would return to Troy (342f.).[1] But as it is, the fates lead him to Italy — here lie his love and his country (*hic amor, haec patria est* 347). Why does Dido who has a city begrudge him his (347ff.)? He leaves because the *imago* of his father warns and terrifies him in dreams (351ff.), as does Jove's messenger (356ff.). So too the thought seriously concerns him of wronging Ascanius by not moving to fated lands in Italy (354f.). He is determined to follow fate and tells Dido tersely not to make complaints (360), for he makes for Italy *non sponte* (361).

The fact that Aeneas' speech forcefully presents his *pietas* — his commitment to following fate, his love for his Trojan land, as well as for his son and father's spirit — did not concern generations of scholars who were virulent in their criticism of the hero in this episode. The criticism of Page[2] is probably the best known: 'To an appeal which would move a stone Aeneas replies with the cold and formal rhetoric of an attorney'. Largely in response to this kind of criticism, R.G. Austin, in his major work on Book 4,[3] stressed the personal cost to Aeneas as well as to Dido of his departure for Italy. In pointing out the narrative references to Aeneas' love for Dido, Austin takes his argument one stage further — that, in his decision to leave Carthage, Aeneas is not a free agent but is compelled into doing so by the gods.[4] Moreover, in a later reference to this episode,[5] Austin argues that Aeneas is actually unwilling to leave Carthage at all. Did Austin take his argument too far? Is Aeneas a free agent or is he a puppet of the gods? Does he leave Carthage willingly or

---

[1] One might have expected Aeneas in the apodosis (342ff.) to have told Dido that he would choose to remain at Carthage; but it is, in fact, his third 'choice' after Troy and Italy. *Sponte* (341) should be aligned with *sponte* (361): in the latter he suggests that it is not his idea that he makes for Italy. He means (as at 340ff.) that were it possible he would return to Troy. All of this, of course, is little comfort to Dido.

[2] Page, XVIII.

[3] R.G. Austin, *Aeneidos Liber Quartus* (Oxford, 1955) XIVff. and *passim*.

[4] *Ibid.*, ad 331.

[5] R.G. Austin, *Aeneidos Liber Sextus* (Oxford, 1977) ad 460.

unwillingly? It is to these questions that we must now briefly direct our attention.

In the underworld Aeneas tells Dido that he was unwilling to leave from her shores — *invitus, regina, tuo de litore cessi* (6,460). This is often equated in its sense with Aeneas' statement to Dido in Carthage — *Italiam non sponte sequor* (4,361), which is commonly rendered 'I go to Italy not of my own free will'.[1] It is a mistake, however, to equate the two. First, as we shall see, Aeneas' words and experiences in the underworld are an inaccurate reflection of events as they happened in the real world. It is, therefore, a dangerous practice to use Aeneas' words to the shade of Dido in the underworld to convey the sense of his words to her in Carthage. Moreover, given that Aeneas spends the most part of his speech (4,333ff.) explaining to Dido the reasons why he has *chosen* to press on to Italy, it seems implausible that the last line of the speech conveys his unwillingness to leave. In fact, Carthage, as he himself tells her, is his third 'choice', Troy and Italy being the first two (340ff.).[2] Aeneas' difficulty is in trying to explain to Dido that his love and his country lie elsewhere (*hic amor, haec patria est* 347)[3] and at the same time to convey the fact that his decision to leave Carthage was taken with much more in mind than his own pleasure or love. When he hears Jupiter's admonition to leave Carthage, Aeneas is characterised not by his fear, but by his burning desire to leave:

---

[1] Williams, ad loc.; see too Austin, ad loc.

[2] See above, p.86 n.1.

[3] I cannot agree with Austin who comments on 347: 'but this is not his real feeling, as 361 shows — it is only what his "nagging gods" have made him feel'. As Aeneas himself points out, his real love is for his Trojan homeland (342ff.). But having heard Mercury's admonition he is reminded that his real love now is Italy and a new land rather than Dido and Carthage: *ardet abire fuga dulcisque relinquere terras* (281). His words at 347 suggest that he has a deeper love in Italy, fulfilling the god's will and founding a fated city for his people, than he has for Dido.

> ardet abire fuga dulcisque relinquere terras,
> attonitus tanto monitu imperioque deorum.
>
> (281–2)

It is this desire[1] to follow fate and the gods' wishes, in spite of personal loss to himself and to Dido, that characterises the *pietas* of the hero. Thus Vergil is able to describe him as *pius* at 393 because he remains firm in his decision to leave Carthage even though the queen is utterly distraught before his eyes. Aeneas' free will to choose his own course is fundamental both to his piety and his impiety; were he to choose Carthage he would be *impius*, but in choosing Italy he is *pius*. W.A. Camps is one of the few critics to make this point: 'Aeneas could have disregarded the bidding to leave his own country and sail into the unknown; his own wish, as he tells Dido, was to stay in the homeland that he knew. He could have stayed at Carthage with Dido and shared the city that she had founded'.[2] But Aeneas' sense of his own destiny — his *pietas* — allows no such possibility. Once he is reminded of heaven's will the matter is closed.[3] The fundamental point is that it is impossible for Aeneas to follow fate against his will and be in a state of *pietas* at the same time. The call to continue his mission brings great regret to Aeneas at Carthage,[4] but there is no case for questioning his willingness to follow it. Thus at 361 Aeneas attempts to convey the fact that he pursues a greater purpose — *Italiam non sponte sequor* (361), 'it's not my idea that I make for Italy'. The difference in this translation from that of Williams and Austin is small, but it is

---

[1] For the use of *ardeo* to convey Aeneas' *pietas*, cf. 1, 515 and 581.

[2] Camps, 23.

[3] On this, see G. Williams, 11ff.

[4] As leaving Troy also brings great regret; but no one would argue that, once sure that his fate lies elsewhere, Aeneas is unwilling to leave his beloved homeland. See too 8, 133 and below, p. 152 n. 4.

nevertheless a significant one for the understanding of Aeneas'
motivation in leaving Carthage.[1]

Dido reacts with anger to his speech, addressing him (365–87)
as *perfide* (366) and sarcastically questioning his whole ancestry.
Love has now turned to hate and she speaks of Aeneas in the third
person (369ff.). She stresses that Aeneas must surely be punished
by the gods who watch over such actions (371f.). She treats with
contempt his reasons for departing from Carthage and recalls her
own gestures of generosity towards the Trojans (373ff.). The
shadow of Dido will follow him even after death (384ff.). Having
fainted with anguish she is then helped by her maids to her room.
Vergil continues as follows:

> at pius Aeneas, quamquam lenire dolentem
> solando cupit et dictis avertere curas,
> multa gemens magnoque animum labefactus amore
> iussa tamen divum exsequitur classemque revisit.

>                                                              (393–6)

We have seen that Aeneas regains his piety in his decision to
follow the fates rather than to remain at Carthage with Dido. The
precise meaning of *pius* here has long been the subject of debate.
Page[2] could scarcely believe that the man who wrote the speech
of Dido (365ff.) could describe Aeneas immediately afterwards as
'the good' (*pius* 393). He describes it as 'one of the puzzles of
literature'. The difficulty which Page had with this passage arose
partly from his rendering of *pius* as 'good'. Any connection in the
poem between *pietas* and goodness, in its full moral sense, is
purely coincidental. Yet the reaction of Page and many of his
contemporaries was not, it seems, altogether unintended by Vergil. For by describing Aeneas as *pius* at a moment when his
actions cause great anguish to the queen, with whom we have

[1] The question of Aeneas' unwillingness to leave Carthage and his statement to that effect (6, 460) are further discussed below, p. 128ff.

[2] Page, XVIII f.

much sympathy, the poet forces the reader to focus on the exact meaning and implications of *pietas*. It is almost as if Vergil sets out to shock the reader. It is a technique which he uses again; in Book 10,510ff.[1] we observe the hero at his most savage, killing without mercy many Italians, some of whom had begged for their lives. Aeneas is shown in a fit of fury almost unequalled in its ferocity anywhere in the poem. Despite these actions he is described as *pius* (10,591) in between his slaying of the two brothers Lucagus and Liger, the latter of whom pleads for mercy (597ff.). Many scholars in more recent times have shown the same amazement at Vergil's use of *pius* at 10,591 as Page did at 4,393.[2] In each case the poet juxtaposes Aeneas' *pietas* and the human suffering which results from it. By describing Aeneas as *pius* as Dido is helped away by her *famulae* (4,391ff.) and as the moribund Lucagus tumbles from his chariot (10,590), Vergil forces us to question the precise meaning of *pietas* against a background of death and despair. Moreover, in each case, Aeneas, for all his piety, is depicted as a most unlikeable figure.

Whereas Aeneas' actions in both episodes have dire human consequences for non-Trojans, in each case the hero acts with the blessing of Jupiter/*Fata* and thus helps his own people to establish their fated city. Despite attempts to show otherwise,[3] in neither case can the piety of the hero be called into question, for *pius* is used specifically both times to show that Aeneas furthers

[1] For a full discussion of Aeneas' *aristeia* in Book 10, 510ff., see below, p. 165ff.

[2] See, for example, Williams, ad 10,510f. and 591. Austin, ad 4,393, seems to feel distinct unease about Vergil's use of *pius* at 10,591. Neither commentator mentions that *pius* in both cases signifies that Aeneas, by his behaviour, furthers the progress of fate.

[3] W.R. Johnson, *C.J.* 60 (1965) 359ff., argues that *pius* in the poem has the meaning of 'compassionate' and thus Vergil uses it with strong irony. This is clearly not the case at 4,393ff., for *pius* belongs to the main clause signifying his decision to follow the *iussa divum* (396). His desire to lessen Dido's agony (393f.) results from his *amor* (395); it is precisely because of his *pietas* that he cannot even attempt to ease her suffering. Contrast Austin, ad 394. It is significant that in the underworld (6,467) Aeneas actually makes the attempt to lessen her grief, for no *pietas* restrains him there; see below, p. 128ff.

the progress of fate. Yet there seems little doubt that, by placing
the epithet at such significant points in the narrative, Vergil
makes us focus more clearly on the cost to others of Aeneas' *pietas*
than on the benefits that will accrue to his own people.

All of Dido's pleas to Aeneas fall on deaf ears. She approaches
Anna (416ff.) in the hope that she may be able to convince Aeneas
at least to delay his departure. The narrative continues as follows:

> talibus orabat, talisque miserrima fletus
> fertque refertque soror. sed nullis ille movetur
> fletibus aut voces ullas tractabilis audit;
> fata obstant placidasque viri deus obstruit auris.            440
> ac velut annoso validam cum robore quercum
> Alpini Boreae nunc hinc nunc flatibus illinc
> eruere inter se certant; it stridor, et altae
> consternunt terram concusso stipite frondes;
> ipsa haeret scopulis et quantum vertice ad auras             445
> aetherias, tantum radice in Tartara tendit:
> haud secus adsiduis hinc atque hinc vocibus heros
> tunditur, et magno persentit pectore curas;
> mens immota manet, lacrimae volvuntur inanes.

(437–49)

Anna attempts repeatedly to persuade Aeneas to postpone his
departure, but he is like a strong oak[1] that not even Alpine
winds can shift. Fate stands in the way and a god seals his ears
(440).[2] Yet despite his strong resolve to depart for Italy Aeneas
feels anguish in his heart (448), as he did after trying to explain to
the queen the reasons for his planned departure (393ff.). For all
Aeneas' concern, however, his mind remains unmoved and the

---

[1] It is part of the reversal of their roles in the underworld that Dido (6, 470f.) is pictured
as like hard flint or Parian rock in response to the pleas of Aeneas.

[2] This may seem like a superfluous gesture (cf. 1, 297ff.) as there is no indication that
Aeneas' resolve is weakening; but heaven is taking no chances.

tears fall in vain (449).[1] Again we see that, having heard the
god's words, Aeneas is determined to leave (*pietas*) and that no
further delay is possible.

In the remainder of the book (450–705) the poet focuses
clearly on the disintegration and death of Dido. In contrast to the
insomnious Dido, who is tormented by love-agonies (522ff.),
Aeneas sleeps peacefully in the knowledge that he is soon to leave
Carthage (554f.). Despite this resolve a vision appears before
him in his sleep (556ff.), who resembles the god Mercury. The
vision tells Aeneas (560–70) to leave forthwith, for Dido is wild
with fury and might bring harm to him and his men.[2] The hero
reacts as follows:

> tum vero Aeneas subitis exterritus umbris
> corripit e somno corpus sociosque fatigat
> praecipitis: "vigilate, viri, et considite transtris;
> solvite vela citi. deus aethere missus ab alto
> festinare fugam tortosque incidere funis          575
> ecce iterum instimulat. sequimur te, sancte deorum,
> quisquis es, imperioque iterum paremus ovantes.

[1] There has been much debate as to who sheds these tears — Dido, Aeneas or even
Anna. I see no reason to question the conclusions of A. Hudson-Williams, '*Lacrimae Illae
Inanes*', *G.&R.* 25 (1978) 16ff., who gives a full discussion and bibliography of the debate, and attributes the tears to Dido. To his argument I add one small point: Aeneas
could certainly be described at times as a lachrymose figure in the first three books of the
poem (see 1,459, 465, 470; 2,279, 790; 3,492), yet in each case they are tears which help
to convey his *pietas* — his great love of his Trojan friends and relatives, many of whom are
now dead. The significance of his tears in Book 6 (455, 468 and 476) is not only that they
signal a reversal of his failure to weep whilst at Carthage, but also that they do not help to
convey his *pietas* (see below, p. 129f.).

[2] On the significance of Mercury's reference to Dido as *certa mori* (564), see below, p. 95,
n. 4 and p. 130f.

adsis o placidusque iuves et sidera caelo
dextra feras." dixit vaginaque eripit ensem
fulmineum strictoque ferit retinacula ferro.                    580
                                                           (571–80)

Aeneas, who is this time scared (*exterritus* 571) by the supernatural appearance, tears himself from sleep and rouses his
fellows (571f.). He follows the god's injunctions by ordering his
men to set sail with haste (573ff.). At the same time he prays to
the god stating that again they obey with joy (*ovantes* 577) the
divine *imperium* (576f.).[1] He also prays for the presence and
assistance of the god during their voyage (578f.). Having said
this he puts words into action by drawing his sword and cutting
the cable (579f.), thus sending them on towards their fated land
(581ff.).

[1] We again see here Aeneas' burning desire to follow the injunctions of heaven (*pietas*) as
we did in his first response to Mercury at 279ff.; note Aeneas' use of *iterum* at 577.

# BOOK 5

In Book 5 the Trojans return to Sicily where they celebrate games to honour Anchises, who died at Drepanum one year beforehand. The book is modelled largely on Book 23 of the *Iliad* in which the Greeks hold games[1] in honour of Patroclus, who had been killed by Hector shortly beforehand. The roles of Achilles (*Il.*) and Aeneas (*Aen.*) as conveners of the games have distinct similarities, but their states of mind are notably different. Achilles is both angry and grief-stricken at the recent loss of Patroclus and realises (23,80ff. and 144ff.) that he too is now destined to fall in the war against the Trojans. Aeneas' period of mourning has passed[2] and he is seen as neither grief-stricken nor angry, but rather shows love and loyalty to the memory of his father (*pietas*).

In his personal involvement in and sense of loss at Patroclus' death Achilles is set apart from the other heroes. Yet even though he does not compete in the games, Achilles is the protagonist of Book 23. We understand that were he to take part he would prevail over the other competitors.[3] Those who do take part are of great and heroic stature — Ajax, Odysseus, Menelaus, Antilochus and Diomedes all compete in the presence of Nestor, Idomeneus, Agamemnon and Achilles, as well as the Greek host. We have no doubts as to the greatness of these competitors whose physical attributes have been stressed throughout the poem. This cannot be said of Vergil's competitors; their greatness is assumed

[1] Homer describes eight different games whereas Vergil describes only four prior to the *Lusus Troiae*. On the games in Vergil and Homer see Heinze, 140–66; H.W. Prescott, *The Development of Vergil's Art* (New York, 1963) 206ff.; W.H. Willis, 'Athletic Contests in the Epic', *T.A.Ph.A.* 72 (1941) 392ff.; E. Mehl, 'Die Leichenspiele in der Äneis als turngeschichtliche Quelle', *R.E.* 8A 2 (1958) 1487–93; Otis, 41ff.; and H.A. Harris, 'The Games in *Aeneid* V', *P.V.S.* 8 (1968–9) 14ff.

[2] See 3,707ff. and above, p. 74f.

[3] See *Il.* 23,274ff.; Highet's point (200) is that this is 'a remark inconceivable for Aeneas'.

by the poet. Most of them have only a small role outside of Book 5;[1] they are shadowy figures created for the purpose of the games, who never attain the reality of their Homeric counterparts. Aeneas, by contrast, has a significant dramatic role in the book uttering 12 direct speeches — 73 lines. Only in Book 6 is his dramatic role greater (12 speeches, 88 lines).

It is to foreshadow Aeneas' important role in Book 5 that Vergil names his hero in the first line.[2] He is pictured holding steadfastly (*certus* 2)[3] to his course and looking back with puzzlement at the flames in Dido's Carthage (1–7).[4] Aeneas' first speech is in response to an appeal from the helmsman Palinurus, who wishes to change direction (17ff.) as a result of the inclement weather:

> tum pius Aeneas: "equidem sic poscere ventos
> iamdudum et frustra cerno te tendere contra.
> flecte viam velis. an sit mihi gratior ulla,
> quove magis fessas optem dimittere navis,
> quam quae Dardanium tellus mihi servat Acesten          30
> et patris Anchisae gremio complectitur ossa?"
>
> (26–31)

Aeneas agrees with his helmsman's suggestion and tells him accordingly to change direction.[5] They will visit the land of Acestes where his father had died one year before. *Pius*, notes

[1] On this see A. Bellessort, *Virgile: son oeuvre et son temps* (Paris, 1920) 166, and J. Glazewski, 'The Function of Vergil's Funeral Games', *C.W.* 66 (1972–3) 92, who both point out that Vergil introduces these minor characters in Book 5 prior to their roles later in the poem. Mnestheus (4, 288), Sergestus (1, 510; 4, 288), Cloanthus (1, 222), and Acestes (1, 195) have been mentioned in passing in earlier books.

[2] Cf. 4, 1 *At regina* and 12, 1 *Turnus ut,* which foreshadow the important roles of Dido in Book 4 and Turnus in Book 12.

[3] This is an echo of *certus eundi* 4, 554.

[4] At 6, 463f. Aeneas claims to be unaware that his departure caused Dido such *dolor* ; but cf. 4, 435f. and 563ff. On the implications of Aeneas' statement of denial at 6, 463f., see below, p. 132f. On the symbolic importance of lines 1ff., see Büchner, 352 and Pöschl, 47f.

[5] Knauer, indices ad loc., cites no Homeric model for the speech of Aeneas.

Williams,[1] shows 'Aeneas' position of responsibility for his men'.
Furthermore, it indicates his love and honour for the memory of
his father. The reference to his piety (26) sets the tone for the
speech and demonstrates this essential quality of Aeneas, which is
seen throughout his direct speeches in Book 5. Aeneas is grateful
for the opportunity to shelter his ships in Acestes' land where lie
the bones of his father.

On landing at Drepanum and being welcomed by Acestes
(35ff.), Aeneas makes a lengthy address to his men as follows:

> "Dardanidae magni, genus alto a sanguine divum,          45
> annuus exactis completur mensibus orbis,
> ex quo reliquias divinique ossa parentis
> condidimus terra maestasque sacravimus aras;
> iamque dies, nisi fallor, adest, quem semper acerbum,
> semper honoratum (sic di voluistis) habebo.               50
> hunc ego Gaetulis agerem si Syrtibus exsul,
> Argolicove mari deprensus et urbe Mycenae,
> annua vota tamen sollemnisque ordine pompas
> exsequerer strueremque suis altaria donis.
> nunc ultro ad cineres ipsius et ossa parentis              55
> haud equidem sine mente, reor, sine numine divum
> adsumus et portus delati intramus amicos.
> ergo agite et laetum cuncti celebremus honorem:
> poscamus ventos, atque haec me sacra quotannis
> urbe velit posita templis sibi ferre dicatis.              60
> bina boum vobis Troia generatus Acestes
> dat numero capita in navis; adhibete penatis
> et patrios epulis et quos colit hospes Acestes.
> praeterea, si nona diem mortalibus almum
> Aurora extulerit radiisque retexerit orbem,                65
> prima citae Teucris ponam certamina classis;
> quique pedum cursu valet, et qui viribus audax

---

[1] Williams (*Aen.* 1–6) ad 26; see also his longer note, *Aeneidos Liber Quintus* (Oxford, 1960) ad loc.

aut iaculo incedit melior levibusque sagittis,
seu crudo fidit pugnam committere caestu,
cuncti adsint meritaeque exspectent praemia palmae.            70
ore favete omnes et cingite tempora ramis."

(45–71)

The piety of Aeneas is stressed throughout the speech and most especially in his intention to perform solemn rites in honour of his father. A year has passed since Anchises' death (46ff.), and now the day has arrived which will always be painful to Aeneas and honoured by him — for the gods will it thus (*sic di voluistis* 50). Aeneas would conduct funeral rites to his dead father were he wandering in obscure parts of the world (51ff.), far away from Sicily, so that he shall certainly perform them when, as now, at Drepanum. He feels that not without divine purpose are they present at a friendly haven (56f.). The task for Aeneas is one of joy (*laetum ... honorem* 58)[1] and he promises to perform such rites each year in his destined city (59f.). Here Vergil evokes the *Parentalia*: Aeneas is, therefore, founder and observer of traditional ritual.[2] He orders his own Penates and those of Acestes to be brought to the feast (62f.). Furthermore, on the ninth day Aeneas will proclaim contests of ships, foot-race, javelin and archery, and boxing (64ff.). All should remain silent to keep good the omens and also wreath their temples with branches (71).

At *Il.* 22,386ff.[3] Achilles vows to mourn Patroclus who is still unwept and unburied. He says that he will never forget him even if he goes down to Hades. He is consoled by the μέγα κῦδος (393) of slaying Hector, but, as we shall see, takes grim satisfaction in the sacrifice of another twelve sons of the Tro-

---

[1] On the mood of joy in Book 5, see P. Miniconi, 'La joie dans l'*Énéide*', *Latomus* 21 (1962) 568, and G. K. Galinsky, '*Aeneid* V and the *Aeneid*', *A.J.P.* 89 (1968) 159.

[2] On the *Parentalia*, see Williams (*Aen.* 5) ad loc.

[3] Knauer, indices ad 53f.

jans.[1] The death of Patroclus leads to funeral games in the *Iliad*,
as that of Anchises does in the fifth *Aeneid*; yet Achilles' reaction
to his friend's death is the model for Aeneas' reaction to the
killing of Pallas (10,510–605). Achilles' vow (22,386ff.) is
made in grief to a dead friend, killed on the battlefield, whereas
Aeneas' is made in a spirit of joyful religious observance to his
father. The former stresses Achilles' exultation in vengeance as a
means of assuaging his grief, the latter Aeneas' joyful piety in the
remembrance of his father.

In *Il.* 23,194ff.[2] Achilles is described as praying for winds,
so that the pyre of Patroclus will burn. Aeneas too asks for winds
(*poscamus ventos* 59) so that the Trojans may reach Italy. Again he
shows his *pietas* in his concern to reach his destined land and
establish a city (*urbe ... posita* 60). The religious rites, which are
so important to the Trojans, will typify the new city. The feast at
Drepanum will be held in the presence of the Penates brought by
the Trojans and those worshipped by Acestes. Aeneas' insistence
that they be present underlines his *pietas* and represents a clear
un-Homeric element.[3] The declaration by Aeneas of a solemn
nine days follows Roman tradition[4] on the one hand and also
resembles the avowal of Priam[5] who has recently recovered the
body of Hector:

> "ἐννῆμαρ μέν κ' αὐτὸν ἐνὶ μεγάροις γοάοιμεν,
> τῇ δεκάτῃ δέ κε θάπτοιμεν δαινῦτό τε λαός,
> ἑνδεκάτῃ δέ κε τύμβον ἐπ' αὐτῷ ποιήσαιμεν,
> τῇ δὲ δυωδεκάτῃ πολεμίξομεν, εἴ περ ἀνάγκη."
>
> (*Il.* 24,664–7)

The period of mourning is similar to that of the solemnities at

---

[1] 23,175ff. On the differences in the presentation of human sacrifice in Homer and Vergil, see above, p. 9f. and below, p. 182ff.

[2] Knauer, indices ad 59a.

[3] Cf. *Il.* 23,10f.

[4] See Williams (*Aen.* 5) ad 64–65.

[5] Knauer, indices ad loc.

Drepanum. Aeneas' *pietas* — the loving memory of son for father
— evokes the same kind of solemn mourning as Priam bestowed
on the dead Hector. It is an apt borrowing: Priam's love for
Hector and his labour to retrieve the body for the proper rites
prefigure Aeneas' love for his father (Anchises) and son
(Ascanius). In this sense a continuity exists in the behaviour of
the Trojans from the Homeric poem into the Vergilian. The piety
of Priam becomes Aeneas' distinctive quality.

Aeneas and the others place on their brows the myrtle, which is
sacred to Venus, whilst the hero himself pours a libation and
cries:

> "salve, sancte parens, iterum; salvete, recepti
> nequiquam cineres animaeque umbraeque paternae.
> non licuit finis Italos fataliaque arva
> nec tecum Ausonium, quicumque est, quaerere Thybrim."
>
> (80–3).

The opening of the speech resembles[1] the speech of Achilles to the
dead Patroclus:

> "χαῖρέ μοι, ὦ Πάτροκλε, καὶ εἰν Ἀΐδαο δόμοισι·
> πάντα γὰρ ἤδη τοι τελέω τὰ πάροιθεν ὑπέστην.       180
> δώδεκα μὲν Τρώων μεγαθύμων υἵεας ἐσθλοὺς
> τοὺς ἅμα σοὶ πάντας πῦρ ἐσθίει· Ἕκτορα δ᾽ οὔ τι
> δώσω Πριαμίδην πυρὶ δαπτέμεν, ἀλλὰ κύνεσσιν."
>
> (*Il*. 23, 179–83)

Comparison of these two passages demonstrates clearly the
careful way in which Vergil selects Homeric material for his own
poem. The salutation of Aeneas to his dead father (80ff.) is
without doubt modelled on that of Achilles to the dead Patroclus
(23, 179); yet the slaughter of the Trojan youths by Achilles
(referred to at 23, 180ff.) is the model for Aeneas' sacrifice of
eight Italian youths following the death of Pallas. It is significant, however, that Achilles' words (23, 180ff.) have no parallel

---

[1] Knauer, indices ad loc. There is also a strong resemblance to Catullus 64, 23.

in the *Aeneid*, for Aeneas utters no speech as he prepares the youths for sacrifice.[1] Vergil carefully avoids giving dramatic reality to the action of his hero in this matter. On the other hand, Achilles' words of piety — his address to his beloved Patroclus (23, 179) — are given dramatic reality and expanded by Vergil in Aeneas' utterance to the spirit of his father (80–3).[2] Thus both in his pious words and in his perpetration of human sacrifice Achilles is the model for Aeneas, yet in characterising his hero Vergil gives full dramatic significance to the former, whilst obscuring the latter in an indistinct narrative. Therefore here too Aeneas' speech underlines his *pietas*: he salutes the spirit of his father and laments that Anchises will not seek Italy with him.

The rites to his father are interrupted by the appearance of a snake (84ff.) which coils and glides around the altar. The sight of the snake induces Aeneas to continue with more eagerness the solemn rites. He kills two sheep, two pigs and two black-backed bullocks, and pours wine at the altar. As preparation for the games begins (104ff.) we may reflect that the portrayal of Aeneas in Book 5 (1–103) demonstrates a single-minded devotion to the memory of his father, the rites in his honour and the eventual foundation of the fated city.

*Pius* (286) refers backwards to the presentation following the ship-race and forwards to his introduction to the foot-race. At 282ff. Aeneas presents to Sergestus his promised gift: the latter had been captain of the barque which struck a rock (202ff.) putting it out of the race.[3] Aeneas is joyful (*laetus* 283) that ship

---

[1] On this, see above, p. 9f. and below, p. 182ff.

[2] J. W. Mackail, *The Aeneid* (Oxford, 1930) ad 5, 81, points out that Aeneas' salutation is given to (1) the buried ashes (2) the spirit (*anima*) in Elysium (3) the ghost (*umbra*) which haunts and revisits this world (as it does at 5, 722ff.).

[3] Otis, 51ff. gives an interesting comparative analysis of *Aen.* 5, 114–243 and *Il.* 23, 287–652.

and crew are able to return (*pietas*) to collect the promised reward.[1] After the ship-race Aeneas prepares to begin the foot-race and, when the contestants appear, he speaks as follows:

> "accipite haec animis laetasque advertite mentes.
> nemo ex hoc numero mihi non donatus abibit.                    305
> Cnosia bina dabo levato lucida ferro
> spicula caelatamque argento ferre bipennem;
> omnibus hic erit unus honos. tres praemia primi
> accipient flavaque caput nectentur oliva.
> primus equum phaleris insignem victor habeto;               310
> alter Amazoniam pharetram plenamque sagittis
> Threiciis, lato quam circum amplectitur auro
> balteus et tereti subnectit fibula gemma;
> tertius Argolica hac galea contentus abito."
>
>                                              (304–14)

As we have seen, the force of *pius* (286) carries forward to Aeneas' speech denoting the hero's position as leader and organiser of the games. *Pietas* excluded, the speech shows few glimpses of his character. Each runner will receive a gift from Aeneas (305); he then elaborates on the minor prizes and those for first, second and third places. In *Il*. 23,262ff.[2] Achilles sets out the prizes for the chariot-race, ranging from a woman skilled in handiwork for the winner to an urn with two handles for fifth place. He then calls on charioteers to come forward and try to win prizes, since he himself will not compete (23,272ff.). Generally speaking, in Homer the elaborate detail of the prizes falls within the narrative rather than the direct speeches.[3] Vergil follows this

---

[1] This episode resembles *Il*. 23,534ff. in which Achilles gives to Eumelus the second prize even though, as a result of an accident, he came last (see also below, p. 102f.). There is no parallel in the Homeric passage, however, for Aeneas' *pietas* in the joy that he shows at the safe return of his men.

[2] Knauer, indices ad 308b–314.

[3] As it does at *Il*. 23,262ff., 653ff., 700ff., 740ff. and 798ff. Achilles does name the prizes for the boxing at 658ff., although he does so less elaborately than Aeneas at 5,304ff.

practice when he describes the earlier presentation following the ship-race (244ff.). Aeneas' speech at 304ff. is vividly descriptive and fulfils a similar function to the various narrative references to prizes in Vergil and Homer. It seems unlikely, however, that such a formal and elaborate speech would ever have been uttered by Achilles; for in the *Iliad* the narrator and characters have roles which are more clearly defined. Aeneas' speech, certainly in Homer's terms, more properly fulfils the role of the narrator – a fact of which there seems little doubt Vergil was aware. The single quality to emerge from the speech is Aeneas' *pietas*, his determination that none of his men will leave without reward (305). Achilles' speeches in Book 23 of the *Iliad* and elsewhere in the poem exude a wide range of human qualities and emotions. As we can see from this speech of Aeneas (304ff.), Vergil makes no attempt to create the same kind of three-dimensional hero as Homer's Achilles. It is purely the *pietas* of Aeneas on which Vergil concentrates.

Salius claims (341f.) that he was cheated of his prize in the foot-race and demands that it be returned to him. Aeneas responds as follows:

> tum pater Aeneas "vestra" inquit "munera vobis
> certa manent, pueri et palmam movet ordine nemo;
> me liceat casus miserari insontis amici."

$$(348–50)$$

The speech is based[1] on that of Achilles to Antilochus:

> "'Ἀντίλοχ', εἰ μὲν δή με κελεύεις οἴκοθεν ἄλλο
> Εὐμήλῳ ἐπιδοῦναι, ἐγὼ δέ κε καὶ τὸ τελέσσω.
> δώσω οἱ θώρηκα, τὸν Ἀστεροπαῖον ἀπηύρων,     560
> χάλκεον, ᾧ πέρι χεῦμα φαεινοῦ κασσιτέροιο
> ἀμφιδεδίνηται· πολέος δέ οἱ ἄξιος ἔσται."

$$(Il.\ 23,558–62)$$

---

[1] Knauer, indices ad loc.

In *Il.* 23,288ff. it is Eumelus who is expected to win the chariot-race because of his well-known ability as horseman. This ability shows forth as he quickly races to the front, only to have Pallas Athena sabotage his chances (391ff.). As a result of this Eumelus comes last and Diomedes wins the race (499ff.). Achilles feels that Eumelus is the best and should have a prize even though he came last (536ff.); and he therefore decides to give him the prize for second place. Antilochus, who came second in the race, objects (543ff.) to the taking of his prize, even though all the Greeks concur with Achilles (ἐπήνησαν γὰρ Ἀχαιοί 540). Achilles accepts Antilochus' argument and fetches for Eumelus a corselet from his tent (558ff.).

In Vergil's foot-race Nisus takes the lead, only to fall on some blood-soaked ground and lose all chance of winning (327ff.). In the process of this accident he remembers Euryalus and purposely causes Salius to fall too, whereby Euryalus wins the race. Salius claims that he has been cheated of his prize; which brings Euryalus to tears (343). Aeneas, in a complete reversal of Achilles' capriciousness, decides that no one alters the order,[1] and he finds another prize for Salius (351ff.).

Whereas Achilles largely creates the air of friction by making a subjective judgement of the heroes' relative worth, regardless of the result of the race, Aeneas is objective and firm. The prizes are to be awarded in the same order as they crossed the line: Aeneas, unlike Achilles, has no part in the precipitation of the argument. The nature of the relationship between Aeneas and his men is emphasised in Vergil's use of *pater* (348) and *pueri* (349). *Pater* is used of Aeneas nine times[2] in Book 5 and considerably less often in the earlier books, indicating a shift in emphasis on Vergil's

---

[1] Note the word order here: *et palmam movet ordine nemo* (349), with the emphasis on *nemo*.

[2] 130, 348, 358, 424, 461, 545, 700, 827, 867.

part.[1] The stress given to Aeneas' paternal role in Book 5 is appropriate, given that the Trojans commemorate the death of *pater* Anchises: Vergil seems to be underlining the fact that Aeneas now has the role of *paterfamilias*. In this instance *pater* (348) reflects his paternal firmness: yet in his pity for the hapless Salius (350ff.) the epithet *pius* could quite happily have been used by Vergil.[2]

Achilles is amused (μείδησεν 555) at Antilochus, who argues strongly from a sense of personal injustice. Achilles' speech has a personal ring to it (ἐγὼ ... τελέσσω 559, δώσω 560), which cannot be said for that of Aeneas (*nemo*... 349, *me liceat* 350). He refers to himself in an oblique case, failing again to use the first person singular.[3]

Nisus too complains (353ff.) that he would have earned first prize, had he a better fortune. The *pater optimus* (358) smiles and gives him also a prize (359ff.), thus demonstrating his *pietas*. He then announces the next event:

> "nunc, si cui virtus animusque in pectore praesens,
> adsit et evinctis attollat bracchia palmis."
>
> (363–4)[4]

---

[1] 1,580, 699; 2, 2 and 3, 716 — all *after* the death of Anchises, who has the role of *paterfamilias* in the long narration. Elsewhere in the poem *pater Aeneas* is used less often: once in 7; 3 times in 8; 3 times in 9; twice in 11; and 3 times in 12. Contrast Glazewski, *C.W.* 66 (1972–3) 87 n. 4, who seems confused about the facts here.

[2] Contrast 5, 700 where Aeneas is described as *pater* but where *pius* could on no account be used.

[3] In his previous 3 speeches (80–3, 304–14 and 348–50) Aeneas uses the first person singular only once — *dabo* (306). In the Homeric parallels to 80–3 and 348–50 (*Il.* 23, 179–83 and 558–62) the first person singular is used 5 times — τελέω (180), ὑπέστην (180), δώσω (183); τελέσσω (559) and δώσω (560). Aeneas' speeches are generally less personal than those of his Homeric counterparts.

[4] Knauer, indices ad loc., compares *Il.* 23, 658ff. where Achilles announces the commencement of the boxing and the two prizes for the contestants.

The boxing event is described at 424ff., the result of which is victory for Entellus over Dares.[1] The winner proceeds to batter the loser until Aeneas intervenes:

> tum pater Aeneas procedere longius iras
> et saevire animis Entellum haud passus acerbis,
> sed finem imposuit pugnae fessumque Dareta
> eripuit mulcens dictis ac talia fatur:
> "infelix, quae tanta animum dementia cepit?                    465
> non viris alias conversaque numina sentis?
> cede deo." dixitque et proelia voce diremit.

> (461–7)

The speech is modelled[2] on that of Achilles to Odysseus and Ajax:

> "μηκέτ' ἐρείδεσθον, μηδὲ τρίβεσθε κακοῖσι·
> νίκη δ' ἀμφοτέροισιν· ἀέθλια δ' ἴσ' ἀνελόντες
> ἔρχεσθ', ὄφρα καὶ ἄλλοι ἀεθλεύωσιν Ἀχαιοί."

> (Il. 23,735–7)

Aeneas' paternal role (pater 461) brings him to stop the fight just as Achilles stopped the wrestling match between Odysseus and Ajax. The tanta dementia of Dares is that he fights against impossible odds since the gods have turned against him. It is noteworthy that Aeneas, unlike Achilles, refers to a divine influence in the contest. This may reflect Aeneas' actual belief, or he may, on a more subtle level, be offering Dares an excuse for his defeat at the hands of Entellus. In either case it is prudent for Aeneas to intervene, for Entellus makes it plain (474ff.) that without such interference he would have battered his opponent to death. Such a conclusion as the result of a boxing match between two of his own people is abhorrent to Aeneas' pietas. The Homeric wrestling match between Odysseus and Ajax is considerably more

---

[1] Note Entellus' reference to pio...Aeneae (418) as an example of indirect characterisation of the hero. Note also pater (424) where his impartiality is stressed.

[2] Knauer, indices ad loc.

even. Achilles needs not and does not attribute victory or defeat to divine factors, but merely comments on the evenness of the match and suggests that the prizes be shared. Aeneas' paternal role (*pietas*) is more strongly emphasised and contrasts with Achilles' more specific role as judge and mediator.

In the archery contest (485ff.) Acestes is the last to take aim; but the target (a dove) has already been shot by Eurytion (513ff.). Acestes still shoots his arrow which catches fire — a great omen. This brings joy to those who watch:

> attonitis haesere animis superosque precati
> Trinacrii Teucrique viri, nec maximus omen          530
> abnuit Aeneas, sed laetum amplexus Acesten
> muneribus cumulat magnis ac talia fatur:
> "sume, pater, nam te voluit rex magnus Olympi
> talibus auspiciis exsortem ducere honores.
> ipsius Anchisae longaevi hoc munus habebis,          535
> cratera impressum signis, quem Thracius olim
> Anchisae genitori in magno munere Cisseus
> ferre sui dederat monimentum et pignus amoris."

(529–38)

This speech is modelled[1] on that of Achilles to Nestor:

> "τῆ νῦν, καὶ σοὶ τοῦτο, γέρον, κειμήλιον ἔστω,
> Πατρόκλοιο τάφου μνῆμ' ἔμμεναι· οὐ γὰρ ἔτ' αὐτὸν
> ὄψῃ ἐν Ἀργείοισι· δίδωμι δέ τοι τόδ' ἄεθλον          620
> αὔτως· οὐ γὰρ πύξ γε μαχήσεαι, οὐδὲ παλαίσεις,
> οὐδ' ἔτ' ἀκοντιστὺν ἐσδύσεαι, οὐδὲ πόδεσσι
> θεύσεαι· ἤδη γὰρ χαλεπὸν κατὰ γῆρας ἐπείγει."

(*Il.* 23,618–23)

In the Homeric games, following the chariot-race, the fifth prize has been left unclaimed; Achilles, therefore, decides spontaneously to give it to Nestor as a personal tribute to his ἀρετή. Achilles feels pity for Nestor now that χαλεπὸν γῆρας (623)

---

[1] Knauer, indices ad 533–538.

afflicts him and that, as a result, he is unable to compete in the
games. The Vergilian situation is quite different in that Acestes
does compete — in the archery contest. At the sight of the omen
all of the Trinacrians and Trojans pray to the gods above; but
Vergil concentrates on *maximus ... Aeneas* (531f.), who not only
accepts the miracle as a good omen but also bestows a gift on
Acestes.[1] No ordinary gift is this, but an engraved bowl given
by the Thracian Cisseus to Anchises as a mark of their friendship.
The repetition of Anchises' name (535, 537 — note *ipsius* 535)
stresses the honour in which Aeneas holds his father (*pietas*).[2]
Achilles' gesture to Nestor has great spontaneity and is not
prompted by an occurrence of any kind; Aeneas, by contrast,
reacts emotionally to the divine signal. In every sense his reaction
demonstrates his *pietas*.[3] He proceeds to call Acestes the victor
(539ff.) and to give him the laurel that Eurytion would otherwise
have won. Thus Aeneas, like Achilles (23, 536ff.), decides on his
own initiative to alter the order, yet it is shown that this is done
out of reverence towards Jupiter who, he believes, has sent the
omen. Achilles' decision (23, 536ff.) shows his capriciousness as
master of the proceedings; Aeneas' decision demonstrates his
*pietas*.[4]

Aeneas now calls for the boys' parade to begin:

> at pater Aeneas nondum certamine misso                    545
> custodem ad sese comitemque impubis Iuli

[1] Moreover, Aeneas embraces joyful Acestes (531).

[2] His *pietas* is also seen as he interprets the omen as the will of Jupiter (533f.).

[3] Thus note again that Vergil chooses to underline his hero's *pietas* where Homer stresses
his hero's spontaneity. Time and again we see Vergil alter Homer's methods of characterisation in such a way.

[4] Whereas Antilochus objects with passion (23, 543ff.) to the intervention of Achilles,
Eurytion does not do so (5, 541f.), even though he shot the bird and is thus entitled to the
prize. The decision of Achilles to interfere is thus contentious, whereas that of Aeneas,
who acts out of *pietas*, is not. Similarly, the *pietas* of all the Trojans and Sicilians, and of Eurytion in particular, is stressed. Where there is often conflict amongst Homer's Greek
characters, there is generally harmony amongst Vergil's Trojans.

> Epytiden vocat, et fidam sic fatur ad aurem:
> "vade age et Ascanio, si iam puerile paratum
> agmen habet secum cursusque instruxit equorum,
> ducat avo turmas et sese ostendat in armis          550
> dic" ait.

(545–51)

Again Aeneas' paternal role is stressed (*pater* 545). The boys' parade (*Lusus Troiae*) is perhaps based loosely on the dancing of the Phaeacians (*Od.* 8, 370ff.).[1] Ascanius too has a role to play in the rites to his grandfather as the leader of the parade. In performing the *Lusus Troiae* the Trojans can be seen as founders and observers of an established Augustan performance.[2] The boys perform the manoeuvres (553ff.), when suddenly (604ff.) the joy of the ceremony turns to disaster. Juno sends Iris who induces the women, tired as they are of the labours of the voyage, to fire the ships. Despite her disguise as Beroë, Iris is recognised as an immortal and revered as such. They then take torches and begin to burn the ships (659ff.). Ascanius is the first to the ships and challenges the actions of the scattering women (670ff.) before Aeneas himself appears:

> tum pius Aeneas umeris abscindere vestem          685
> auxilioque vocare deos et tendere palmas:
> "Iuppiter omnipotens, si nondum exosus ad unum
> Troianos, si quid pietas antiqua labores
> respicit humanos, da flammam evadere classi
> nunc, pater, et tenuis Teucrum res eripe leto.          690
> vel tu, quod superest, infesto fulmine morti,
> si mereor, demitte tuaque hic obrue dextra."

(685–92)

It scarcely needs to be stated that *pietas* is Aeneas' fundamental quality in this speech. *Pius Aeneas* (685) stretches out his hands to

---

[1] Knauer, indices ad loc.
[2] On the *Lusus Troiae*, see Williams (*Aen.* 5) ad 545f.

the heavens in a gesture of prayer[1] asking Jupiter to show his *pietas antiqua* and implying that he himself is deserving of respite from further tribulation. He prays that Jupiter will save the fleet from the flames, or else, if Aeneas does not deserve this, that he will destroy them with his right hand. The god hears him and the prayer is fulfilled: storm showers begin to fall from the sky (693ff.). Thus Aeneas' *pietas* is shown to save the Trojans from disaster.[2]

Although his prayers are answered, Aeneas lapses into despondency:

> at pater Aeneas casu concussus acerbo
> nunc huc ingentis, nunc illuc pectore curas
> mutabat versans, Siculisne resideret arvis
> oblitus fatorum, Italasne capesseret oras.                    (700–3)[3]

Vergil's use of *pater* (700) stresses that the *ingentis curas* (701) rest solely on Aeneas' shoulders. However, in his consideration of residing in Sicilian fields, forgetful of the fates (*oblitus fatorum* 703), Aeneas is in a temporary state of *impietas*. In his passing moment of despair, he contemplates the abandonment of his mission in Italy. Thus here, unlike earlier instances, Vergil would not have considered using the epithet *pius* instead of *pater* (700)[4] to describe Aeneas. The use of *pater* captures the hero's sense of social responsibility and yet does not detract from his *impietas* in temporarily forgetting the fates.

An ardent admirer of Aeneas' character in the poem saw his behaviour here as one of the three cases 'when by the highest

---

[1] On the gesture of stretching out hands in prayer, see above, p. 19 n. 4.

[2] Knauer, indices ad loc., compares Nestor's prayer to Zeus at *Il.* 15, 372ff. not to allow the Greeks to be defeated by the Trojans. Zeus hears Nestor's prayer (377ff.) and the Greeks are not defeated in battle.

[3] Knauer, indices ad loc., compares *Od.* 10, 497f. which is not, however, a close parallel.

[4] As, for example, at 348, where *pius* could quite easily replace *pater*.

standards he fails'.[1] He suggests that 'it seems almost incredible that Aeneas should at this juncture think of abandoning his quest. Yet he does, and it shows how deeply his emotions still rule him'. Following Heinze,[2] who saw this episode as an important turning point in the character of Aeneas, some scholars refer to 5,700ff. as the beginning of the second phase in the narration of his experiences.[3] It is argued that Aeneas' despondency here is a final hesitation prior to his journey to the underworld from where he emerges a man of greater vision and purpose.[4] Thus the meaning and implications of Aeneas' sudden despondency — *oblitus fatorum*[5] — have been the subject of considerable conjecture, whereas Vergil's method of presenting Aeneas at this point has not, to my knowledge, been discussed.

It is significant that prior to this episode Aeneas utters 10 direct speeches in Book 5, all of which, to varying degrees, underline his *pietas*. It is not the work of chance that Aeneas' single moment of *impietas* in Book 5 is described indirectly by the poet. Clearly, Vergil deems Aeneas' sentiments as unsuitable for a direct speech. He thus withdraws the hero from the dramatic spotlight by conveying his sentiments indirectly thereby depicting Aeneas' quiet contemplation of his misfortune. The reader is not in a position to know clearly Aeneas' words or thoughts because Vergil at this point has deliberately blurred his role; the hero's *curae* are not given the dramatic reality which, were he in a state of *pietas*, we might reasonably have expected. The dichotomy in the presentation of Aeneas could scarcely be more explicit

[1] Bowra, *From Virgil to Milton* (London, 1945) 60ff.

[2] Heinze, 269ff.; cf. Büchner 356f. who argues that the incident is Aeneas' greatest test.

[3] Camps, 25f., cites three phases in Aeneas' experiences: 1, 1–5,699; 5,700–8, 731; and 10, 1–12,952. I would agree with Camps that there is 'no probable indication' of a change in the hero's character throughout these changing situations.

[4] See Pöschl, 37f.

[5] Cf. 4,221 where Aeneas and Dido are described as *oblitos famae melioris amantis*, and 4,267 where Mercury addresses Aeneas, *heu, regni rerumque oblite tuarum!*

than in Book 5 where Vergil consistently highlights his hero's *pietas* by direct methods and obfuscates his *impietas* by indirect methods.[1] In contemplating the abandonment of his mission in Italy after Jupiter's favourable action in putting out the fire (693ff.), Aeneas is in a state of *impietas*, but, by using his indirect method, Vergil seeks not to stress the point.

Nautes encourages Aeneas to follow the course of fate (709ff.) whilst allowing those exhausted by their labours to remain in Sicily. During the night the ghost of Anchises appears before Aeneas reiterating the words of Nautes and telling him (724ff.) to seek the aid of the Cumaean Sibyl in entering the underworld.[2] Anchises then suddenly disappears in front of Aeneas' eyes like smoke into thin air (740). Aeneas reacts as follows:

> Aeneas "quo deinde ruis? quo proripis?" inquit,
> "quem fugis? aut quis te nostris complexibus arcet?"
>
> (741–2)[3]

Aeneas' love for (the ghost of) his father emphasises his *pietas* as does his reverence towards the Trojan Lar and Vesta (743ff.). He performs the ritual worship in order to expiate any ill-omen after the supernatural appearance.[4] Aeneas assists those of his people who wish to remain in Sicily (746ff.), marking out the city and allotting homes (755f.).[5] A shrine is founded on Eryx to his mother Venus (759f.) and a priest is assigned to Anchises' tomb (760f.). Moreover, *bonus Aeneas* (770) assuages the fears of those who wished not to depart for Italy, reluctant as they were to

---

[1] We might compare the poet's use of indirect methods to describe Aeneas' dilemma at 4, 279ff. — a dilemma which does not exemplify his *pietas*; see above, p. 79ff.

[2] It is fitting after Aeneas' exemplary *pietas* in Book 5, particularly towards the spirit of his father, that Anchises' ghost should appear in order to give him advice and encouragement following his only moment of despair.

[3] Knauer, indices ad loc., compares *Od.* 11, 210–12 where the shade of Odysseus' mother flees from her son.

[4] Page, ad loc.

[5] Cf. 3, 132ff. where his *pietas* is also stressed in this way.

endure such labours at sea again. In tears (771–note the *pietas* here) he commends them to his kinsman Acestes. He then orders sacrifice to Eryx and the Tempests (772f.), throwing the entrails and pouring wine into the sea (774ff.). The *pietas* of Aeneas is thus, in every sense, forcefully underlined in this section as the hero prepares to leave Sicily.

Venus asks Neptune (781ff.) that the Trojans be given safe passage on the sea so that they may establish their fated city. Neptune (800ff.) replies that he too shares her concern for Aeneas, as he has shown in the battles at Troy; only one person shall die — one in place of many:

> "unum pro multis dabitur caput."          (815)

Neptune calms the sea, bringing joy to father Aeneas (*patris Aeneae* 827). All the fleet follows the course made by Palinurus, helmsman of Aeneas' ship. When night arrives the god Somnus (as Phorbas) induces Palinurus to sleep and to forget about the tiller (843ff.). 'Phorbas' himself will take over the watch. Palinurus, however, distrustful of the sea, will have none of this idea and clings fast to the tiller; he will not allow Aeneas to be subjected to the treacheries of the sea (848ff.). The god causes Palinurus to become drowsy and, despite all his efforts, the helmsman falls asleep. Having put him to sleep, Somnus throws him overboard (857ff.) into the clear waters (*liquidas undas* 859).[1] Aeneas soon discovers that his helmsman has gone missing and responds as follows:

> cum pater amisso fluitantem errare magistro
> sensit, et ipse ratem nocturnis rexit in undis
> multa gemens casuque animum concussus amici:
> "o nimium caelo et pelago confise sereno,          870
> nudus in ignota, Palinure, iacebis harena."

>                                        (867–71)

---

[1] There are inconsistencies in the Palinurus episodes of Books 5 and 6 (337ff.) which are discussed more fully below, p. 121ff.

Most readers will agree with Williams' point that 'it is a most effective piece of irony that Aeneas in his last farewell to Palinurus attributes his death to the very thing which he had so resolutely refused to do'.[1] *Pater* (867) again signifies the nature of Aeneas' role as he takes charge of the fleet (an important image) having discovered to his sorrow that Palinurus has gone overboard.[2] The hero groans and is sick at heart at the mischance that befalls his friend (869). The text implies that it is under the auspices of Neptune that Somnus kills Palinurus,[3] who as it turns out suffers further in the land of the dead for his lack of burial (6,337ff.). Aeneas regrets the fact that Palinurus will lie unburied, and also attributes his helmsman's death to natural causes. It is an important inconsistency that later, in the underworld (6,341ff.), Aeneas asks Palinurus which of the gods killed him. This and other inconsistencies must be looked at more fully in the following chapter.

[1] Williams (*Aen.* 1–6) ad 870–1.

[2] Knauer, indices ad loc., offers no close Homeric parallel to this speech.

[3] It is another example of Vergilian 'framing' that the story of Palinurus begins and ends Book 5 (12ff. and 833ff.). For what reason is Palinurus singled out for death by Neptune (815) and Somnus (833ff.)? It is most likely that the answer to this is to be found in his speeches earlier in the book when he is confronted by the storm. In this episode he utters sentiments which could conceivably give grounds for divine vindictiveness:

*quidve, pater Neptune, paras?* (14), *non, si mihi Iuppiter auctor spondeat, hoc sperem Italiam contingere caelo* (17–18), *superat quoniam Fortuna, sequamur, quoque vocat vertamus iter* (22–3); cf. Nautes' words to Aeneas at 5,709f. Whether or not Palinurus is put to death for some such statement, Vergil stresses his innocence (*insonti* 841) and his loyalty to Aeneas. For a bibliography of Palinurus' role in the poem, see G. Thaniel, '*Ecce...Palinurus*', *Acta Classica* 15 (1972) 149 n. 3 and n. 6.

# BOOK 6

For the purpose of analysing the character of Aeneas we shall divide Book 6 of the poem into two sections: the first is his preparation for the underworld (1–263), and the second his experiences in the underworld itself (264–901).[1] In the first section Aeneas is described as *pius* on three occasions (9, 176, 232), whereas in the second section the word is not used of him at all.[2] The hero is more verbose in his preparation for the underworld in which he utters four speeches totalling 47 lines. In the underworld itself he utters 8 speeches, 41 lines. The tendency towards longer speeches in the first section is designed partly to underline the piety of Aeneas as he imprecates Phoebus and the Sibyl.

We are reminded immediately of Aeneas' *pietas* at the very beginning of Book 6 where he is pictured shedding tears at the loss of his helmsman Palinurus (*sic fatur lacrimans* 1).[3] On their arrival at Cumae Aeneas' men hastily search for fuel and water but the hero himself (*at pius Aeneas* 9) searches immediately for the cave of the Sibyl, prophetess of Apollo. Unlike his men Aeneas thinks first of his religious duties.[4] He observes the temple built by Daedalus with its pictures which tell the stories of Androgeos, the children of Cecrops, Pasiphaë, the minotaur and Daedalus

---

[1] Some scholars divide the underworld section into two — 264–675 and 675–901; see R. D. Williams, 'The Sixth Book of the *Aeneid*', *G. &R.* 11 (1964) 50.

[2] This fact may be more significant than it at first appears; see below, p. 125ff. and p. 128 n. 2.

[3] Thus, as in the earlier books, his tears stress his *pietas*; see above, p. 35 and below, p. 129f.

[4] His men, it seems, are carried away with the excitement of their arrival in Italy (note 5f.); Vergil contrasts Aeneas' scrupulous behaviour (9ff.).

himself (14ff.).[1] The priestess tells him (37ff.) that he would do
better to perform sacrifice than observe the sights on the doors.
The Trojans immediately follow her commands and enter the
temple (40f.). The Sibyl now goes into a prophetic trance and
asks Aeneas (51ff.) why he is slow to vow and pray. The hero
proceeds to do so as follows:

> funditque preces rex pectore ab imo:                     55
> "Phoebe, gravis Troiae semper miserate labores,
> Dardana qui Paridis derexti tela manusque
> corpus in Aeacidae, magnas obeuntia terras
> tot maria intravi duce te penitusque repostas
> Massylum gentis praetentaque Syrtibus arva:              60
> iam tandem Italiae fugientis prendimus oras.
> hac Troiana tenus fuerit fortuna secuta;
> vos quoque Pergameae iam fas est parcere genti,
> dique deaeque omnes, quibus obstitit Ilium et ingens
> gloria Dardaniae. tuque, o sanctissima vates,            65
> praescia venturi, da (non indebita posco
> regna meis fatis) Latio considere Teucros
> errantisque deos agitataque numina Troiae.
> tum Phoebo et Triviae solido de marmore templum
> instituam festosque dies de nomine Phoebi.               70
> te quoque magna manent regnis penetralia nostris:
> hic ego namque tuas sortis arcanaque fata
> dicta meae genti ponam, lectosque sacrabo,
> alma, viros. foliis tantum ne carmina manda,

---

[1] Some argue that there are affinities between Aeneas and Daedalus: see Pöschl, 149f.;
Otis, 284f.; C. P. Segal, '*Aeternum per saecula nomen*, The Golden Bough and the Tragedy of
History: Part 1', *Arion* 4 (1965) 643ff.; D. E. Eichholz, 'Symbol and Contrast in the
*Aeneid*', *G. &R.* 15 (1968) 108ff.; A. J. Boyle, *Ramus* 1 (1972) 116ff. See also E. Norden,
*P. Vergilius Maro Aeneis Buch VI* (Stuttgart, 1957) 120ff.; Prescott, 266 and 365f.; H. C.
Rutledge, 'Vergil's Daedalus', *C.J.* 62 (1967) 309–11; H. C. Rutledge, 'The Opening of
*Aeneid* 6', *C.J.* 67 (1971) 110–5; J. W. Zarker, 'Aeneas and Theseus in *Aeneid* 6', *C.J.* 62
(1967) 220–6; W. Fitzgerald, 'Aeneas, Daedalus and the Labyrinth', *Arethusa* 17 (1984)
51–65.

ne turbata volent rapidis ludibria ventis:          75
ipsa canas oro."

(55–76)[1]

The repeated description of Aeneas as *rex* (36,55) seems to indicate his role as *rex sacrorum*.[2] In this role he prays to the Sibyl from the very bottom of his heart (*pectore ab imo* 55),[3] emphasising his earnestness here. Apollo has pitied and helped the Trojans before, and Aeneas prays that he will continue to do so. He prays too for the acquiescence of the other gods who have been Troy's enemies in the past (63ff.). He pays his respect to the *sanctissima vates* (65), the priestess of Apollo, hopeful that the Trojans will fulfil their destiny by establishing their fated city. Aeneas will build a marble temple to Apollo and Diana, and establish festal days in Apollo's name; he will also build a shrine for the prophecies of the Sibyl.[4] In keeping with the instructions of Helenus (3,456f.) Aeneas asks the Sibyl not to entrust her prophecy to leaves, but rather to sing it herself. Thus it scarcely needs to be stressed that this first speech of Aeneas in Book 6 forcefully underlines his *pietas*. His prayer 'marks the divinity of Phoebus as supreme, and also recognizes the authority vested in the Sibyl: he vows to both a tangible sign of his gratitude when his prayer is granted'.[5] He also prays to those gods formerly hostile to Troy and demonstrates his determination to follow the course of fate by establishing a city for his people in Italy.

In her reply (83ff.) the Sibyl foresees the arrival of the Trojans

[1] Knauer, indices ad loc., cites no close Homeric parallel for Aeneas' speech.

[2] Vergil does not describe Aeneas elsewhere in the narrative of the Odyssean *Aeneid* as *rex*, although he is described as such by other characters in Book 1 — Juno 1,38; Ilioneus 1,544 and 553; and Dido 1,575.

[3] See above, p. 28.

[4] On the significance of these references, see Norden's note, ad loc.

[5] R.G. Austin, *Aeneidos Liber Sextus* (Oxford, 1977) ad 55. By 'supreme' Austin presumably has the Augustan connection in mind. He prays to Phoebus because he is at the oracle of Apollo and it is by the Sibyl's assistance that he can enter Avernus. Apollo is also the god of colonists (cf. Book 3) and they have now reached Italy.

into the kingdom of Lavinium and the *horrida bella* to be fought
with the Italians. There will be another Achilles (89) and another
Helen in Latium (93ff.). Despite the ills that confront them they
should go forward boldly where fortune allows them, even to
befriend a Greek city (95ff.). Aeneas replies to the Sibyl as
follows:

> incipit Aeneas heros: "non ulla laborum,
> o virgo, nova mi facies inopinave surgit;
> omnia praecepi atque animo mecum ante peregi.               105
> unum oro: quando hic inferni ianua regis
> dicitur et tenebrosa palus Acheronte refuso,
> ire ad conspectum cari genitoris et ora
> contingat; doceas iter et sacra ostia pandas.
> illum ego per flammas et mille sequentia tela               110
> eripui his umeris medioque ex hoste recepi;
> ille meum comitatus iter maria omnia mecum
> atque omnis pelagique minas caelique ferebat,
> invalidus, viris ultra sortemque senectae.
> quin, ut te supplex peterem et tua limina adirem,           115
> idem orans mandata dabat. gnatique patrisque,
> alma, precor, miserere (potes namque omnia, nec te
> nequiquam lucis Hecate praefecit Avernis),
> si potuit manis accersere coniugis Orpheus
> Threicia fretus cithara fidibusque canoris,                 120
> si fratrem Pollux alterna morte redemit
> itque reditque viam totiens. quid Thesea, magnum
> quid memorem Alciden? et mi genus ab Iove summo."

$$(103-23)^1$$

In his plea to the Sibyl Aeneas concentrates not on the prospect
of future wars but on his urgent desire to meet with his dead

---

[1] Knauer, indices ad loc., compares *Od.* 11, 139–144 in which Odysseus asks Teiresias
why the shade of his mother will not look at him or speak to him; it is not, however, a close
parallel.

father in the underworld.[1] In this request only the Sibyl can help him. The speech stresses Aeneas' great love for his father — his filial *pietas*. He carried him from flaming Troy, from the midst of the enemy (110f.). His father, though an old man, was his companion throughout all adventures on land and sea. The strength and urgency of Aeneas' appeal to the Sibyl should not be underestimated.[2] The *mandata* (116) to which Aeneas refers are those of Anchises' ghost at 5,724ff., who told him that the Sibyl will lead him to Elysium where they will be reunited. Aeneas' urgent desire to follow these *mandata* and visit the shade of his beloved father underlines his *pietas*. He stresses his own immortal descent (from Venus and Jupiter) and that he too, like Orpheus, Pollux, Theseus and Hercules, should be permitted to enter the underworld. Vergil's main concern in the first section of the book and his main divergence from Homer is the stressing of the *pietas*-element as Aeneas seeks pleadingly for entry to Avernus.[3]

The Sibyl explains the things that Aeneas must do to gain entry to the underworld (125–55). He must find and pluck the golden bough and give funeral rites to a dead comrade who lies unburied on the shore. The Trojans find the body of Misenus and mourn him[4] — especially Aeneas (*praecipue pius Aeneas* 176) — before preparing the funeral rites:

> nec non Aeneas opera inter talia primus
> hortatur socios paribusque accingitur armis.

---

[1] His lack of concern for future *labores* as a result of his haste to imprecate the Sibyl demonstrates his *pietas*. Cf. 1,326f. where he gives a perfunctory reply to the disguised Venus in order to show reverence towards her.

[2] Note especially 115–7; it is noteworthy that, when in the underworld, Aeneas claims (458ff.) that he is actually there against his will. On this inconsistency, see below, p. 131f.

[3] Cf. *Od.* 11,23–36 where Odysseus pours libations, utters vows and prayers, and performs sacrifice prior to the *Nekuia*.

[4] Quinn, 164f., has a good discussion of this episode.

atque haec ipse suo tristi cum corde volutat                185
aspectans silvam immensam, et sic forte precatur:
"si nunc se nobis ille aureus arbore ramus
ostendat nemore in tanto! quando omnia vere
heu nimium de te vates, Misene, locuta est."
vix ea fatus erat geminae cum forte columbae             190
ipsa sub ora viri caelo venere volantes,
et viridi sedere solo. tum maximus heros
maternas agnovit avis laetusque precatur:
"este duces, o, si qua via est, cursumque per auras
derigite in lucos ubi pinguem dives opacat               195
ramus humum. tuque, o, dubiis ne defice rebus,
diva parens."

                                                    (183–97)[1]

It is noticeable that Aeneas' first two speeches in Book 6
(56–76 and 103–23) are of equal length (20$^5$/$_{12}$ lines),[2] and
that his third and fourth speeches (187–9 and 194–7) are of
similar length (3 lines and 3¼). When told that one of his
number is dead (149ff.), Aeneas reacts immediately with sadness
(156ff.) and, on finding Misenus, joins in the mourning (175f.)
and preparation for the funeral rites (176ff.). Whilst exhorting
his men in their work (183f.), he looks about the forest in a mood
of despondency at Misenus' death (185), and prays that the golden bough may appear just as certainly as did the body of his
friend (187ff.).[3] His *pietas* brings the hoped-for result when two
doves appear before him (190ff.). *Maximus* (192) Aeneas immediately recognises their significance (*pietas*) and joyfully (*laetus* 193)
proceeds again to pray for guidance.[4] Again his *pietas* effects the

---

[1] Knauer, indices ad loc., cites no Homeric models or parallels to this scene of the poem.

[2] See Highet's numerical classification, 328.

[3] Austin, ad loc., notes the heavy spondaic rhythm of 186–7, which expresses Aeneas' sorrow at the loss of Misenus.

[4] Note *precatur* at 186 and 193, which stress Aeneas' piety at this point.

desired result[1] when the doves lead him to the bough hidden in the forest (197ff.). In performing funeral rites to Misenus (212ff.),[2] the Sibyl's *mandata* are fulfilled.

From the very outset of Book 6 where Aeneas sheds tears for his lost helmsman (*sic fatur lacrimans* 1) until his actual entrance into the underworld (268ff.), the *pietas* of the hero is forcefully emphasised. In his first two speeches the *pietas* of Aeneas is directed first to the gods and then to his kin. The next two utterances, both introduced by *precatur*, convey a strong commitment to his men (Misenus) and a further determination to find the bough and enter Avernus. The threefold use of *pius* (9, 176, 232) helps to convey this fundamental quality of Aeneas. As we follow the hero into the land of the dead, we should remember Vergil's portrayal of him in the first section of Book 6 and the fact that it is utterly consistent with that in Books 1, 3, 4 and 5, in all of which *pietas* is the central underlined feature of Aeneas' *dramatic* (direct speech) role.

Sacrifices are made to Hecate and libations poured (243ff.), whilst Aeneas himself (249ff.) sacrifices to Night, Terra and Proserpine before solemnly inaugurating an altar to Pluto. The ground bellows underfoot, and Deiphobe tells the uninitiated to depart (258ff.) and calls upon Aeneas to have courage and draw his sword from the sheath. On entering the underworld Aeneas and the Sibyl are confronted by personified forms of suffering (273ff.) and various terrifying creatures (285ff.). Aeneas is *trepidus formidine* (290) at the sight of the Gorgons, Harpies, Geryon and others. He would have rushed forward fruitlessly (292ff.) waving his naked sword had not the Sibyl prevented him. Aeneas' first experience in Avernus thus stresses the insub-

---

[1] Cf. 5, 685ff. where Aeneas' *pietas* (note *pius* 685) saves the Trojans from possible disaster.

[2] Note the part played by *pius Aeneas* (232) in the rites to Misenus (232ff.).

stantial nature of the figures.[1] His behaviour here is not unlike that at Troy (*arma amens capio...* 2,314ff.), where he automatically reaches for arms; it is, so to speak, his 'heroic impulse'.[2]

At the Styx Aeneas sees Charon the boatman and a throng of shades waiting to cross the river (295ff.). He transports some of them, but not others, prompting the following questions from Aeneas:

> Aeneas miratus enim motusque tumultu
> "dic," ait, "o virgo, quid vult concursus ad amnem?
> quidve petunt animae? vel quo discrimine ripas
> hae linquunt, illae remis vada livida verrunt?"
>
> (317–20)[3]

On hearing that these are the shades of the unburied who must wait one hundred years before crossing, Aeneas dwells much on the inequity of their lot (332). He then sees Leucaspis and Orontes who died in the storms that washed the Trojans onto the African coast. Aeneas also sees Palinurus who died recently (*nuper*) on the journey to Italy (337ff.). He had tried desperately to stay awake out of duty to Aeneas (5,847ff.), but was overpowered by Somnus (5,854ff.); he fell asleep and was then cast headlong overboard (5,857ff.).[4] Aeneas, whilst lamenting Palinurus' death (5,869; 6,1), suggests, by his comment (5,870f.), that the helmsman brought about his own fate by allowing himself to fall asleep. It is significant, and relevant for

---

[1] It is perhaps for this reason that Vergil devises the apparent inconsistency in the Sibyl's behaviour at this point; for she tells Aeneas (260), prior to entering Avernus, to take his sword from the sheath, only to point out when they first enter (292ff.) that his weapon serves no purpose against the insubstantial figures of the underworld. Circe, likewise, tells Odysseus (*Od.* 10, 535ff.) to fend off the spirits of the dead with his sword, which the hero is able to do (11,48ff.). The apparent inconsistency in the Vergilian episode, which is not to be found in the Homeric parallel, seems to highlight the incorporeal nature of Avernus. Cf. Austin's plausible suggestion, ad 260.

[2] See Quinn, 1ff.

[3] Knauer, indices ad loc., gives no Homeric model or parallel for Aeneas' speech.

[4] See discussion above, p. 112f.

our discussion of Aeneas' role in the underworld, that inconsistencies now emerge in the circumstances of Palinurus' death and the hero's response to it. Aeneas speaks to the shade of Palinurus as follows:

> "quis te, Palinure, deorum
> eripuit nobis medioque sub aequore mersit?
> dic age. namque mihi, fallax haud ante repertus,
> hoc uno responso animum delusit Apollo,
> qui fore te ponto incolumem finisque canebat          345
> venturum Ausonios. en haec promissa fides est?"

(341–6)

In response Palinurus tells the story (347ff.) of his agonising death: Aeneas was not deceived by Phoebus nor did any god plunge him into the sea, but the seas were rough and he was washed overboard, floating in the water for three nights before sighting Italy. He might have reached land and safety, had not local inhabitants attacked him as he tried to climb the rocks. He seeks now to cross the Stygian marsh with the help of Aeneas, thereby avoiding a wait of one hundred years.

In a comparative analysis of the episodes in Books 5 and 6, a number of inconsistencies arise which have been listed as follows: '(i) In Book V the god Sleep throws Palinurus overboard, but in Book VI there is no mention by Palinurus of divine intervention; in fact he explicitly says *nec me deus aequore mersit*. (ii) Conversely, in Book V Aeneas thinks Palinurus' death was an accident, but in Book VI asks what god was responsible. (iii) In Book V the sea is calm, in Book VI stormy. (iv) In Book V Palinurus was on the journey from Sicily to Italy, but in Book VI we read *qui Libyco nuper cursu...* (v) In Book VI Palinurus says that he was on the sea for three days and nights, but in fact only one day has passed since the events at the end of Book V'.[1] One further inconsistency could have been listed — that the depiction of Aeneas in the Palinurus episode of Book 6 is inconsistent with the characterisation of the hero elsewhere in the poem; but more of this later.[2] Williams' view is that the discrepancies would have been rectified had Vergil undertaken his intended revision.[3] He argues that the death of Palinurus, as explained in Book 6, may have been suppressed, not yet written, or implied in the storm in Book 1. He notes that Book 6 was read to Augustus in 23 B.C. and that Palinurus' death in Book 5 (779–871) was probably composed later than Book 6 and possibly later than the rest of Book 5.[4]

Before discussing these inconsistencies and putting forward suggestions which might help to explain them, let us observe the Palinurus episodes against the Homeric background. The story of Palinurus is clearly based on that of Elpenor in Books 10 and 11 of the *Odyssey*.[5] Odysseus narrates (10,550ff.) the story that Elpenor, one of his men, fell asleep heavy with wine (οἰνοβαρείων 555), and in the morning was startled by a noise, fell from the roof and broke his neck. Elpenor's death occurs immediately before the *Nekuia* in which he is the first of the shades to approach Odysseus (11,51ff.). Odysseus asks him

[1] R.D. Williams, *Aeneidos Liber Quintus* (Oxford, 1960) XXV. P. Jacob, 'L'Épisode de Palinure', *Ét. Cl.* 20 (1952) 163ff., considers the same five problems and argues that the Palinurus of Book 6 and the helmsman of Orontes (1,115f.) are the same person. Both scholars omit the reference (6,345) to a guarantee by Apollo that Palinurus would reach Italy: no such reference appears earlier. See also Heinze, 141 n. 1; Norden, ad 337–383; M. Crump, *The Growth of the 'Aeneid'* (Oxford, 1920) 64f. and 71f.; W.F.J. Knight, *Roman Vergil* (London, 1944) 291f; T. Berres, *Die Entstehung der Aeneis* (Wiesbaden, 1982).

[2] See below, p. 125ff.

[3] Williams (*Aen.* 5) XXVff.

[4] In his discussion of the Palinurus episodes, G. Williams, 281, follows the same line: 'The discrepancies are such as to make it certain that the two accounts were composed independently and never received the necessary revision. It is clear, too, that the account in Book 5 is the later...'.

[5] See Knauer's discussion of the two episodes, 135ff., and M. Lossau, 'Elpenor und Palinurus', *Wiener Studien* 14 (1980) 102–24.

(57f.) how he came to the land of darkness and with such haste. Elpenor replies as follows:

$$\text{"}\grave{\alpha}\sigma\acute{\epsilon}\ \mu\epsilon\ \delta\alpha\acute{\iota}\mu\text{ovo}\varsigma\ \alpha\grave{\iota}\sigma\alpha\ \varkappa\alpha\varkappa\grave{\eta}\ \varkappa\alpha\grave{\iota}\ \grave{\alpha}\vartheta\acute{\epsilon}\sigma\varphi\alpha\text{ro}\varsigma\ \text{o}\grave{\iota}\text{vo}\varsigma.\text{"}$$

(11,61)

He proceeds to explain how he fell and broke his neck. He then asks Odysseus (72ff.) not to leave him unwept and unburied but to perform funeral rites. This Odysseus agrees to do (80).

There are two main points of comparison between the Homeric episodes and the Vergilian. First, there is a certain inconsistency, albeit of different importance, between the narrative descriptions of the characters' deaths and the accounts of the shades themselves given in the *Nekuiai*. Elpenor's reference to the part played by a δαίμων (61) in his death, strictly speaking, contradicts the account of Odysseus who explained it purely as a result of natural causes. The Vergilian inconsistency is more glaring: the poet clearly explains in the narrative of Book 5 that Palinurus' death was the result of divine machination, whereas in the underworld Palinurus says the very opposite. Vergil reverses the Homeric cause of death (i.e. a god instead of wine or carelessness), yet retains and magnifies the inconsistency between narrative and *Nekuia*.

The second point of comparison concerns the structure of the Elpenor and Palinurus episodes. In each case the death of the man concerned is described at the end of the book preceding the *Nekuia*, and in each case his is the first shade with whom the hero holds conversation. Moreover, the lack of burial preoccupies both shades (*Od.* 11,72ff. and *Aen.* 6,365ff.). In these circumstances there seems no doubt that for all the inconsistencies in the Palinurus episodes in Books 5 and 6, in its modelling on the episodes of Elpenor, Vergil was deliberate and judicious. This close modelling on the Homeric episodes in *Od.* 10 and 11 would seem to discount the suggestion that the Palinurus of Book 6 is in

any way connected with the obscure helmsman of Orontes' ship
(1,115f.) who died in the storm.[1] Moreover, the order in which
the shades speak to him (Palinurus, Dido and Deiphobus) is, it
seems, deliberately retrogressive,[2] further indicating that the
poet always envisaged the story of Palinurus' death as to be told at
the end of Book 5.

Thus we can state at this point that Vergil conceived the figure
Palinurus as a direct parallel to the Homeric Elpenor; from which
we can infer that the Palinurus of Book 6 is the shade of the
unfortunate helmsman of Book 5. Such an inference, however,
fails to answer the fundamental problem of the inconsistencies in
the two accounts. Were these to be ironed out in revision? Or was
the poet who wrote and left such glaring inconsistencies so
woolly-headed that he was actually unaware of the problems?
Vergil seems to have made no attempt to rationalise the episodes;
was he too busy working on the later books, content to leave it
until his planned revision of the poem? Many critics have argued
for affirmative answers to these questions, suggesting implicitly
that all such speculations are feasible, yet not so the possibility
that Vergil was aware of the discrepancies, actually intended
them, and was content to leave them in this form to posterity. It
is this possibility that we must now consider.

Let us begin by comparing Aeneas' behaviour at 341–6 with
his more general presentation throughout the poem. The
portrayal of the hero in Books 1, 3, 4, 5 and 6 (section 1) is
consistent throughout in that his direct speeches underline his

---

[1] It is worth noting that Orontes' helmsman is described as *magister* (1,115) whereas
Palinurus is *gubernator* at 5,12 and 6,337; moreover, in the latter two cases, *gubernator
Palinurus* appear in the same position in the lines. This would seem to support the view
that the same Palinurus appears in Books 5 and 6, and he is not to be confused with the unfortunate helmsman in Book 1. See G. Thaniel, '*Ecce ... Palinurus*', *Acta Classica* 15 (1972)
149ff.

[2] See B. Otis, 'The Originality of the *Aeneid* ', in *Virgil*, D. R. Dudley ed. (London,
1969) 40f.

*pietas*,[1] whereas his occasional *impietas*,[2] or any ambivalence which would not reflect *pietas*,[3] is presented indirectly (narrative or *oratio obliqua*). This statement was forcefully reaffirmed in the first section of Book 6 (1–263) where Aeneas' four speeches take the form of imprecations. He shows particular reverence towards Apollo, Diana and the Sibyl, and also a great love of kin. When he sees the shade of Palinurus it is a different story — 'Which of the gods took you from us and plunged you into the sea?... Apollo deluded my mind in this one response... is this his promised *fides*?' Aeneas, of course, is quite right, for Palinurus was in fact plunged into the sea by a god; yet his questions here contradict his response to the death of Palinurus (5,870f.), where he assumes that the helmsman had been careless in going to sleep and falling overboard. Whereas his first reaction to the death of Palinurus had shown his *pietas*,[4] his meeting with the helmsman's shade reflects only *impietas*. Moreover, it is significant that this latter speech is inconsistent with Vergil's *general* portrayal of the hero. Far from praying to the gods by means of the direct speech, as we have come to expect, Aeneas openly questions their morality, lacking reverence rather than demonstrating it. In his questions to Palinurus in the underworld, he goes much further than does Odysseus to Elpenor:

> "'Ελπῆνορ, πῶς ἦλθες ὑπὸ ζόφον ἠερόεντα;
> ἔφθης πεζὸς ἰὼν ἢ ἐγὼ σὺν νηΐ μελαίνῃ."
>
> (*Od.* 11,57–8)

We begin to see that Vergil alters his methods of characterising Aeneas as the hero moves through the underworld from those used to characterise him in the upper world. This is shown by the

---

[1] Book 2 is, of course, an exception in that on Troy's last night Aeneas only gradually comes to terms with his destiny and thus acquires *pietas* only in the third section of the book; see above, p. 45ff.

[2] As, for example, at 5,700ff.

[3] As, for example, at 4,279ff. See also Aeneas' implicit response to Dido at 1,494ff.

[4] His *pietas* was shown in his sorrow at the loss of his helmsman at 5,868ff. and 6,1.

fact that there is no close connection, as in the other books, between the direct presentation of Aeneas and his *pietas*. As we shall see, this is also the case in his next encounter — with the shade of Dido at 6,450ff.[1] It is surely unlikely to be mere chance that the connection between direct speech and *pietas*, which is so true for the hero in the physical world (Books 1, 3, 4, 5, 6 section 1), is false for his experience in the underworld. In fundamentally altering the presentation of Aeneas here, Vergil seems to be telling us something about the hero and something about the nature of the world through which he currently moves. We expect Aeneas to question Palinurus' shade in a way which somehow aligns itself with his previous nature and behaviour; but Vergil denies our expectation. As a result Aeneas' address to the dead Palinurus is not only inconsistent with Book 5, but also with the rest of the poem. Thus 'ironing out'[2] the inconsistencies relating to Book 6 might have involved more comprehensive changes than some scholars suspect.

The statement of Palinurus in reply is also the exact opposite of what we might reasonably have expected: no god plunged him into the sea, but the weather was rough (rather than calm, 5,835ff.) and he was swept overboard, although he did his best to hold the tiller. On the basis of Vergil's narrative in Book 5 we expect Palinurus to say that he was put to sleep by a god and cast headlong in calm seas over the side of the ship; but again Vergil denies our expectation. It is as if the incident of Palinurus' death in the physical world, and the behaviour of those involved, are utterly transformed when perceived in the environment of the underworld. It is difficult to see how Vergil could have created more gaping inconsistencies without actually intending to do

---

[1] See below, p. 128ff.
[2] I use Otis' words, 292. See also his discussion, 417f.

so.[1] The possibility of this intention must now be examined in a wider context.

Aeneas and the Sibyl are now challenged (384ff.) by Charon. She describes him to the boatman as *Troius Aeneas, pietate insignis et armis* (403) and as *tantae pietatis imago* (405).[2] After the Sibyl shows the boatman the golden bough they are ferried across the Styx (406ff.). They proceed to enter the *Lugentes Campi*, where Aeneas sees many heroines who died as a result of love (442ff.). He sees Dido herself and reacts as follows:

> demisit lacrimas dulcique adfatus amore est:                455
> "infelix Dido, verus mihi nuntius ergo
> venerat exstinctam ferroque extrema secutam?
> funeris heu tibi causa fui? per sidera iuro,
> per superos et si qua fides tellure sub ima est,
> invitus, regina, tuo de litore cessi.                       460
> sed me iussa deum, quae nunc has ire per umbras,
> per loca senta situ cogunt noctemque profundam,
> imperiis egere suis; nec credere quivi
> hunc tantum tibi me discessu ferre dolorem.
> siste gradum teque aspectu ne subtrahe nostro.              465
> quem fugis? extremum fato quod te adloquor hoc est."
> talibus Aeneas ardentem et torva tuentem
> lenibat dictis animum lacrimasque ciebat.
> illa solo fixos oculos aversa tenebat
> nec magis incepto vultum sermone movetur                    470
> quam si dura silex aut stet Marpesia cautes.

$$(455-71)^3$$

---

[1] See Lossau, *W.S.* 14 (1980) 120f., who notes the chiasmus-structure of the Palinurus episodes in Books 5 and 6.

[2] One wonders if there is any significance in his description as *tantae pietatis imago* (405), given both the lack of any apparent *pietas* in his dealings with Palinurus, Dido and Deiphobus and the ubiquity of *imagines* in Avernus.

[3] The Homeric parallel to the Dido episode of Book 6 is *Od.* 11,541–67 where Odysseus describes his meeting with the shade of Ajax. Odysseus speaks to Ajax (553ff.) giving him great praise, but Ajax, still remembering his defeat at Odysseus' hands in the contest for the arms of Achilles at Troy, turns from him in silence (563ff.). The Homeric encounter (Odysseus and Ajax) has less impact on the reader than the Vergilian (Aeneas and Dido) chiefly because Ajax is not a familiar dramatic figure from earlier in the poem as is the tragic figure of Vergil's Dido.

Happily, there have been no suggestions that, had he completed his planned revision, Vergil would have reworked the
Dido episode. There is a general feeling that, although 'relations
have been exactly reversed',[1] the essential detail of the encounter
remains consistent in Books 4 and 6. If we look more closely,
however, especially at the presentation of Aeneas in the two
episodes, we see that a similar alteration in Vergil's methods of
characterisation occurs to that in the Palinurus episode. Aeneas'
retrospective perception in the underworld of the incident at
Carthage does not exactly accord with Vergil's own narrative in
Book 4. It is because of this and Dido's aggrieved silence that
some of the difficulties in the Palinurus episode are compounded
rather than clarified.

*Adfari* (455) is often used in Vergil to describe tenderness or
affection.[2] The verb is used of Dido (speaking to Barce 4,632)
and by her (when telling Anna to speak to the *hostem ... superbum*
4,424). *Adfatus* (6,455), describing Aeneas, helps to convey the
hero's emotional reaction to the sight of Dido's shade. He even
sheds tears (*lacrimas* 455) at the sight of her. *Lacrimae* in its
various cases occurs on seven occasions in Book 4 – in each case in
reference to Dido.[3] As we have seen, Aeneas, like his Homeric
counterparts, is not above the shedding of tears, yet in every case
they are tears which help to emphasise his *pietas*.[4] This is not the
case at 455, 468[5] or 476 where his tears are shed out of *amor* for
the woman who died on his departure from Carthage. In Book 4
the *lacrimae* are those of Dido, whereas in Book 6 they belong to
Aeneas: this is one of the many reversals in the latter episode. Yet

---

[1] E. K. Rand, *The Magical Art of Virgil* (Cambridge Mass., 1931) 368.

[2] R. G. Austin, 'Virgil, *Aeneid* VI. 384–476', *P.V.S.* 8 (1968–9) 57. See also 1,663;
2,700; 7,544; 8,126; 9,198. The use of the verb at 10,591 is a notable exception.

[3] 30,314, 370, 413, 449, 548, 649. For the reference to the *lacrimae ... inanes* at
4,449, see above, p.92.

[4] See 1,459, 465, 470; 2,279, 790; 3,10, 492; 5,771; 6,1, and above, p.35.

[5] For a brief discussion of *lacrimas ... ciebat* (468), see below, p. 133 n. 1.

more importantly his weeping in the underworld is indicative of a purely emotional response which has nothing to do with *pietas*. In other words here again we see the shift in the presentation of Aeneas in the underworld away from the type of hero who passes through the physical world. Vergil here in Book 6 allows the reader to see Aeneas displaying the same spontaneous emotion of love which in Book 4 he revealed in Dido and denied to Aeneas. This can be seen in the use of the word *amor* itself. At 6,455 it is clear that Aeneas speaks from love (*amore*). As we would expect, *amor* is used frequently in Book 4, generally in reference to Dido and her love for Aeneas.[1] On one particular occasion, however, the *amor* is that of Aeneas for Dido:

> at pius Aeneas, quamquam lenire dolentem
> solando cupit et dictis avertere curas,
> multa gemens magnoque animum labefactus amore
> iussa tamen divum exsequitur classemque revisit.
>
> (4,393–6)

The *amor* of Aeneas here is never given dramatic reality by Vergil in Book 4.[2] At Carthage Aeneas actively desires to lessen the suffering of the queen (393–4), but his *pietas* (393ff.) — his determination to follow the *iussa ... divum* (396) and return to his fleet — stops him from doing so. In the underworld he actually makes the attempt to lessen her suffering (cf. *lenire ... cupit* 4,393f. and *lenibat dictis animum* 6,468), for no *pietas* clouds the issue here.

Aeneas realises (456ff.) that the report was true that Dido had died and that he himself was the cause. He calls her *infelix*, thereby echoing her own self-address (4,596) and other narrative references.[3] Austin suggests that the *nuntius* was the message conveyed by the flames at Carthage (5,4), and that Vergil

---

[1] See 4,17, 28, 38, 54, 85, 171, 307, 414, 516, 532, 624.

[2] For a discussion of this passage, see above, p. 89f.

[3] 1,712, 749; 4,68.

'intends us to know ... that Aeneas in his heart of hearts, knew what he had done to Dido'.[1] Perhaps Aeneas is genuinely shocked or feigns surprise or gives voice to an uneasy conscience. In any case, he claims that unwillingly he left her shores:

> "invitus, regina, tuo de litore cessi.
> sed me iussa deum, quae nunc has ire per umbras,
> per loca senta situ cogunt noctemque profundam,
> imperiis egere suis."                              (460–3)

We saw in the context of Book 4 that Aeneas claims it is not his idea that he makes for Italy (*Italiam non sponte sequor* 4,361).[2] He means that he has heard the *mandata* of Jupiter (note 4,222, 270 and 357) and feels compelled to act instantly and definitely upon them. It is for this reason that he is described as *pius* at 4,393 — because he chooses to follow fate and the *iussa divum* in preference to the calling of his own heart. We saw that it is a mistake to read *Italiam non sponte sequor* (4,361) and *invitus, regina, tuo de litore cessi* (6,460) as expressing the same sentiments. The former explains a choice which the hero makes (*hic amor, haec patria est* 4,347) whereas the latter claims an utter reluctance to have left Carthage at all. In fact remaining at Carthage is, all things considered, the last choice that Aeneas would make.[3] Aeneas' claim to the shade of Dido (460ff.) contradicts the evidence of the text of Book 4;[4] Aeneas cannot be *pius* and unwilling to leave Carthage at the same time.

A similar kind of inconsistency is seen in his suggestion to Dido's shade that also against his will is the journey he undertakes into Avernus. This statement too conflicts with the evidence of the text. At 5,722ff. the ghost of Anchises appears

---

[1] Austin, *P.V.S.* 8 (1968–9) 57f.

[2] See above, p. 84ff.

[3] See 4,340ff. and above, p. 86, n. 1.

[4] See 4,281f. (esp. *ardet* ... 281) and 4,576f.: "sequimur te, sancte deorum, quisquis es, *imperioque iterum paremus ovantes*."

suddenly before Aeneas reaffirming the counsel of Nautes (5, 709ff.) and telling him to visit the land of the dead after first consulting the Cumaean Sibyl. When he reaches Cumae he prays with great reverence to Apollo (6, 56–76) and then imprecates the Sibyl (103–23) to allow him into the underworld. The urgency of Aeneas' supplication should not be underestimated (note 108ff. and esp. 115ff.). [1] Aeneas follows the *mandata* of his father with such ardour that it makes false his claim to be in Avernus 'against his will'. Aeneas cannot be *pius* (which he unquestionably is throughout the first section of Book 6) and unwilling to enter Avernus to see his father at the same time. *Pietas* can impose hard choices on a man, as it does on Aeneas, yet neither at Carthage nor at Cumae does he display any unwillingness to follow the injunctions issued to him.

Aeneas proceeds to claim that he could not believe that his leaving Dido would cause her such great *dolor*. He could not know for certain that Dido would commit suicide (although see 4, 436 and 564), yet he is awake to the despair that his departure causes (4, 448) but is like a strong oak which refuses to give way (4, 438ff.). His refusal to do so underlines his *pietas*. As Austin implies, the death and suffering of Dido can hardly have come as a shock to him. [2] Here again Aeneas' sentiments echo those of Dido at Carthage:

> "hunc ego si potui tantum sperare dolorem,
> et perferre, soror, potero."                (4, 419–20)

Aeneas' claim to ignorance of her *dolor* makes Dido turn away

---

[1] As Otis, 286, points out, 'Aeneas in his request for admission to the underworld (103–23) dwells far more on his own affection for Anchises than on the *mandata patris* (116) or the commands of Jupiter. He who has undergone so many ordeals, is now ready for the greatest of all, but it is not fate; it is love and filial piety that motivate him'. At 294 Otis contradicts his own statement: 'He (Aeneas) tries to explain (to Dido): it was against *his* will he left her; he was then, as now, the hapless agent of the gods (461ff.)'.

[2] Austin, *P.V.S.* 8 (1968–9) 58: 'In the words "nec credere quivi…" Aeneas had returned to the *nuntius* and to the naggings of his conscience'.

from him. He cries out to her *quem fugis?* (6,466) in tears,[1] echoing again her words to him at Carthage (*mene fugis?* 4,314). She turns away from him, eyes fixed to the ground, silently hostile. In Book 4 she is overwhelmingly the dominant character (9 speeches, 189 lines), whereas Aeneas has a comparatively small dramatic role (2 speeches, 35 lines). Moreover, Dido 'is an open book',[2] allowed by the poet to express dramatically the full range of her emotions: by contrast, Vergil expresses indirectly the thoughts and emotions of Aeneas in Book 4 and obfuscates all those which do not underline his piety. Here in Book 6 the presentation of the two is reversed: Dido is silent, like hard flint or rock (469ff.) just as Aeneas at Carthage had been deaf to her pleas, like a sturdy oak withstanding the wind (4,441ff.). Conversely, Aeneas in the underworld, like Dido at Carthage, gives voice to his deepest emotions pouring forth tears.

We must now pause to reflect upon the issues we have discussed in the context of the Palinurus and Dido episodes. Two main points arise in each comparison. The first is that in the Palinurus episode the retrospective accounts of Aeneas and Palinurus conflict with the narrative detail of the helmsman's death and with their own behaviour in it. The second is that the presentation of Aeneas as he addresses Palinurus' shade (341–6) is inconsistent with that of Books 1, 3, 4, 5 and 6, section 1. The two main points that arise from comparison of the Dido episodes

[1] There is some doubt as to whose tears are meant; is Aeneas shedding tears, or attempting to arouse tears (i.e. Dido's)? *Lenibat* (468) is clearly conative, but is *ciebat*? Servius, Austin, and Williams (ad loc.) think not, referring to the fact that *ciere* is used of the emotions of the subject rather than of another person (cf. Andromache at 3,344). The other references to Aeneas' tears in this episode (455, 476) help to support this view: Vergil is attempting to portray forcefully the lachrymose state of the hero as a reversal of his earlier behaviour, hence the reference to tears both before and after his speech. Attempting to soothe her anger as a conscious effort (468a) is understandable, but an equally conscious attempt to arouse tears from Dido would seem rather strange after the regrets he has just shown (456ff.). For the opposite argument, see O. Seel, 'Um einen Vergilvers (*Aeneis*, VI, 468)' in *Hommages à M. Renard* (Coll. Latomus, 1969) 677ff.

[2] Austin (*Aen.* 4) ad 393.

are similar; first, some of Aeneas' statements to Dido's shade conflict with the actual detail of events at Carthage as Vergil presents them. The second is that the roles of Aeneas and Dido are completely reversed and the portrayal of the former in this episode is inconsistent with that in Books 1, 3, 4, 5 and 6 (i). For all the obvious difficulties and incongruities, there is a consistency in Vergil's methods indicative of a deeper purpose. The presentation of the episodes is too alike, too contrived to be accidental. Events and behaviour which are true for the physical world are seen in a false perspective in the underworld.[1] Only in the underworld is Aeneas characterised primarily by his *humanitas*, for in the real world, from his dealings with Dido at Carthage till the death of Turnus in Italy, his *humanitas* is buried under the obligations brought on by his *pietas*.[2] Thus Aeneas' nature in Avernus is a false reflection of his real nature in the physical world as Vergil presents it, just as the events of his past with Palinurus and Dido are not perceived accurately when he meets with their shades in the underworld.

At 494ff. Vergil describes Aeneas' encounter with the shade of Deiphobus, the son of Priam, who has terrible wounds such that Aeneas can scarcely recognise him:

> "Deiphobe armipotens, genus alto a sanguine Teucri,        500
> quis tam crudelis optavit sumere poenas?
> cui tantum de te licuit? mihi fama suprema
> nocte tulit fessum vasta te caede Pelasgum
> procubuisse super confusae stragis acervum.
> tunc egomet tumulum Rhoeteo in litore inanem        505
> constitui et magna manis ter voce vocavi.

---

[1] For the connection between Aeneas' encounter with Palinurus, Dido and Deiphobus, and his exit via the gate of false dreams (6, 893ff.), see below, p. 136ff.

[2] Thus at 4, 393ff. he desires to ease her suffering but does not attempt to do so, because his *pietas* obliges him to follow the *iussa ... divum* and return to his fleet. *Pietas* prevails over *humanitas* at Carthage, but not so in the underworld. For the concept of *humanitas* in the *Aeneid* see below, p. 217, n. 1.

> nomen et arma locum servant; te, amice, nequivi
> conspicere et patria decedens ponere terra."

(500–8)[1]

Deiphobus narrates the story (509ff.) of Helen's *scelus exitiale*. It was she who led the Greeks to his bedroom from which she had already removed his weapons. The enemy burst into the room and brutally killed him; and he now prays (529f.) that the Greeks will, in recompense, suffer similar penalties. Deiphobus and Aeneas hold conversation until the Sibyl tells Aeneas that night passes and he must press on with his journey (539–43).

In Book 2 Deiphobus is mentioned only once:

> "iam Deiphobi dedit ampla ruinam
> Volcano superante domus, iam proximus ardet
> Ucalegon."                                    (2, 310–2)

This reference to Deiphobus is made merely in passing by the hero as he narrates his first view of the flaming city. No mention is made by Aeneas in Book 2 that Deiphobus had died in great slaughter of Greeks (6, 502ff.), nor is reference made to the conducting of funeral rites by Aeneas (6, 505ff.). The reply of Deiphobus to Aeneas is no less difficult. Like Palinurus (347ff.), he contradicts Aeneas' understanding of events, telling him that his recollection is false. Far from dying in great heroic fashion, Deiphobus points out (509ff.) that he was treacherously betrayed by his wife Helen, and killed in his bed by the Greeks. This is inconsistent with the portrayal of Helen in Book 2, 567ff., where she is described as desperately frightened of possible

---

[1] The Homeric parallel to the Deiphobus episode of Book 6 is *Od.* 11, 385ff. in which Odysseus encounters the spirit of his former ally Agamemnon. Odysseus asks him (397ff.) what caused his death; did Poseidon stir up the winds or was he killed by hostile men on land? Agamemnon replies (405ff.) with the story of his death at the hands of Aegisthus. Vergil's episode is considerably different, yet Deiphobus falls victim to Helen's monstrous guile just as Agamemnon is destroyed by that of Clytemnestra (421ff.). Odysseus, when he sees Agamemnon, does not evince the same apparent guilt as does Aeneas on seeing his former friend.

revenge at any moment either from Trojans or Greeks.[1] At Troy she is *deserti coniugis iras praemetuens* (2,572f.), beside Vesta's shrine, whereas Deiphobus in the underworld describes her (511ff.) as calling the Greeks to the room where he slept heavily, opening the doors, and thus allowing him to be slaughtered. Deiphobus points out that by acting in this way Helen hoped to redeem herself in Menelaus' eyes (526f.). Thus we see that Aeneas' recollection of Helen at Troy as described in Book 2 is inconsistent with that of Deiphobus in Book 6.

The Deiphobus episode is the third in succession in which discrepancies arise with other parts of the poem. This supports the view that there is a consistency in these inconsistencies — that the delineation of the characters and the circumstances of the episodes in the earlier books are deliberately distorted when Vergil recalls them in the second section of Book 6. In suggesting that Vergil would have ironed out these inconsistencies in his revision of the poem, scholars may be doing the poet a disservice and at the same time may be failing to grasp the significance of these episodes. To find an explanation as to why the poet devises these discrepancies the scholar need not go outside the framework of the poem: Vergil has himself in Book 6 given us a clue as to what is their meaning and significance. At the end of the book Aeneas and the Sibyl leave the underworld, which is described by the poet as follows:

> sunt geminae Somni portae, quarum altera fertur
> cornea, qua veris facilis datur exitus umbris,
> altera candenti perfecta nitens elephanto,                    895
> sed falsa ad caelum mittunt insomnia Manes.
> his ibi tum natum Anchises unaque Sibyllam
> prosequitur dictis portaque emittit eburna,
> ille viam secat ad navis sociosque revisit.

(893–99)

---

[1] For a discussion of the Helen episode of Book 2, see above, p. 52ff.

The exact meaning of these enigmatic lines has never been clear and perhaps never will be.[1] The plethora of critical discussion on the subject of Aeneas' exit from Avernus has possibly made the issues more complicated than they ought to be.[2] One important viewpoint as to why Aeneas and the Sibyl leave via the ivory gate is that on the one level of meaning they are not true shades (*verae umbrae*) and thus cannot leave via the gate of horn.[3] The reference to them as *falsa ... insomnia* (896) together with the Homeric parallel[4] induces us, on another level, to think of the whole experience as a dream: 'his journey through the underworld was in some way analogous to sleeping and dreaming. This means that the passage on the Gates of Sleep is intended to compel a re-reading and a retrospective interpretation; in fact, the whole concept of a physical journey through the Underworld by a living man is called into question'.[5] If there is a case for such a view, and many scholars would argue that there is, then surely there must be something in the text to complement the enigmatic ending of the book. There is little point in referring to the gate of false dreams if it bears no relevance to the description of Aeneas in

---

[1] See Austin, ad loc.: 'The matter remains a Virgilian enigma (and none the worse for that)'.

[2] For a summary of the earlier views on this subject see B. Otis, 'Three Problems of *Aeneid* 6', *T.A.Ph.A.* 90 (1959) 173ff. For some more recent views, see W. Clausen, 'An Interpretation of the *Aeneid*', *H.S.C.P.* 68 (1964) 146f.; J. J. Bray, 'The Ivory Gate' in *For Service to Classical Studies: Essays in Honour of Francis Letters* (Melbourne, 1966) 55–69; Boyle, *Ramus* 1 (1972) 120ff.; N. Reed, 'The Gates of Sleep in *Aeneid* 6', *C.Q.* 23 (1973) 311–5; E. C. and N. M. Kopff, 'Aeneas: False Dream or Messenger of the *Manes* (*Aeneid* 6, 893ff.)', *Philologus* 120 (1976) 246–50; B. C. Verstraete, 'The Implication of the Epicurean and Lucretian Theory of Dreams for *Falsa Insomnia* in *Aeneid* 6,896', *C.W.* 74 (1980–1) 7–10; A. K. Michels, 'The *Insomnium* of Aeneas', *C.Q.* 31 (1981) 140–6.

[3] J. van Ooteghem, '*Somni Portae*', *Ét. Cl.* 16 (1948) 386–90. See also Austin, ad 893–901 and Williams, ad 893f.

[4] See *Od.* 19, 562ff. where Penelope describes the gate of horn from which true dreams issue and the gate of ivory for false dreams; see below, p. 138 n. 1.

[5] G. Williams, 48f.; cf. Otis, *T.A.Ph.A.* 90 (1959) 173ff.

the underworld that precedes it.[1] In this context it seems plausible that the inconsistencies in the earlier episodes of Palinurus, Dido and Deiphobus are closely related to the enigmatic end of the book. By ending Book 6 as he does Vergil complements and clarifies the incongruities which have characterised it. Aeneas leaves by the gate reserved for false dreams because his dream-experience is 'false' in the sense that it does not accurately reflect the realities of the upper world. His vision is of the nature of dreams[2] in that his own personality and recollection of events, and that of those whom he once knew, are not perfect representations of actuality. As Vergil points out later in the poem, the nature of dreams is to delude the sleeping senses.[3] Palinurus, Dido, Deiphobus, and Aeneas himself are thus to be seen as dream-figures whose utterances and recollections need not be taken as accurately reflecting true experience.

In the remainder of Book 6 (548ff.), which describes Aeneas' experiences after leaving Deiphobus at the Sibyl's prompting (539ff.), the emphasis is on the future rather than the past. Aeneas is comparatively silent in this part of the book, uttering only 13 lines prior to his exit from Avernus. His last four speeches are interrogative in nature. He looks back (548ff.) to the entrance to Tartarus and Phlegethon, the burning river, and hears a noise coming from within. He asks the Sibyl to explain:

---

[1] Penelope's description of the two gates is prompted by a dream which she has had (19,535ff.). In *Aen.* 6 the connection between the gates and the preceding narrative is less obvious: 'The Gates of Sleep come now as a total surprise', Austin, ad 893–901.

[2] See Verstraete, *C.W.* 74 (1980–1) 9: '*Falsa*, then, in Vergil's *falsa insomnia* ... is a generic epithet pointing to the illusory and counterfeit nature of all dream-experience. Thus the contrast between the Gate of Horn and the Gate of Ivory hinges upon a contrast between real apparitions (*veris umbris*) of the dead and false, unreal dreams — all dream-experience being only a counterfeit simulation of waking experience'. No one has, to my knowledge, linked this interpretation of the ivory gate to the inconsistencies which occur earlier in the book.

[3] Note the simile used by the poet to describe the phantom Aeneas: *morte obita qualis fama est volitare figuras aut quae sopitos deludunt somnia sensus.* (10,641–2).

"quae scelerum facies? o virgo, effare; quibusve
urgentur poenis? quis tantus plangor ad auras?"

$(560-1)^1$

The questions of Aeneas prompt a long explanation by the Sibyl
(562ff.) on the nature of Tartarus. All the different sinners are
punished in various ways — all described vividly by the Sibyl.
The two proceed to the groves of the blessed in Elysium, where
the Sibyl asks the poet Musaeus (669ff.) for directions to find
Anchises. These they receive, and they find Anchises, who is
telling the story of Troy and the Trojans' descendants (679ff.).
Anchises sheds tears as he sees his son (686) and shows great relief
(687ff.) that Aeneas has escaped from the *pericula* of his journey
— most notably in Libya. Aeneas replies to his father as follows:

ille autem: "tua me, genitor, tua tristis imago            695
saepius occurrens haec limina tendere adegit;
stant sale Tyrrheno classes. da iungere dextram,
da, genitor, teque amplexu ne subtrahe nostro."
sic memorans largo fletu simul ora rigabat.
ter conatus ibi collo dare bracchia circum;               700
ter frustra comprensa manus effugit imago,
par levibus ventis volucrique simillima somno.

$(695-702)^2$

Aeneas' attempt to grasp the fleeing *imago* is a common motif
in the first half of the poem. At 1,405f. Venus disappears before
her son's eyes just as he recognises her; at 2,790ff. Creusa's ghost
flees as he attempts to embrace her;[3] and at 5,741ff. Anchises'
ghost departs from in front of his son.[4] Aeneas' reaction to the
sight of Anchises' shade at 6,695ff. is consistent with his more

---

[1] Knauer, indices ad loc., cites no Homeric model for Aeneas' speech.

[2] This episode is not unlike *Od.* 11,204ff. in which Odysseus attempts to clasp the spirit of his dead mother. For Aeneas' statement (695f.) that the *tristis imago* of his father instructed him to journey to the underworld, see 5,731ff. and discussion above, p. 111.

[3] 6,700–2 is a repetition of 2,792–4.

[4] Cf. Dido's flight from Aeneas at 6,466.

general portrayal throughout the poem.[1] His willingness to follow the *mandata* of his father (695ff.), his profuse tears (699), and his desire to embrace Anchises' shade, all serve to underline his *pietas*.

Vergil does not dwell for long on Aeneas' desire to embrace his father's shade; for the hero sees a multitude of shades at the river Lethe. Anchises explains (713ff.) that these souls are waiting to be reborn at some future time. This prompts further questions from Aeneas:

> "o pater, anne aliquas ad caelum hinc ire putandum est
> sublimis animas iterumque ad tarda reverti
> corpora? quae lucis miseris tam dira cupido?"
>
> (719–21)[2]

Aeneas is clearly amazed that souls return to the upper world. Why do they have such a dread desire? This seems to reflect his own view of life and his despondency in it. Anchises now tells of the purification and transmigration of souls based largely on the Stoic doctrine (724–51). This leads Anchises to observe the future heroes of Rome waiting to be re-born, who will bring greatness to Aeneas' destined city (756–859). He helps to teach Aeneas his fate (759) in a passage which has been described as 'the most sustained of all the patriotic passages in the *Aeneid*'.[3] The pageant of heroes includes many Roman historical figures up to and including Augustus himself (791ff.). Yet at the end of the pageant it is a young man on whom Aeneas concentrates:

[1] Similarly there is nothing openly incongruous or untrue about what he is told by Anchises (756ff.) on the subject of Aeneas' descendants (the pageant of heroes). We should be cautious, therefore, in accepting lightly Boyle's claim, *Ramus* 1 (1972) 123 (following Servius, ad 893: 'vult ... intellegi falsa esse omnia quae dixit'), that Aeneas' exit via the ivory gate 'is but a harbinger of tragedy, death, and the non-fulfilment of empire's dream'.

[2] Knauer, indices ad loc., compares *Od.* 11, 210–214 which is not, however, a close parallel; see above, p. 139 n. 2.

[3] Williams, ad 752f.

"quis, pater, ille, virum qui sic comitatur euntem?
filius, anne aliquis magna de stirpe nepotum?
qui strepitus circa comitum! quantum instar in ipso!
sed nox atra caput tristi circumvolat umbra."

(863–6)[1]

This prompts Anchises to lament the fate of the young Marcellus (868ff.), Augustus' nephew, who died in 23 B.C., the year in which Vergil performed a *recitatio* of Book 6 for the imperial family.[2] Anchises then proceeds to show his son (886ff.) the whole region, and tells him of the wars which he will fight in Italy (Books 7–12). Having been instructed in these Aeneas and the Sibyl depart via the ivory gate. Aeneas then returns to his ship.

[1] Knauer, indices ad loc., compares *Il.* 3,166–70 in which Priam asks Helen who is the man of great stature amongst the Achaeans. Helen replies (178ff.) that it is Agamemnon. In situation, the parallel is not a close one.

[2] See Austin's note, ad 868.

# BOOK 7

If the vision or experience of Aeneas, which was described in the sixth book, has a profound effect upon him, then it is not shown in the narrative of Book 7.[1] Aeneas has a minor role in the book, uttering only one speech of 15 lines.[2] Moreover, Vergil's presentation of him takes a familiar form, underlining the community aspects of his role and his careful observance of religious ritual. Both of these aspects of his character are seen at the opening of the book as Aeneas scrupulously conducts the funeral rites for the dead Caieta:

> at pius exsequiis Aeneas rite solutis,
> aggere composito tumuli, postquam alta quierunt
> aequora, tendit iter velis portumque relinquit.
>
> (5–7)

One wonders why Vergil makes reference to the death of Caieta at all at the outset of Book 7, other than to demonstrate Aeneas' *pietas* in response to it. We might infer that the Roman reader too is less than interested, after some of the haunting passages in Book 6, in the fact that a gulf on the Italian coast was named after the heretofore unmentioned figure of Caieta. The story of her death and Aeneas' proper response to it convey, at the outset, both a sense of loss and the *pietas* of the hero.[3] Aeneas conducts the last rites for his former nurse and builds a funeral mound before continuing the voyage. The Trojans then skirt the shore of Circe's island from which monstrous noises are heard (10ff.). By filling

---

[1] On this subject, see A. Michels, *C.Q.* 31 (1981) 140–46.

[2] Aeneas has a far less significant dramatic role in the Iliadic half of the poem than in the Odyssean half — 182 as opposed to 345 lines; see below, p. 219f.

[3] Vergil is certainly fond of concentrating on the deaths of individuals at the end of books: cf. Creusa (2), Anchises (3), Dido (4), Palinurus (5), Marcellus (6), Mezentius (10), Arruns (11), Turnus (12). The openings of some books too show a similar sense of loss, although it is less striking: cf. Orontes' helmsman (1), Polydorus (3), Misenus (6), Caieta (7).

their sails with winds, however, Neptune ensures that the
Trojans do not draw close to the shore of the island (21ff.).[1]
Aeneas sees a large wood through which the Tiber flows into the
sea and about which many different kinds of birds flit (29ff.).
Aeneas joyfully (*laetus* 36) changes course and enters the shady
river (35f.).[2]

Vergil now sets the scene for the Iliadic *Aeneid* by narrating the
story of King Latinus whose daughter Lavinia is sought by
Turnus, the young Rutulian prince, in noble wedlock. The
portents, however, for such a marriage are bad, for the oracle of
Faunus makes it clear that Lavinia must take a husband from
foreign stock (58ff.). Rumour at the same time flies to Latium
that the Trojans have landed on Ausonian shores (104ff.). At this
point the Trojans begin their meal, in response to which Iulus
asks if they are eating their tables (*heus, etiam mensas consumimus?*
116) in reference to the cakes that they eat. Aeneas responds to
Ascanius' words as follows:

> ea vox audita laborum
> prima tulit finem, primamque loquentis ab ore
> eripuit pater ac stupefactus numine pressit.
> continuo "salve fatis mihi debita tellus          120
> vosque" ait "o fidi Troiae salvete penates:
> hic domus, haec patria est. genitor mihi talia namque
> (nunc repeto) Anchises fatorum arcana reliquit:
> 'cum te, nate, fames ignota ad litora vectum
> accisis coget dapibus consumere mensas,          125
> tum sperare domos defessus, ibique memento
> prima locare manu molirique aggere tecta.'
> haec erat illa fames, haec nos suprema manebat
> exitiis positura modum.

---

[1] Note the description of the Trojans as *pii* (21): it is their *pietas* that prompts Neptune's
assistance.

[2] Aeneas' joy here reflects his anticipation that he has reached the Tiber; for not until
151 is he certain. On the earlier references to the Tiber, see Conington's note, ad 35.

> quare agite et primo laeti cum lumine solis                130
> quae loca, quive habeant homines, ubi moenia gentis,
> vestigemus et a portu diversa petamus.
> nunc pateras libate Iovi precibusque vocate
> Anchisen genitorem, et vina reponite mensis."

> (117–34)

Aeneas recognises immediately the significance of Ascanius' words and stops him from further utterance lest it is ill-omened. He himself is *stupefactus numine* (119), 'astonished by the divine revelation',[1] and he begins with religious formulae a pious imprecation in response. He recognises that he has reached the land owed to him by fate[2] and also greets the faithful Penates. Aeneas now knows that here is his home and his country;[3] for his father Anchises had told him that they would be compelled to eat their tables and that this would be a signal to hope for homes and to establish dwellings. That Aeneas refers to a prophecy made by Anchises, of course, helps to convey the corporate nature of his family: Iulus, the son, utters the crucial words and Aeneas, the father, recognises their significance and the fact that they were once told to him by his own father Anchises.[4] Moreover, all of this happens with the goodwill of the father of the gods.[5]

The problem is, of course, that the prophecy is presented in Book 3, 250ff. as emanating from the Harpy Celaeno. Anchises

---

[1] Williams, ad loc.

[2] Cf. *debita moenia* (145) which further stresses the fact that they are about to establish a city owed to them by fate.

[3] *hic domus, haec patria est* (122) — a clear echo of 4, 347, *hic amor, haec patria est*. We are reminded that in the earlier speech of Aeneas Vergil could easily have substituted *domus* for *amor*; yet the poet wanted to convey the notion that Aeneas, although in love with Dido, has a deeper longing to establish his city; see above, p. 84ff.

[4] Knauer, indices ad loc., compares Aeneas' speech at 120ff. to that of Odysseus at *Od.* 13, 356–60, in which the hero rejoices at the first clear sight of Ithaca. We are reminded that, whereas Odysseus has been attempting to return home, Aeneas has been attempting to find his fated land.

[5] See 110, 133, 141ff.

does respond to the prophecy with an immediate prayer
(3,265f.), but he makes no mention of it elsewhere in the poem.
Furthermore, the prophecy of Celaeno is greeted with great
trepidation[1] as an ill omen for the Trojans,[2] whereas that of
Anchises (124ff.) emphasises the good fortune to be associated
with its fulfilment. Not surprisingly, Ascanius' words (*mensas
consumimus* 116) agree more readily with Anchises' (*consumere
mensas* 125) than with Celaeno's (*absumere mensas* 3,257). The
significance of Anchises' role in Book 3 may go some way to
explaining the inconsistency and the lack of any reference to
Celaeno in Book 7.[3] Conversely, Vergil may have felt that poetic
licence gave him scope to quote a prophecy from outside the
framework of his own text. Vergil here in Book 7 seeks to place
the emphasis on the optimism which fulfilment of the prophecy
will bring (note *sperare* 126) rather than Aeneas' relief at having
survived a fearful omen. The wording of Anchises' prophecy and
the fulfilment of it propel Aeneas into a new-found ardour to
continue the *labores* and establish their fated city.[4] The negative
nature of Celaeno's prophecy does not so easily suit Vergil's
purpose in Book 7 as it did in Book 3.[5]

It is in this mood of hope and anticipation that Aeneas tells his
men to learn details of the neighbouring lands, the people and
their city (130ff.). The last five lines of Aeneas' speech stress his
*pietas* in two different ways. It is first seen as he organises his men
to ascertain the facts of the land (130–2). Moreover, his religious
piety is shown as he calls on his men to pour libations to Jupiter

[1] See 3,258–66 and 3,365ff.
[2] Although Helenus attempts to mollify their fears: "*nec tu mensarum morsus horresce fu-
turos: fata viam invenient aderitque vocatus Apollo.*" (3,394–5).
[3] See Williams, ad 107f.
[4] See 130–59.
[5] See Mackail's note, ad 124, where he argues that the discrepancy 'is only superficial'.
The fact that Aeneas actually quotes the prophecy of Anchises (124–7) may signify that
Vergil was aware that it did not appear in this form earlier in the poem.

and give prayers to his father Anchises (133f.). He tells them also to renew the banquet (134) as a fitting response to the joyful fulfilment of such a prophecy.

Aeneas' earnest commitment to perform such rituals is shown immediately (135ff.) as he places a wreath on his forehead, prays to the god of the locality (*genius loci*), to Mother Earth, to the nymphs and the rivers. He then prays (138ff.) to Night and her rising signs, to Jupiter, to Cybele, to his father in Erebus and his mother Venus in heaven. Aeneas takes great care to worship both local and greater gods. Both his reverence and his pursuit of a fated course are confirmed by a response from Jupiter himself who thunders three times from a clear sky and himself makes 'a cloud blazing with golden rays of light'.[1] Jupiter's sign of approval is notably forceful, and the Trojans continue their feast with a sense of expectation that the day has come to found their fated city (144ff.). Aeneas' impeccable response to the fulfilment of the prophecy draws a response from Jupiter himself and is shown to benefit all the Trojans.[2]

The next morning the Trojans learn details of the country and its inhabitants (148ff.) as they had been instructed. With this done Aeneas (*satus Anchisa* 152) chooses one hundred envoys to bear gifts to Latinus and seek peace for the Trojans. Aeneas himself again begins to build his city (157ff.),[3] thus demonstrating that his first task lies here (*pietas*) rather than in the diplomatic initiative.

Aeneas takes no further part in the action of Book 7, although he is characterised indirectly throughout much of what follows. Although his role in the book is small Aeneas is presented consistently and forcefully, in both speech and narrative, as a model of *pietas*. His actions show his desire to build the city owed

---

[1] Williams, ad 142f. Conington, ad loc., has a detailed note on the prodigy.

[2] Cf. his prayer to Jupiter at 5,687ff. which results in the saving of the Trojan fleet.

[3] Cf. 3,132ff. and 5,746ff.

to the Trojans by fate and to live in harmony in the new land with gods and men. That this latter objective cannot be achieved is shown to be no fault of Aeneas, nor, for that matter, of Turnus. Again he cannot build his city, but instead must go to war, in which we see his character in another light from that of Book 7.

# BOOK 8

Aeneas has a more important role in Book 8 than in Book 7 (4 speeches, 46 lines as opposed to 1 speech, 15 lines), yet his dramatic role is vastly overshadowed by that of Evander, who utters 7 speeches, 219 lines — almost one third of the book. Thus, whilst Aeneas is present in the action of the book from beginning to end, the poet strictly limits his dramatic role. The reason for this is clear; Book 8 is the most Roman of all the books in the *Aeneid*, and, as such, it is the implications of what Aeneas sees and hears at Pallanteum and near Caere on which Vergil focuses. In short, Aeneas has a passive role in this book; the poet concentrates three of his four speeches into the preliminary section, prior to Evander's long utterances[1] on the subject of his and Pallanteum's past. In the remainder of the book (152–731) Aeneas utters only one speech — in response to the sign from his mother Venus (532ff.). In the main body of Book 8 Vergil turns our attention to Hercules, forebear of Aeneas, and his victory over the monstrous Cacus, to Saturn, to Evander and his kin, and lastly to events in Rome's future and to Augustus himself. Thus Aeneas, who is introduced to the 'continuum of Roman history',[2] needs not have an active, dramatic role in the book.

At the outset Aeneas (*Laomedontius heros* 18)[3] is described as

---

[1] 154–74; 185–275; 314–36; 351–58; 362–65. Much of the Roman-historical theme in Book 8 centres on the role of Evander.

[2] See P.G. Walsh's introduction to C.J. Fordyce, *Aeneidos Libri VII–VIII* (Oxford, 1977) XXV.

[3] *Laomedontius heros* (18) seems here to foreshadow the attention paid to lineage in the early section of the book. Note the indirect characterisation of Aeneas at 11ff., on which see Fordyce's note, ad 12.

greatly troubled by events in Latium (19ff.).[1] In his sleep he sees a
vision of the god of the place, Tiberinus, who tells him (36ff.)
that he has reached his homeland and not to be frightened by
threats of war, for the anger of the gods has abated. Aeneas will
find a huge white sow with thirty young under a tree; from this
spot (where Lavinium is destined to be built) Ascanius will
venture to establish a city, Alba Longa, in thirty years. The god
tells him (51ff.) of the Arcadians and their king, Evander, who
dwell at Pallanteum and war ceaselessly with the Latin race.
Tiberinus encourages Aeneas (56ff.) to join with the Arcadians as
allies and form a treaty with them; Tiberinus himself will guide
the Trojans to Pallanteum. He also tells him to pray to Juno and
appease her wrath (59ff.). Aeneas soon awakes and responds to
Tiberinus as follows:

> surgit et aetherii spectans orientia solis
> lumina rite cavis undam de flumine palmis
> sustinet ac talis effundit ad aethera voces:                          70
> "Nymphae, Laurentes Nymphae, genus amnibus unde est,
> tuque, o Thybri tuo genitor cum flumine sancto,
> accipite Aenean et tandem arcete periclis.
> quo te cumque lacus miserantem incommoda nostra
> fonte tenent, quocumque solo pulcherrimus exis,                       75
> semper honore meo, semper celebrabere donis
> corniger Hesperidum fluvius regnator aquarum.
> adsis o tantum et propius tua numina firmes."

---

[1] Binder, 13, n.25, lists similar descriptions of Aeneas in other books. Otis, 332, is
clearly troubled by Constans' suggestion, L'Énéide de Virgile (Paris, 1938) 269ff., that
Aeneas is in the same kind of despair here as he is at 1,94ff. and 5,700ff. Vergil is not
specific, yet it would seem significant that he uses indirect methods here. Cf. 8,520ff.
where Vergil presents Aeneas' despondency indirectly and his *pietas* directly (532ff.), following the divine signal (523ff.).

sic memorat, geminasque legit de classe biremis
remigioque aptat, socios simul instruit armis.        80
                                                    (68–80)[1]

Aeneas ceremonially glances to the sunrise and washes his
hands in the water before praying earnestly to the Laurentine
nymphs and Father Tiber that he may receive their blessing and
be kept from harm.[2] In return the horned river, Tiberinus, king
of the western waters, will be worshipped and given offerings by
Aeneas.[3] The hero prays finally for the god to be with him and
desires confirmation of the divine revelation. After his prayer,
Aeneas further shows his *pietas* by following immediately the
directions of Tiberinus; he chooses two ships and makes ready the
crews for the trip to Pallanteum. Aeneas' *pietas* — his formal
prayer to Tiberinus and the Nymphs, and his willingness to
follow the god's instructions — effects the desired result, for
suddenly they see a white sow with her young beside the shore
(81ff.). *Pius Aeneas* (84), as suggested by Tiberinus (59ff.), offers
her as sacrifice to Juno in order to appease her anger. Following
this Tiber calms its waters for the hero's journey to Pallanteum —
the site of the future Rome. The waters and woods are amazed
(*mirantur ... miratur* 91f.)[4] at the flashing shields of the warriors
and painted boats on the river. When the Trojans arrive at
Evander's city the king is paying homage to Hercules and the
other gods. Evander, his son Pallas, the senators and young men

[1] Knauer, indices ad loc., cites the Homeric model as *Od.* 13,356–60 in which Odysseus, when first being told that he is back in Ithaca, prays to the Naiads. Knauer also cites this prayer as the model for 7,120ff., where Aeneas realises the significance of Ascanius' question *heus, etiam mensas consumimus?* 7,116 (on which see above, p. 143ff.). The parallel seems more relevant to Aeneas' earlier speech given the excitement of both heroes at arriving finally in their homeland (*hic domus, haec patria est* 7,122).

[2] Cf. Turnus at 9,16ff. and esp. 9,22ff. As Aeneas is prompted by a deity at the outset of Book 8, so too is Turnus at the beginning of Book 9. Both heroes respond with *pietas* and according to the Roman practice.

[3] Binder, 30, points out that Aeneas' prayer is 'Dank, Lobpreis und Bitte zugleich'.

[4] On *mirari* as a key-word in Book 8, see Walsh (op. cit. p. 148, n. 2) XXIVf.

are described (102ff.) as offering incense and performing sacrifice. When they see the Trojans, they all break off from the
ceremony; but *audax ... Pallas* (110) forbids them to do so and
himself goes to meet Aeneas.[1] In response to the challenge of
Pallas (112ff.) Aeneas speaks as follows:

> tum pater Aeneas puppi sic fatur ab alta                    115
> paciferaeque manu ramum praetendit olivae:
> "Troiugenas ac tela vides inimica Latinis,
> quos illi bello profugos egere superbo.
> Euandrum petimus. ferte haec et dicite lectos
> Dardaniae venisse duces socia arma rogantis."               120
>                                                    (115–20)[2]

Aeneas bears the olive branch and stresses that they as Trojans are
hateful to the Latins who have attacked them with insolent
warfare, although they are exiles. They seek Evander and wish to
inform him of their desire for an alliance. After shaking hands
with the young Pallas, Aeneas addresses Evander as follows:

> tum regem Aeneas dictis adfatur amicis:
> "optime Graiugenum, cui me Fortuna precari
> et vitta comptos voluit praetendere ramos,
> non equidem extimui Danaum quod ductor et Arcas
> quodque a stirpe fores geminis coniunctus Atridis;          130
> sed mea me virtus et sancta oracula divum
> cognatique patres, tua terris didita fama,
> coniunxere tibi et fatis egere volentem.
> Dardanus, Iliacae primus pater urbis et auctor,
> Electra, ut Grai perhibent, Atlantide cretus,               135
> advehitur Teucros; Electram maximus Atlas
> edidit, aetherios umero qui sustinet orbis.

---

[1] For the use of *audax* here, see Servius, ad loc., where he compares the adjective when
used of Turnus. It is noticeable that Vergil stresses the commitment of Pallas and Evander
(172ff.) to performing at all costs the ceremonial rites to Hercules. The piety of the indi-
genous population is thus firmly emphasised at the outset.

[2] Knauer, indices ad loc., cites no Homeric model for Aeneas' speech.

vobis Mercurius pater est, quem candida Maia
Cyllenae gelido conceptum vertice fudit;
at Maiam, auditis si quicquam credimus, Atlas,          140
idem Atlas generat caeli qui sidera tollit.
sic genus amborum scindit se sanguine ab uno.
his fretus non legatos neque prima per artem
temptamenta tui pepigi; me, me ipse meumque
obieci caput et supplex ad limina veni.          145
gens eadem, quae te, crudeli Daunia bello
insequitur; nos si pellant nihil afore credunt
quin omnem Hesperiam penitus sua sub iuga mittant,
et mare quod supra teneant quodque adluit infra.
accipe daque fidem. sunt nobis fortia bello          150
pectora, sunt animi et rebus spectata iuventus."

(126–51)

Aeneas speaks warmly to the king,[1] addressing him as *optime
Graiugenum*, one to whom Fortune wished him to pray and bear
the olive branch decked with the chaplet. Nor does he fear the
fact that Evander is a leader of Greeks, an Arcadian, and related
by blood to the Atridae.[2] Aeneas now states clearly the factors
that motivate him; his own *virtus*, *sancta oracula divum*,[3] the kinship of their fathers — Dardanus and Mercury — and Evander's
fame join him, a willing servant of fate,[4] to the king. Aeneas now
stresses to Evander the fact that they are both descended from the
one blood (i.e. Atlas) and that in their enmity towards the Rutuli
they have a common interest. The bulk of the speech — by far
Aeneas' longest in Book 8 — is devoted to stressing their com-

[1] For *adfari* to express warm feelings, see above, p. 129f.

[2] See Servius' note, ad loc.

[3] Binder, 51ff., has a detailed discussion on the *virtus* and *pietas* of Aeneas here and
stresses the connection with Augustus' principate: 'Aeneas ist in seiner *pietas* Urbild des
Augustus' (54). See P.T. Eden's criticism of Binder here, *J.R.S.* 62 (1972) 222. Cf.
W. Warde Fowler's interesting discussion, *Aeneas at the Site of Rome* (Oxford, 1918) 50ff.

[4] *fatis egere volentem* (133). Aeneas' willingness to follow fate is fundamental to his *pietas*.
For a discussion of this fact in the context of the Dido episodes of Books 4 and 6, see above,
p. 86ff. and p. 131.

mon lineage. The Trojans trace their ancestry through Dardanus and Electra to Atlas, and the Arcadians through Mercury and Maia also to Atlas. Aeneas seeks to emphasise their kinship most strongly by referring to Atlas four times in seven lines.[1] He stresses the point that relying on his kinship he himself came to Pallanteum rather than send envoys;[2] and as such he places his life in Evander's hands as a suppliant (143ff.). He points out finally that the Trojans, like the Arcadians, are persecuted in war by the Rutuli who, he argues, wish to bring the whole of Hesperia, from coast to coast, under their yoke. He seeks an exchange of *fides*; his men have brave hearts, good spirit and are tried in action.[3] The *pietas* of the hero is shown in his willingness to follow the wishes of fate and the gods by visiting Evander and in his attempt to join hands in friendship and good faith with the king. Aeneas' speech is a skilful one,[4] in which he stresses forcefully their common lineage, underplays the Trojan aversion towards Greeks, and points out that they have everything to gain by an alliance.

In his response (154ff.) Evander infers that the hero before him is Aeneas,[5] the son of Anchises, whom he once met and greatly admired when a youth in Arcadia. Anchises gave gifts to Evander

[1] 135, 136, 140, 141. Note *Atlas, idem Atlas* ... (140–1). See P. McGushin, 'Virgil and the Spirit of Endurance', *A.J.P.* 85 (1964) 225ff.

[2] Aeneas sends envoys to Latinus (7, 152ff.) so that he is able to begin what he considers a more important task — the establishment of a camp (7, 157ff.).

[3] Knauer, indices ad loc., cites *Od.* 3, 79–101 as the Homeric parallel for Aeneas' speech. In this speech Telemachus explains to Nestor the reason for his journey and seeks news of Odysseus. In situation, however, the parallel is not a close one. See also K. W. Gransden, *Aeneid Book VIII* (Cambridge, 1976) ad 126–51.

[4] For the formal rhetorical structure of the speech, see Highet, 79.

[5] Aeneas did not actually introduce himself in his speech to Evander.

which his son Pallas now owns.[1] Evander states (169ff.) that he will send the Trojans forth the following day, but he must now continue the *sacra* in which he invites Aeneas and his men to share.

Evander proceeds to describe at length (185–275) the story of the monster Cacus and the battle with Hercules which the latter wins, thereby freeing the people from fear.[2] It is, says Evander, in gratitude to Hercules for his great feats in destroying Cacus that each year the Arcadians perform these solemn rites (described at 276–305). Following these rites the host shows his city to Aeneas, who marvels at the scenes around him and joyfully asks questions about the memorials of earlier men (310ff.). Evander tells his guest about the early kings. The role of Saturn in the book is as a forebear of Aeneas; like the Trojan hero he is exiled from his lost kingdom, following which he brought together the unruly race, gave them laws and began a golden age of peace.[3] Yet disorder again beset the country (326ff.) until Evander, another outcast and 'type' of Aeneas and Augustus, arrived at the prompting of Carmentis and Apollo. The poet then describes the places destined to become famous in the future Rome — the Porta Carmentalis, the Asylum, the Lupercal, the Argiletum and the Capitol. Evander describes to Aeneas (351ff.) the religious significance of the areas destined to become the Capitol, Janiculum and *arx Saturnia*. Aeneas then sees the area of the Forum and Carinae — then cow paddocks — before entering

---

[1] One wonders if Vergil considered listing the *balteus*, which Turnus takes from Pallas' body (10,495ff.), amongst the gifts of Anchises (166ff.). Had he done so it would have added a further incentive to the killing of Turnus at 12,938ff. We can only speculate on his reason for not doing so; one possibility is that it might have clarified the issues and given a strong sense of righteousness to Aeneas' act (12,938ff.), neither of which Vergil desired.

[2] For the battle between Hercules and Cacus as a representation and anticipation of that between Aeneas and Turnus, and that between Augustus and Antonius, see V. Buchheit, *Vergil über die Sendung Roms* (Heidelberg, 1963) 116ff.; Otis, 330ff.; Binder, 2ff. and *passim*.

[3] See Binder's discussion on Evander, *Romanae conditor arcis*, and on the *aurea Saturni saecula* in his Chapter 3, 76ff.; see also that of Buchheit, 92ff.

Evander's house which Hercules once entered. The role of Hercules as prototype of Aeneas (and Augustus) is further emphasised as Evander calls upon Aeneas (362ff.) to emulate the god in humble living and in *pietas*. Thus, in a short space of time, we see a close connection between Saturn, Hercules, Aeneas and Evander — all outsiders who come into Latium, live a life of *frugalitas,* and impose peace and order by their efforts.

Vergil maintains the tempo of his narrative by switching his attention, as night falls, to the divine realm, where Venus appeals for new armour for her son with which to fight in the war that approaches (370ff.). Vulcan readily agrees to her request and orders the Cyclopes to begin the work (395ff.). As the work on the armour continues the morning breaks and Evander tells his guest (470ff.) of the cruel reign of Mezentius in neighbouring Caere, the rebellion against him, and his shelter with Turnus. Whereas Evander the day before had concentrated solely on the past, with the new day he switches his attention to the present.[1] He points out that with just fury Etruria has risen demanding punishment for the king. He sees Aeneas as the foreign leader, referred to in a soothsayer's prophecy, who will lead them in war. Moreover, the king entrusts his son Pallas to Aeneas and two hundred horse with a further two hundred coming from Pallas himself. As *Aeneas Anchisiades*[2] and Achates are pondering many hard thoughts with sad hearts (520ff.),[3] a sign comes suddenly from heaven — a flash in the sky and thunder (524ff.).

[1] On the relationship between the three days in which the action of the book takes place and the poet's concentration on past, present and future, see Otis, 330ff. For earlier views on the structure of Book 8, see F. Bömer, 'Studien zum VIII. Buche der Aeneis', *Rh.M.* 92 (1944) 319ff. and D.L. Drew, *The Allegory of the 'Aeneid'* (Oxford, 1927) 6ff. G.K. Galinsky, 'The Hercules-Cacus Episode in *Aeneid* VIII', *A.J.P.* 87 (1966) 21ff., questions Otis' tripartite division of Book 8.

[2] Reference to Aeneas here as *Anchisiades* may foreshadow the sign from his mother at 524ff.

[3] On Aeneas' despondency here, see above, p. 149 n. 1.

They look up and see arms flashing in the sky and clashing like thunder. The response of Aeneas and the others is as follows:

> obstipuere animis alii, sed Troius heros                              530
> agnovit sonitum et divae promissa parentis.
> tum memorat: "ne vero, hospes, ne quaere profecto
> quem casum portenta ferant: ego poscor Olympo.
> hoc signum cecinit missuram diva creatrix,
> si bellum ingrueret, Volcaniaque arma per auras      535
> laturam auxilio.
> heu quantae miseris caedes Laurentibus instant!
> quas poenas mihi, Turne, dabis! quam multa sub undas
> scuta virum galeasque et fortia corpora volves,
> Thybri pater! poscant acies et foedera rumpant."       540
>                                                                    (530–40)[1]

Whereas all the others remain stunned Aeneas recognises the divine signal (*pietas*) and tells Evander not to ask what these portents mean.[2] He recognises that he is summoned by heaven; for his goddess mother foretold to him that if war should threaten she would assist his cause with arms from Vulcan. The hero foresees the carnage to result from the war as well as his own victory in it. The end of his speech is particularly effective in evoking his sorrow at the general loss of life in the war to come and his unquestioning belief in victory. Turnus too has this belief at the outset of the war, but he is deluded by Allecto and Iris.[3] There is nothing delusive about this portent in the sky which

---

[1] Knauer, indices ad loc., compares *Od.* 15,172–8 in which Helen interprets an omen as meaning that Odysseus after his long wanderings will return home. The content of the parallels is thus quite different. For the promise by Thetis of arms for Achilles, see *Il.* 18,134ff.

[2] Cf. the reaction of Turnus and the others to the miracle of the ships at 9,123ff. Whereas all the Rutuli are stunned (*obstipuere* 9,123), Messapus is terrified, and Tiberinus recoils, Turnus does not lose faith. Vergil seems to have drawn a clear parallel in his presentation of Aeneas in Book 8 and Turnus in Book 9 in their reactions to divine appearances and signals.

[3] See 7,445ff. and esp. 9,1–24.

signals victory for Aeneas. The hero's *pietas* is again shown
following his speech, where he is described (541ff.) renewing the
fires on Hercules' altar, and joyfully (*laetus* 544) approaching the
household god and humble Penates, which (we are to infer) he
worshipped the day before. Moreover, Evander and the Trojans
make sacrifice of chosen ewes (544f.). Aeneas' final speech in
Book 8 and his behaviour afterwards thus show his impeccable
response to the divine signal. Whereas he was sad shortly
beforehand (520ff.), he is now joyful in his *pietas*.

The remainder of the book concerns Evander's tearful farewell
to his son (554ff.) and Aeneas' receiving of the armour made by
Vulcan. As Trojans and Arcadians prepare to depart, Evander
clasps his son's hand, sheds tears, and prays to Jupiter for his
survival (560–83). Following this prayer, the swooning Evander
must be helped into his palace. The reader may already anticipate
worse to come with the death of the young Pallas on the
battlefield. As *pater Aeneas* (606) and his men approach Tarchon
and the Etruscan camp, Venus appears with the armour made by
Vulcan (608ff.). In joy (*laetus* 617) Aeneas rolls his eyes over the
armour — a helmet with plumes that pours out flames,[1] a
death-bearing sword, a huge blood-red corselet, greaves of
electrum and gold, a spear and a mighty shield. It is on the shield
(*clipei non enarrabile textum* 625) that Vergil focuses; for on its
surface Vulcan has fashioned the story of Italy and the triumphs of
the Romans (626f.).[2] The pictures begin with scenes from early
Roman history, telling the story of Romulus and Remus, Rome
and the Sabines, Mettus Fufetius of Alba, Porsena and Cloelia,

[1] For the imagery of fire in the armour of Aeneas, see below, p. 162ff.

[2] For detailed analysis of the pictures on the shield, see Fowler (op. cit. p. 152 n. 3),
100ff.; Drew, 26ff.; J. R. Bacon, 'Aeneas in Wonderland', *C.R.* 53 (1939) 97ff. and esp.
101ff.; C. Becker, 'Der Schild des Aeneas', *W.S.* 77 (1964) 111–27; M. Wigodsky, 'The
Arming of Aeneas', *C. & M.* 26 (1965) 192–221; D. E. Eichholz, 'The Shield of Aeneas',
*P.V.S.* 6 (1966–7) 45–9; Otis, 341f. A discussion of the shield occupies the largest section of Binder's book, 150–282.

Manlius and the Gauls. There follows a religious tableau, the Salii, Luperci and *matres*, and then a picture of Catiline in Tartarus and Cato in Elysium. These pictures precede that of the battle between Augustus and Antonius at Actium on which the entire scene centres. In the battle, conducted on a human and divine level, Augustus and Apollo are shown to prevail over Antonius and the gods of discord. As Aeneas looks at the last scene — the list of conquered peoples in Augustus' triumph — he shows amazement and joy, although ignorant of the events shown on the shield, and then he raises 'high on his shoulder the glory and destiny of his children's children'.[1]

---

[1] See Williams ad loc., who notes the wider significance of Aeneas' lifting of the shield.

# BOOK 9

In Book 9 Turnus attempts, in the absence of Aeneas, to burn the Trojans' ships. When he fails in this aim he turns his attention to the enemy camp, only to be forced by nightfall to call an end to the day's fighting (156ff.). During the night the two Trojan youths, Nisus and Euryalus, creep into the camp of the Rutuli and slaughter many of the sleeping enemy (176–502). On the next day the fighting resumes with Turnus pre-eminent in battle. It is made clear (756ff.) that had Turnus not been so consumed with battle-fury, he might well have gained victory for the Italian cause.

Thus Vergil concentrates his attention in Book 9 on the characterisation of Turnus.[1] Some attempt is made to characterise Aeneas indirectly, through the eyes of Turnus;[2] but Vergil's aim in the book is to develop the Rutulian's heroic stature in battle in anticipation of Aeneas' return to the scene. The absence of Aeneas is as significant for the action of Book 9 as is his return for Book 10: in the former Turnus is allowed pre-eminence on the battle-field, whereas in the latter he is eclipsed by his Trojan counter-part.[3] Even Turnus' highest point in battle (503–818) is tainted with failure because of a wasted opportunity (756ff.). The reader understands at the end of Book 9 that if Turnus cannot achieve victory in Aeneas' absence, he will certainly fail to do so after his return.

[1] For an analysis of Turnus' role in Book 9, see my doctoral thesis (University of Glasgow, 1984) 33ff.

[2] See Turnus' *cohortatio*, 128–58, and especially 136ff.

[3] It is an interesting example of Vergilian 'framing' that Juno (via Iris) prompts Turnus into battle (9, 6ff.) and then withdraws him when the going gets too rough (10, 633ff.). In both cases Turnus responds emotionally and with piety, and raises his hands to the heavens (9, 16f., and 10, 667).

# BOOK 10

In Book 2 we saw Aeneas in a war situation prior to the acquisition of *pietas* in the full sense. We saw that at Troy he had a propensity towards heroic violence and irrationality.[1] In the books that describe his adventures after the fall of Troy (Books 3, 1, 4, 5, 6(i), 7 and 8), Vergil concentrates on projecting forcefully the hero's *pietas* by use of his direct and indirect methods of characterisation. Apart from Book 2 we have not seen Aeneas in a situation of war. This has allowed Vergil to place full emphasis on some of the more noble aspects of the hero's character. Yet as he now approaches war again for the first time since Troy, how will he react? Or, more pertinently, how will Vergil present *pius Aeneas* in the war situation?[2]

Following the *concilium deorum* (1–117), and a restatement of the *status quo* in battle (118–45), Vergil's attention switches briefly to Aeneas. He has by this time left Pallanteum and proceeds to see Tarchon (148ff.), king of the Lydians, who, now free from fate (*libera fati* 154),[3] join forces with the Trojans. Following this Aeneas returns towards Latium, notably with Pallas close beside him (159ff.), asking about the stars and his labours on land and sea.

Vergil now digresses from the action (163–214) to give an account of the Etruscan forces who sail with Aeneas. This account pre-empts his reappearance at the Trojan camp. Aeneas sits at his post holding the rudder and looking after the sails, for his concern for his men and their situation allows no rest (215ff.).

---

[1] See above, p. 48ff.

[2] One obvious difference is in the nature and length of Aeneas' speeches: in Book 10 he utters 10 speeches totalling only 29 lines. Unlike Homer, Vergil writes notably short speeches for his heroes in battle.

[3] This is a reference to the oracle (8, 499ff.) that the Etruscan cause requires a foreign leader. Vergil thus emphasises Aeneas' role here (10, 154ff.) as in keeping with the fated will (*pietas*).

His *cura* here (217) underlines his *pietas*. Suddenly (219ff.) the nymphs, whom Cybele had metamorphosed from ships,[1] appear before him swimming beside his ship. One of these, Cymodocea, informs him (228ff.) of the happenings in his absence — the Trojans including Ascanius are penned up in their camp by Turnus and the Rutuli. She urges him into action and promises him (244f.) great slaughter of the enemy. Aeneas reacts as follows:

> tum breviter supera aspectans convexa precatur:
> "alma parens Idaea deum, cui Dindyma cordi
> turrigeraeque urbes biiugique ad frena leones,
> tu mihi nunc pugnae princeps, tu rite propinques
> augurium Phrygibusque adsis pede, diva, secundo."    255
>                                                      (251–5)[2]

*Precatur* (251) introduces the tone of the speech.[3] The prayer is addressed to Cybele, who, as we have seen, saved the Trojan fleet from the flames of the Rutuli. He prays that she will lead him in battle, that the omen will be fulfilled, and that she will be present amongst the Phrygians with a favouring step. Aeneas' portrayal here is consistent with the more general presentation, in that he utters this speech as an *exemplum* of *pietas*. He now prepares his men for battle and lifts high the blazing shield which Vulcan himself had made. This brings a roar of approval and anticipation from his men who, with new hope, cast their spears. Turnus and his captains turn to see the waters filled with ships, but attention focuses on Aeneas:

---

[1] 9,77ff.

[2] Knauer, indices ad 252f., compares Achilles' prayer to Zeus at *Il.* 16,233f. in which the hero prays that Patroclus may win glory in battle and also return safely to the ships. The speeches are alike in that they are both prayers before battle, although Aeneas, unlike Achilles, leads his men and takes part in the battle.

[3] *Precatur* is used regularly of Aeneas; cf. 6,186, 193; 7,137; 10,874; 12,175.

> ardet apex capiti cristisque a vertice flamma          270
> funditur et vastos umbo vomit aureus ignis:
> non secus ac liquida si quando nocte cometae
> sanguinei lugubre rubent, aut Sirius ardor
> ille sitim morbosque ferens mortalibus aegris
> nascitur et laevo contristat lumine caelum.          275
> (270–5)

In the *Iliad*[1] Priam sees Achilles dressed in his armour which is described as follows:

> τὸν δ' ὁ γέρων Πρίαμος πρῶτος ἴδεν ὀφθαλμοῖσι,          25
> παμφαίνονθ' ὥς τ' ἀστέρ' ἐπεσσύμενον πεδίοιο,
> ὅς ῥά τ' ὀπώρης εἶσιν, ἀρίζηλοι δέ οἱ αὐγαὶ
> φαίνονται πολλοῖσι μετ' ἀστράσι νυκτὸς ἀμολγῷ·
> ὅν τε κύν' Ὠρίωνος ἐπίκλησιν καλέουσι.
> λαμπρότατος μὲν ὅ γ' ἐστί, κακὸν δέ τε σῆμα τέτυκται,   30
> καί τε φέρει πολλὸν πυρετὸν δειλοῖσι βροτοῖσιν.
> (*Il.* 22,25–31)

The sight of Achilles is a bad omen for Hector whom he is about to face in single combat. Priam becomes distraught[2] and pleads with his son (38ff.) not to fight the mighty Achilles. The meaning of πολλὸν πυρετὸν δειλοῖσι βροτοῖσιν (31) thus becomes clear: Achilles is like the dog-star of Orion; and Hector, Priam, Hecuba and the Trojans are the wretched mortals who must bear the affliction. A similar effect is conveyed by Vergil: 'The effect of Aeneas' return to the scene of battle is to bring as certain disaster on his enemies as Achilles' return did'.[3] This, however, is only half of the effect, for the picture of Aeneas (10,270–5) is more elaborate than that of Achilles. In the Homeric case it is Achilles himself who is like the dog-star,

---

[1] Knauer, indices ad loc. Cf. *Il.* 5,4ff. where Diomedes is pictured in battle with a flame coming from his helmet.

[2] Contrast the reaction of Turnus to the sight of Aeneas: *haud tamen audaci Turno fiducia cessit* (10,276).

[3] Williams, ad 272f.

whereas in Aeneas' case flames are actually pictured flowing from the armour: the simile which follows this description belongs, as in Homer, to the narrator (272–5).

Vergil's description of Aeneas in his armour prefigures the *furor* of the hero.[1] This is seen especially at 270f.: *ardet ... flamma funditur et vastos umbo vomit aureus ignis.* As surely as fire-imagery helps to convey the demonic *furor* of Turnus,[2] so here it foreshadows the *furor* of Aeneas in the Italian war. It is Aeneas' *furor* that is the ill omen, one that soon finds reality in his *aristeia* following the death of Pallas (10,510–605). Thus the description of Turnus in his armour (7,783ff.) and that of Aeneas in his (10,270ff.) both perform the same function in foreshadowing the heroes' rage and violence in battle.

There is, however, an important difference. The picture of Turnus conveys a furious monster on the one hand and an unfortunate metamorphosis, divinely inspired, on the other. This reflects the reality of Turnus' infection by Allecto (7,445ff.) — that he is the unwilling agent of a demonic force. The simile, which likens Aeneas to blood-red comets or to fiery Sirius, however, conveys an altogether different source for the hero's *furor*, yet one which aptly reflects Aeneas' character as he is presented throughout the poem. Aeneas' *furor* is like fiery Sirius in the sky, in that it rises from within him bringing disaster to the Italians.[3] The imagery thus communicates the nature of

[1] On the armour of Aeneas, see W.H. Semple, 'War and Peace in Virgil's *Aeneid*', *B.R.L.* 36 (1953–4) 216; J.P. Poe, 'Success and Failure in the Mission of Aeneas', *T.A.Ph.A.* 96 (1965) 330; M. Wigodsky, *C.&M.* 26 (1965) 213ff.; Boyle, *Ramus* 1 (1972) 66f.

[2] See e.g. 7,462ff.; 9,65ff.; 9,535ff.; 9,731ff.

[3] Note *rubent*, 273 and esp. *nascitur*, 275. Cf. below, p.174, and the rising anger of Aeneas at 12, 494ff.

Aeneas' *furor*[1] — that it rises from within him in response to circumstances. Whereas Turnus' *furor* is demonic and implanted externally, Aeneas' is to be seen as internally based and having no demonic source. Aeneas is, in this sense, like Achilles whose anger comes from within.[2] Turnus' demonic *furor* is, by contrast, an essentially un-Homeric element in the poem. Thus we see that the descriptions of Aeneas and Turnus in their armour do not simply foreshadow their rage in battle, but also indicate fundamental differences in the natures of their *furor*.[3]

Aeneas and the Etruscans land on the shore and immediately join battle (287ff.). After killing many men (310ff.), Aeneas speaks to Achates as follows:

> "suggere tela mihi, non ullum dextera frustra
> torserit in Rutulos, steterunt quae in corpore Graium
> Iliacis campis."                                        (333–5)[4]

There is little of note in the speech. Aeneas will not fail to hit the Rutuli with spears thrown from his right hand. We are reminded that he was on the battlefield at Troy and that he is commencing another war. Aeneas now seizes a spear and kills Maeon (335ff.) before striking others. As the battle continues Vergil focuses on the combat between Turnus and Pallas. We see the latter bravely leading his men (362ff.) with considerable success before encountering Turnus, who eventually kills him in their subsequent

[1] Boyle, (op. cit. p. 163 n. 1) 67, argues that the birth image of fiery Sirius and Aeneas' connection with it 'provide a suitable analogue for the birth of Rome itself '. The implication is that the rise of Rome brings 'drought, pestilence and gloom' as does the rise of *Sirius ardor*. This seems difficult to accept; the image refers to Aeneas and only through him can it refer to Rome. Vergil is foreshadowing the *furor* of Aeneas, not writing anti-Roman propaganda.

[2] Note εἶσιν, *Il.* 22, 27.

[3] Cf. the words of Nisus: "*dine hunc ardorem mentibus addunt, Euryale, an sua cuique deus fit dira cupido?*" (9, 184–5). Turnus, it could be argued, represents the former and Aeneas, the latter.

[4] Knauer, indices ad loc., cites *Il.* 8, 297–9; 13, 260–5; 14, 454–7 as Homeric parallels, the closest being 13, 260–5 where Idomeneus tells Meriones that he will find spears for battle in his hut.

combat (474ff.). When rumour of his death reaches him Aeneas becomes wild with anger and, as a result, causes carnage on the battlefield (510ff.).

It is worth considering in detail the behaviour of Aeneas here.[1] When first hearing of the death of Pallas, he seeks to reach and assist the routed Trojans and, at the same time, to kill Turnus:[2]

> proxima quaeque metit gladio latumque per agmen
> ardens limitem agit ferro, te, Turne, superbum
> caede nova quaerens.                                    (513–15)

Aeneas is described as *ardens* — part of Vergil's vocabulary of *furor*[3] — and Turnus is *superbum caede nova*. Vergil proceeds to give a reason for the rising fury in Aeneas:

>                              Pallas, Euander, in ipsis
> omnia sunt oculis, mensae quas advena primas
> tunc adiit, dextraeque datae.                           (515–17)

There is method in Aeneas' madness: he had given pledges to his *hospes* Evander at Pallanteum about the safety of Pallas. It is of these pledges that Aeneas now thinks as he prepares for a more gruesome act:

>                              Sulmone creatos
> quattuor hic iuvenes, totidem quos educat Ufens,
> viventis rapit, inferias quos immolet umbris
> captivoque rogi perfundat sanguine flammas.

>                                                          (517–20)

---

[1] The *aristeia* of Aeneas (510–605) in response to the death of Pallas parallels that of Achilles at *Il.* 21, 1–210 (Knauer's indices, ad loc.). Vergil, however, uses different techniques from those of Homer, on occasions projecting vividly the brutality of Aeneas and on other occasions obfuscating it; see below, p. 166ff. and p. 183ff.

[2] From this moment until the end of the poem Aeneas burns with an implacable desire to kill Turnus. Only at the poem's climax (12,938ff.) does he hesitate for a moment in this intention.

[3] See Camps, 38.

The preparation for human sacrifice is no mere threat but is actually carried through.[1] *Immolare* (519) is used on only three occasions in the entire poem, in each case to describe an action of Aeneas.[2] Moreover, Aeneas is the only character in the poem to perform human sacrifice. In this too he is like Achilles who takes twelve sons of the Trojans for sacrifice as a revenge for the death of Patroclus.[3] Vergil, of course, need not have included this act in his own poem; the fact that he has chosen to do so 'must be accorded its full significance'.[4] Aeneas in his battle-fury has a striking resemblance to the heroes in the *Iliad*.

The narrative reverts to the battlefield where the slaughter continues. Aeneas had thrown a spear at Magus and, after it misses, the latter instantly clasps the knees of the hero[5] and as suppliant (*supplex* 523) pleads for his life (524ff.). He prays (*precor* 525) by Anchises' spirit and the hope of growing Iulus that Aeneas will spare his life for the sake of his father and son. To this end he offers him silver and gold and says that victory for the Trojans does not turn on him. Aeneas' reply is that the killing of Pallas makes such mercy impossible:

> "argenti atque auri memoras quae multa talenta
> gnatis parce tuis. belli commercia Turnus
> sustulit ista prior iam tum Pallante perempto.
> hoc patris Anchisae manes, hoc sentit Iulus."

(531–4)

In *Il.* 21,67ff.[6] Achilles holds a spear over Lycaon about to deal the death blow when the latter pleads for his life. He had

---

[1] See 11,81f. where we see the youths again with their hands tied behind their backs ready for sacrifice. The question of human sacrifice is discussed above, p.9f. and below, p.183ff.

[2] S. Farron, 'The *Furor* and *Violentia* of Aeneas', *Acta Classica* 20 (1977) 208.

[3] *Il.* 18,333–7; 21,26–33; 23,19–23; 23,175–83.

[4] Williams, ad 519.

[5] The deaths of Magus and Turnus (12,930ff.) are compared below, p.210ff.

[6] Knauer, indices ad loc.

been captured previously by Achilles and had bought his freedom and now curses his fortune that he is again in Achilles' grasp. Achilles replies to his plea as follows:

"νήπιε, μή μοι ἄποινα πιφαύσκεο μηδ' ἀγόρευε·
πρὶν μὲν γὰρ Πάτροκλον ἐπισπεῖν αἴσιμον ἦμαρ,          100
τόφρα τί μοι πεφιδέσθαι ἐνὶ φρεσὶ φίλτερον ἦεν
Τρώων, καὶ πολλοὺς ζωοὺς ἕλον ἠδὲ πέρασσα·
νῦν δ' οὐκ ἔσθ' ὅς τις θάνατον φύγῃ, ὅν κε θεός γε
Ἰλίου προπάροιθεν ἐμῆς ἐν χερσὶ βάλῃσι,
καὶ πάντων Τρώων, πέρι δ' αὖ Πριάμοιό γε παίδων."          105
                                                    (Il. 21,99–105)

Achilles' argument is clear; until Patroclus died he would take prisoners alive, but now that he is dead, mercy is impossible. Lycaon must die, says Achilles (106ff.), for Patroclus died, who was a far better man than he (Lycaon) is. A day will come (111ff.) when Achilles himself, born from a πατὴρ ἀγαθός and a θεά will die prematurely in battle. In Achilles' terms it is right that Lycaon should die in battle given that Patroclus is dead and that the pleading man at the end of the spear is of a lower social status. It is with a sense of natural justice that Achilles deals the death blow.

Aeneas feels less inclined to justify his actions. His speech lasts for four lines, whereas Achilles' lasts for fifteen. Essentially, however, Aeneas' behaviour here is Homeric. Magus had appealed to him by Aeneas' father and son, and had offered him silver and gold. Aeneas' reply picks up the appeal and the offer, and rejects them totally out of hand. In having Aeneas dismiss the appeal and kill Magus, the poet underlines the hero's *furor* and his lack of *ratio, clementia* and *humanitas*.[1]

---

[1] It is remarkable that Otis, 357, interprets the *aristeia* of Aeneas (10,510–605) as symbolising the *humanitas* of the hero. There is no reference in his discussion of this section to the *furor* of Aeneas. Cf. his discussion of the death of Turnus (379ff.) where he scrupulously avoids reference to Aeneas' irrational rage (12,938ff.).

Aeneas' next victim (537ff.) is Haemonides, *Phoebi Triviaeque sacerdos*.[1] The point is emphasised by Vergil (538–9) that the priest is wearing his sacred garb.[2] Haemonides does bear arms (541f.) and is therefore a legitimate target in war; yet in having Aeneas kill him (*immolat* 541), Vergil is clearly making great play with the uncontrolled violence of his hero. No priest, to my knowledge, is killed in the *Iliad*,[3] suggesting perhaps that Aeneas here has transcended the limits of behaviour of a Homeric hero.

The slaughter continues (543f.) with Aeneas still in a state of uncontrolled fury.[4] He now gloats over the dead Tarquitus as follows:

"istic nunc, metuende, iace. non te optima mater
condet humi patrioque onerabit membra sepulcro:
alitibus linquere feris, aut gurgite mersum
unda feret piscesque impasti vulnera lambent."

(557–60).

This too is modelled[5] on the vaunting of Achilles over the dead Lycaon:

"ἐνταυθοῖ νῦν κεῖσο μετ' ἰχθύσιν, οἵ σ' ὠτειλὴν
αἷμ' ἀπολιχμήσονται ἀκηδέες· οὐδέ σε μήτηρ
ἐνθεμένη λεχέεσσι γοήσεται, ἀλλὰ Σκάμανδρος
οἴσει δινήεις εἴσω ἁλὸς εὐρέα κόλπον.          125
θρῴσκων τις κατὰ κῦμα μέλαιναν φρῖχ' ὑπαΐξει
ἰχθύς, ὅς κε φάγῃσι Λυκάονος ἀργέτα δημόν."

(*Il.* 21, 122–7)

[1] Cf. 6,35 where the same formula is used of the Sibyl, to whom Aeneas shows great reverence, and 6,69 where he displays reverence to the two deities. The echo, it would seem, is deliberate.

[2] Particularly so if we follow Probus' reading of *albis* for *armis* at 539; see Williams, ad loc.

[3] Knauer, indices ad loc., offers no Homeric parallel for the killing of Haemonides.

[4] Note *furit* 545; *ardenti* 552; *inimico pectore* 556.

[5] Knauer, indices ad loc.

The two speeches are notably similar: in each case the dead man's mother will be unable to provide proper burial, and instead fish will now lick their wounds. Vergil, however, has added new elements to the Homeric model. The fish which Aeneas envisages will be hungry (*impasti*), whereas no such adjective is used in Homer.[1] Tarquitus will fall victim to the fish in the sea only if he happens not to be subjected to birds of prey (559f.);[2] this too is a Vergilian variation. Aeneas mentions the bereft mother (557f.) before the birds of prey and the fish, thus making the contrast more stark and heightening the cruelty of his intentions. Tarquitus' mother will not have the opportunity to retrieve the body — a fact which makes the impact of death more terrible. Moreover, Aeneas describes her as *optima mater* (557) which is a variation of Achilles' simple μήτηρ (123). Here again Aeneas' words heighten his cruelty, in that the mother of the victim is suffering all the more because of her devotion to her son.

Aeneas continues the slaughter of many of the enemy (561ff.): he is like Aegaeon, who had a hundred arms and hands, and from whom fire (a significant touch) flashed from fifty mouths and breasts when battling against the thunderbolts of Jupiter (565ff.).[3] Aeneas' sword grows warm (570) as he rages over the plain (569). He now encounters Lucagus and Liger (575ff.), two brothers who ride together in a chariot. Liger chides him (581ff.) that he is not in Phrygia now, nor does he fight Diomede or

[1] Farron, (op. cit. p. 166 n. 2) 207.

[2] The Homeric model makes no mention of birds of prey, which may come from *Il.* 11, 452ff. (Odysseus to Socus), *Il.* 16, 836 (Hector to Patroclus), or *Il.* 22, 335 & 354 (Achilles and Hector).

[3] Whilst the reference to Aegaeon clearly helps to convey the *furor* of Aeneas in battle, I see no particular significance in the reference to Jupiter here. I would argue, in fact, that Aeneas is described as *pius* (591) because he furthers the progress of fate and thus follows Jupiter's will. D.A. Little, 'The Death of Turnus and the Pessimism of the *Aeneid* ', *A.U.M.L.A.* 33 (1970) 69, argues that 'in comparing Aeneas with Aegaeon, Virgil has condemned this brutality clearly enough'. I see no reason to support the view that Vergil 'condemns' either Aeneas or Turnus anywhere in the poem.

Achilles, but now his life will soon be ended. Aeneas hurls a spear (585) which catches Lucagus who falls dead from the chariot. Vergil continues as follows:

> quem pius Aeneas dictis adfatur amaris:
> "Lucage, nulla tuos currus fuga segnis equorum
> prodidit aut vanae vertere ex hostibus umbrae:
> ipse rotis saliens iuga deseris." haec ita fatus
> arripuit biiugos; frater tendebat inertis                595
> infelix palmas curru delapsus eodem:
> "per te, per qui te talem genuere parentes,
> vir Troiane, sine hanc animam et miserere precantis."
> pluribus oranti Aeneas: "haud talia dudum
> dicta dabas. morere et fratrem ne desere frater."        600
> tum latebras animae pectus mucrone recludit.
>
> (591–601).[1]

Perhaps the most striking thing about this passage is Vergil's description of Aeneas as *pius* (591), when he speaks with bitter words and acts with uncontrolled rage both beforehand and afterwards.[2] We could attempt to explain the use of the word here by stressing that Aeneas is motivated by feelings of guilt and responsibility following the death of Pallas. There is no doubt that, both now and later, the death of Pallas has a strong effect upon Aeneas.[3] Nevertheless, it seems unlikely that this alone is Vergil's reason for using the epithet here. Vergil is drawing our attention to the fact that, despite being as brutal as any hero in

[1] Knauer indices ad loc., cites no close parallel for this episode. In my view Aeneas' words to the pleading Liger (599f.) are the most savage in either Vergil or Homer. The brutality of Aeneas thus reaches a climax with this speech.

[2] For a comparison between this use of *pius* at 10,591 and that at 4,393, see above, p. 89f. There is on the whole remarkably little comment on Aeneas' description as *pius* at 10,591. For some different views on the reference, see Mackail, ad loc.; Austin (*Aen.* 4) ad 393; R. Beare, 'Invidious Success', *P.V.S.* 4 (1964–5) 24; Quinn 225, n. 2; and Williams, ad 510f.

[3] See Books 11 and 12, *passim* and esp. 12,938ff. R.S. Conway, 'Vergil's Creative Art', *P.B.A.* 17 (1931) 28f., was one of the first to stress the connection between the death of Pallas (10,479ff.) and Aeneas' *furor* (10,510ff.).

either *Iliad* or *Aeneid*, Aeneas is still in a state of *pietas*. The reason
for this is unlikely to be that piety in the poem is gained by one's
brutality conducted in the name of a just vengeance.

When analysing Aeneas' behaviour here in Book 10, we should
always keep in mind that this is the first time we have seen him in
the war situation since his own narration of the fall of Troy. In
this earlier battle, he was characterised by his irrationality (*arma
amens capio...* 2,314) and his 'heroic impulse'.[1] When he sees
Helen lurking silently, close to Vesta's shrine in fear of her life,
he becomes possessed with *furor* (2,575f.) and decides to kill her
(577ff.) as revenge for all the pain and hardship she has caused his
people. We saw that at this point (2,594ff.) Venus appears and
stops him from doing so, stressing that it is the gods who destroy
the city — forces so great that Aeneas, for all his desire, can do
nothing to stop them. *Quid furis?* she asks Aeneas (2,595), 'why
(to what purpose, for what reason) do you rage?' Venus does not
concern herself with the morality of his contemplated action; her
point is that Aeneas' plan is bound to be fruitless. He must follow
fate, not fight against it. Aeneas is *impius* in the Helen episode (1)
because he is forgetful of family, *sacra* and Penates, and (2)
because his mad rage conflicts with the course of fate. He is not
*impius* simply because of his state of *furor*, but because of the
direction in which that *furor* is applied.[2] On hearing that his
future lies elsewhere,[3] Aeneas finally acts in accordance with the
will of fate, leaves Troy to the conquering Greeks, and becomes
*pius* accordingly.

Aeneas' behaviour in his *aristeia* here in Book 10 is no different

---

[1] See Quinn, 1ff. and discussion above, p. 48ff.

[2] Many of the modern views on the *Aeneid* rest on the assumption, misguided in my
opinion, that *furor* and *pietas* are incompatible opposites, and that Dido, Mezentius and
Turnus represent the former, and Aeneas the latter. Such a dichotomy cannot be justified
from the text and leads to considerable confusion of the issues at the end of the poem; see
below, p. 209ff.

[3] 2, 268ff.; 589ff.; 692ff.

from that at Troy when he decides to murder Helen.[1] The reason for this is that *furor* is of the nature of war — a fact that Aeneas himself recognises: *nec sat rationis in armis* (2,314). Aeneas does not mean that at Troy he acted wrongly and has now learnt his lesson: he means that *furor* is the dominant characteristic in man's psyche in the war situation, and that this is as true for him as it is for anyone.

Yet whereas Aeneas' behaviour is the same at Troy and in Latium, the direction of it has altered. There is no Venus to intervene in the latter situation because destiny is in the process of being fulfilled. Aeneas is, therefore, given full rein to act according to his natural passions, without divine constraint,[2] because he does not fight against the will of heaven nor is he acting against his or his family's best interests. Aeneas is entirely consistent in his behaviour in Books 2 and 10; it is his relationship to divine circumstances that has changed.

It is for this reason that he is described as *pius* at 10,591: because in slaughtering the enemy he furthers the progress of fate.[3] The concept of *pietas* here, as elsewhere[4] in the *Aeneid*, is divorced from the brutality of action. Aeneas is brutal in the extreme and Vergil strenuously highlights the fact, yet there is no justification for the view that he lacks *pietas* as a result. Here, and even at the very end of the poem, Aeneas lacks *ratio, clementia* and *humanitas*, but his *pietas* results from the direction of his actions, not the conduct of them.

---

[1] Except that in Book 10 he *acts* with brutality, rather than merely expressing an intention to do so.

[2] Cf. E. Kraggerud, *Aeneisstudien, Symb. Osl.* Suppl. 22 (Oslo, 1968) 22f. and R. Coleman, *G. &R.* 29 (1982) 154.

[3] Note the way that the conversation between Jupiter and Juno (606–32) helps to convey the fact that Aeneas is destined to conquer and Turnus is doomed to die. This conversation helps to clarify the meaning of *pius* at 591. Vergil uses Jupiter and the *Dira* to convey a similar effect at 12,843ff.

[4] Cf. 4,393 and 10,783, on which see above, p. 89f. and below, p. 174 n. 2.

We begin to see therefore that our preconceptions of *furor* must be qualified. In Book 1 it was presented as follows:

> "Furor impius intus
> saeva sedens super arma et centum vinctus aënis
> post tergum nodis fremet horridus ore cruento." (1, 294–6)

This passage has led to many misconceptions about the nature of *furor* in the poem. The logic runs as follows: (1) *furor* is *impius* (1, 294); (2) Dido and Turnus, in hindering Aeneas, oppose fate and show the strongest symptoms of *furor*: they are therefore *impii*; (3) Aeneas does occasionally appear to show symptoms of *furor*, but he is clearly *pius* and the poem is the victory of *pietas* over *furor*. Aeneas, therefore, cannot be *pius* and have *furor* at the same time, because *furor* is *impius* (1, 294).

Although this summary of the argument is clearly simplistic, we are now in a position to see that the logic falters because the premise is false: *furor* is not necessarily *impius*. The *furor* of Turnus is *impius*; it is implanted against his will, yet its effect is to enrage him to oppose Aeneas and the course of fate. It is the direction of his *furor* more than anything else that causes it to be *impius*. Aeneas in Books 10 and 12 possesses *pius furor* (note 591) because the direction of his actions aligns itself with the will of heaven. This is seen again at the very end of the poem when Aeneas in a fit of rage immolates the pleading Turnus. Although we react with horror at this action, it is clearly indicated that it aligns itself with Jupiter's will.[1] Thus, at the end of the poem, the hero's *furor* is presented forcefully, but there is no justification whatever for the view that he is *impius* because of it. The point at the poem's conclusion, and here in Book 10, is that a man can perform an act or acts of extreme barbarity, and at times lack the scarcest trace of humanity, yet still be described as *pius*.

Such fierce fighting on Aeneas' part causes Juno to have

---

[1] 12, 843ff.; 894f.; 914.

concern for Turnus,[1] whom she now proceeds to remove by deceit from the battlefield (636ff.). Aeneas' next encounter is with Mezentius whom he sees active in battle (769ff.). Mezentius boasts (773ff.) that he will have Aeneas' armour as spoils. He casts his spear, yet it misses Aeneas and hits instead Antores in the side (776ff.). Then *pius Aeneas* hurls his spear, wounding but not killing Mezentius (783ff.).[2] Aeneas is joyful (*laetus* 787) at the sight of his enemy's spouting blood, and *fervidus* (788) as he attempts to complete his victory. Thus here again we see Aeneas' *pius furor* (783 and 788). Lausus, however, groans as he sees his father (789f.); he rushes forth to challenge Aeneas and forces the hero to shelter from a shower of javelins. Aeneas then rebukes and threatens Lausus:

> sustinet et Lausum increpitat Lausoque minatur:
> "quo moriture ruis maioraque viribus audes?
> fallit te incautum pietas tua."          (810–12)[3]

The speech, however, has no effect on Lausus (*nec minus ille exsultat demens* 812f.). Aeneas' anger rises (*saevae ... irae... surgunt* 813f.)[4] and the Fates take up Lausus' final thread (814f.). He is then killed by Aeneas who drives his sword into the youth's breast. When he sees the look on the dying boy's face Aeneas groans and feels pity and stretches out his hand as the *patriae ... pietatis imago* (824) rises in his mind. He then addresses the dead Lausus as follows:

[1] This concern of Juno is a measure of how far Aeneas has furthered the progress of fate by the slaughter he wreaks on the battlefield.

[2] Why *pius* here? Certainly not for the reason given by Mackail, ad 10,591, or that by Williams, ad 783: 'the epithet concentrates our attention on the contrast between the godless Mezentius (773f.) and the god-fearing Aeneas'. There is little that is godless about Mezentius' speech (773ff.), just as there is nothing god-fearing about Aeneas' hurling of the spear (783ff.). They are in battle, each intent on killing the other. The same factors apply as at 10,591.

[3] Knauer, indices ad loc., offers no Homeric parallel for this speech.

[4] The description of the rising anger of Aeneas is consistent with the picture of the hero in his armour at 10,270ff.; see above, p. 163f.

"quid tibi nunc, miserande puer, pro laudibus istis,        825
quid pius Aeneas tanta dabit indole dignum?
arma, quibus laetatus, habe tua; teque parentum
manibus et cineri, si qua est ea cura, remitto.
hoc tamen infelix miseram solabere mortem:
Aeneae magni dextra cadis."                        (825–30)[1]

Aeneas' reaction to Lausus' death emphasises his *pietas*, in the sense that the hero thinks of his own family. It is this love for his father and son that prompts him to treat kindly the body of Lausus.[2] He sees the young man as *pius* (812) and stresses his own piety and greatness (826, 830). The description of him as *Anchisiades* (822)[3] helps to convey his filial *pietas*. It is important to remember that he is *pius* here because of love of family, not because of pity shown for a dead *hostis*.[4] His *pietas* determines the kind of treatment which will be given to the dead Lausus, and not vice-versa. The comparison with Turnus' treatment of Pallas is valid only in so far as no such *patriae pietatis imago* comes into Turnus' thoughts. This is the crucial difference in the two episodes: Aeneas thinks of his own family, whereas Turnus does not. The argument that Aeneas is Turnus' moral superior, however, must be seen as tenuous, given Vergil's recent portrayal of him as morally repugnant (510–605).[5] The difference is that

[1] Knauer, indices ad 829f., compares *Il.* 21,106–8 in which Achilles utters sarcastic words to Lycaon prior to killing him. The pathos of Aeneas' words has no Homeric parallel. Note that Marcellus (6,882) and Pallas (11,42) are also described as *miserande puer*; the phrase seems to be used to depict a boy's impotence in the face of fate.

[2] We might compare 12,938ff. where Aeneas' ferocity abates for a moment in response to Turnus' reference to Anchises and his other pleas (12,931ff.).

[3] For *Anchisiades* here, see Conington, ad loc.; Glover, 223f.; Warde Fowler, *Aeneas at the Site of Rome* (Oxford, 1918) 86ff.; E. A. Hahn, 'Note on Vergil's Use of *Anchisiades*', *C.W.* 14 (1920–21) 3f.

[4] Contrast Glover, 224; W. R. Johnson, *C.J.* 60 (1965) 361.

[5] Otis, 359f., amongst many others, stresses the *pietas* of Aeneas here and argues that it is a direct contrast to Turnus' behaviour in killing and despoiling Pallas. There is a case for this view, although it seems to me to be taking the contrast too far by arguing that 'the moral justification of (Aeneas') final victory is here'. Cf. Thornton, *G.&R.* 22 (1953) 82ff.; E. Klingner, *Virgil* (Zurich, 1967) 577ff.

Turnus does not think of his family until his *furor* has passed and until he feels Aeneas' sword at his chest (12,931ff.). Aeneas, by contrast, is seen to dwell suddenly (10,821ff.) on his own family when he sees the behaviour and visage of the dying Lausus.

Mezentius clasps the corpse of his son and plans to avenge his death. He calls three times to Aeneas (873), who recognises the call and joyfully makes prayer:

> Aeneas agnovit enim laetusque precatur:
> "sic pater ille deum faciat, sic altus Apollo!
> incipias conferre manum."                                    (874–6)[1]

After he has spoken thus, the fighting commences with Aeneas gaining the upper hand. He holds the sword over Mezentius and speaks as follows:

> "ubi nunc Mezentius acer et illa
> effera vis animi?"                                            (897–8)[2]

Having said this Aeneas kills Mezentius, yet not before the latter asks to be given burial beside his son, where he may be guarded from the rage of his own people. Aeneas then cuts Mezentius' throat and his blood spills out all over his armour.

---

[1] The encounter between Aeneas and Mezentius resembles that between Achilles and Hector at *Il*. 20,419–38 (Knauer's indices, ad loc.). Both Mezentius and Aeneas act fully in accordance with the Homeric tradition.

[2] Knauer, indices ad loc., compares *Il*. 5,472; 8,229; 13,219b; 22,331–6: the closest parallel is the last of these in which Achilles mocks Hector prior to killing him.

# BOOK 11

Following the great slaughter on the battlefield described in Book 10, the mood is calm at the outset of Book 11 as both sides prepare to take up their dead. Vergil focuses upon Aeneas in this early section; he utters the first four speeches of the book. The first of these (14–28) is an exhortation to his men to continue battle, but only after the funeral rites have been completed. His next two speeches are addressed to the dead Pallas (42–58 and 96–8) whom the Trojans prepare to be taken on a bier to Pallanteum. His fourth speech (108–19) is addressed to the Latin envoys who have come to request a moratorium. This said, Aeneas is withdrawn by the poet from the drama of the book, which centres largely on Turnus' attempt to hold the support of his people, and Camilla's valiant but fatal *aristeia*. Aeneas' dramatic role in Book 11 is therefore a short one;[1] Vergil characterises him indirectly, through the eyes of the enemy, throughout much of the book.[2]

Although his actual dramatic role in the book is short Aeneas' *pietas* is underlined emphatically throughout. This is clear from the very outset of the book (2–4) where Aeneas is conscious of his two duties — to perform funeral rites for the dead and to give thank-offerings for his victory in battle over Mezentius.[3] Without hesitation he gives the offering first (4ff.).[4] This he does by attaching the armour of Mezentius to an oak tree which has had its branches cut from it. Having constructed the offering Aeneas addresses the leaders of his men as follows:

[1] Aeneas utters 4 speeches, 46 lines in Book 11. The hero's comparative taciturnity in the Iliadic *Aeneid* is shown by the fact that only in Book 12 does he speak more — 47 lines.

[2] See the debate of the Latins at 225–444 and especially the reply of Diomede at 252ff.

[3] He seems to dedicate them to the god Mars (*bellipotens* 8), although Mackail, ad loc., referring to 8,61 and 10,423, argues for Tiberinus.

[4] Aeneas' own desire would have been to bury his comrades first (2f.), but, out of piety and according to Roman ritual, he pays his vow first.

"maxima res effecta, viri; timor omnis abesto,
quod superest; haec sunt spolia et de rege superbo          15
primitiae manibusque meis Mezentius hic est.
nunc iter ad regem nobis murosque Latinos.
arma parate, animis et spe praesumite bellum,
ne qua mora ignaros, ubi primum vellere signa
adnuerint superi pubemque educere castris,          20
impediat segnisve metu sententia tardet.
interea socios inhumataque corpora terrae
mandemus, qui solus honos Acheronte sub imo est.
ite," ait "egregias animas, quae sanguine nobis
hanc patriam peperere suo, decorate supremis          25
muneribus, maestamque Euandri primus ad urbem
mittatur Pallas, quem non virtutis egentem
abstulit atra dies et funere mersit acerbo."
sic ait inlacrimans...

(14–29)

Aeneas begins the speech in a spirit of confidence and ends it in
tears — the two moods reflecting his two duties. With Mezentius dead and his armour in the hands of the victor, Aeneas now
sees the way to Latium itself. Turnus is given no mention. They
must prepare arms with courage and anticipate the war with
hope, for there must be no delay when the gods[1] grant that they
pluck out the standards to recommence battle.

At line 22 the mood changes. They must now bury the bodies
of those killed in battle, but only after they have prepared the
body of Pallas to be sent to Pallanteum. Aeneas knows that the
city will be in mourning (*maestam* 26) for the young man who, as
he says, lacked nothing in *virtus* (27). The thought of Pallas'

---

[1] For the Roman practice of plucking up the standard only after the auguries have been
taken, see Conington's note, ad loc. The reference to *superi* here helps to convey Aeneas'
*pietas* as he scrupulously observes the Roman practice.

death brings tears to Aeneas' eyes even as he is speaking (29). The
speech is modelled[1] on that of Achilles over the dead Hector:

"ὦ φίλοι, Ἀργείων ἡγήτορες ἠδὲ μέδοντες,
ἐπεὶ δὴ τόνδ' ἄνδρα θεοὶ δαμάσασθαι ἔδωκαν,
ὃς κακὰ πόλλ' ἔρρεξεν, ὅσ' οὐ σύμπαντες οἱ ἄλλοι,        380
εἰ δ' ἄγετ' ἀμφὶ πόλιν σὺν τεύχεσι πειρηθέωμεν,
ὄφρα κ' ἔτι γνῶμεν Τρώων νόον, ὅν τιν' ἔχουσιν,
ἢ καταλείψουσιν πόλιν ἄκρην τοῦδε πεσόντος,
ἠὲ μένειν μεμάασι καὶ Ἕκτορος οὐκέτ' ἐόντος.
ἀλλὰ τίη μοι ταῦτα φίλος διελέξατο θυμός;                385
κεῖται πὰρ νήεσσι νέκυς ἄκλαυτος ἄθαπτος
Πάτροκλος· τοῦ δ' οὐκ ἐπιλήσομαι, ὄφρ' ἂν ἔγωγε
ζωοῖσιν μετέω καί μοι φίλα γούνατ' ὀρώρῃ·
εἰ δὲ θανόντων περ καταλήθοντ' εἰν Ἀΐδαο,
αὐτὰρ ἐγὼ καὶ κεῖθι φίλου μεμνήσομ' ἑταίρου.             390
νῦν δ' ἄγ' ἀείδοντες παιήονα κοῦροι Ἀχαιῶν
νηυσὶν ἔπι γλαφυρῇσι νεώμεθα, τόνδε δ' ἄγωμεν.
ἠράμεθα μέγα κῦδος· ἐπέφνομεν Ἕκτορα δῖον,
ᾧ Τρῶες κατὰ ἄστυ θεῷ ὣς εὐχετόωντο."

(Il. 22,378–94)

Aeneas' role here parallels that of Achilles whilst the crucial
role of Mezentius in battle is modelled on that of Hector. We are
reminded that the killing of Hector helps substantially the Greek
war effort, but it does not end the war. The killing of Turnus,
however, whose role in the *Aeneid* is often compared to that of
Homer's Hector, is seen as the final blow of the war — the final
fulfilment of Aeneas' mission. The death of Mezentius is, therefore, an important step in this direction[2] — a fact which Aeneas
himself recognises (14ff.). The latter is notably conscious, not
just of the victory recently achieved, but of the necessity to

---

[1] Knauer, indices ad loc., cites *Il.* 22,378–94 as the Homeric parallel.
[2] Hence the reason for Aeneas' description as *pius* (10,783) as he casts the spear that
wounds Mezentius. See above, p. 174.

continue the war in the suitable way until the successful outcome has been reached (*pietas*).

Achilles in his speech (*Il.* 22,378ff.) also changes in mood as he remembers (385ff.) that Patroclus is unwept and unburied. The role of the dead Pallas parallels that of Patroclus: the latter, however, is mourned and buried only after Hector has been killed. The mourning and funeral of Pallas precede the death of Turnus and emotionally prepare us for it. The preparation and funeral of Pallas (11,29ff.) make us anticipate strongly the revenge of Aeneas: in this sense it parallels the reaction of Achilles when he first hears of Patroclus' death (*Il.* 18).

Yet whereas Achilles mourns the death of Patroclus (*Il.* 22,386ff.), and Aeneas that of Pallas (26ff.), their grief is conveyed in noticeably different ways. Achilles is preoccupied with the death of Patroclus alone and utters his love for him by means of the direct speech.[1] Furthermore, his sense of personal loss at the young man's death is presented in the first person singular.[2] It is thus conveyed vividly and directly to the reader. The last third of the *Iliad* is anchored to Achilles' enormous sense of personal loss at the death of Patroclus. Aeneas, by contrast, takes thought for those of his men who died as well as Pallas (22ff.). Vergil highlights the community elements in Aeneas' behaviour (*pietas*). Aeneas' speech, unlike Achilles' (*Il.* 22,378ff.), is devoid entirely of the first person singular: his sense of personal loss is thus presented less vividly and less directly. That Aeneas laments the death of the young man is clear from this early section of Book 11, yet we must recognise that his tears (29) are shed as a general response to his dead allies, not simply for the dead Pallas.

Aeneas enters the royal building (*regia* 38) which is filled with

[1] See, e.g. 18, 79ff.

[2] In the Homeric parallel to Aeneas' speech at 11, 14–28 Achilles uses the first person singular to express his sense of personal loss; see *Il.* 22, 387; 388; 390.

mourning and lamentation. When he sees the head and face of
Pallas and the wound which caused his death, Aeneas reacts as
follows:

> lacrimis ita fatur obortis:
> "tene," inquit "miserande puer, cum laeta veniret,
> invidit Fortuna mihi, ne regna videres
> nostra neque ad sedes victor veherere paternas?
> non haec Euandro de te promissa parenti                    45
> discedens dederam, cum me complexus euntem
> mitteret in magnum imperium metuensque moneret
> acris esse viros, cum dura proelia gente.
> et nunc ille quidem spe multum captus inani
> fors et vota facit cumulatque altaria donis,               50
> nos iuvenem exanimum et nil iam caelestibus ullis
> debentem vano maesti comitamur honore.
> infelix, nati funus crudele videbis!
> hi nostri reditus exspectatique triumphi?
> haec mea magna fides? at non, Euandre, pudendis            55
> vulneribus pulsum aspicies, nec sospite dirum
> optabis nato funus pater. ei mihi quantum
> praesidium, Ausonia, et quantum tu perdis, Iule!"
> haec ubi deflevit...                                    (41–59)

The mood of Aeneas' lamentation is stressed by his welling
tears (*lacrimis ... obortis* 41) and by *deflevit* (59). Narrative
references to his sorrow thus introduce and conclude the speech.
Aeneas stresses the loss to himself (42f.), to his city (44, 57f.), to
Iulus (58), and especially to Evander (49ff.). He feels strongly his
own *promissa* to Evander (45ff. and 55, *haec mea magna fides?*).
Aeneas' regret for the promises made to Evander, yet not
fulfilled, is modelled[1] on Achilles' sorrow that he had heartened
Patroclus' father prior to leaving for Troy:

---

[1] Knauer, indices ad loc.

"ὦ πόποι, ἦ ῥ' ἅλιον ἔπος ἔκβαλον ἤματι κείνῳ
θαρσύνων ἥρωα Μενοίτιον ἐν μεγάροισι·                    325
φῆν δέ οἱ εἰς 'Οπόεντα περικλυτὸν υἱὸν ἀπάξειν
Ἴλιον ἐκπέρσαντα, λαχόντα τε ληΐδος αἶσαν.
ἀλλ' οὐ Ζεὺς ἄνδρεσσι νοήματα πάντα τελευτᾷ·
ἄμφω γὰρ πέπρωται ὁμοίην γαῖαν ἐρεῦσαι
αὐτοῦ ἐνὶ Τροίῃ."                                      (Il. 18,324–30)

Achilles realises that he too will die at Troy, yet it still pains him
that he gave heart to Menoetius that Patroclus would return to
Opoeis. Achilles does not swear vengeance on Hector and the
Trojans out of obligation to Menoetius,[1] but from his own grief
and personal loss at the death of Patroclus. Aeneas' words, by
contrast, are spoken more out of remorse than from the personal
loss of a friend and comrade. It is the loss to Evander, and Aeneas'
obligation to the father, that characterise the speech. Thus we see
that it is the Roman concept of *fides* (cf. 55) which is behind the
remorse, a concept not to be found in the Homeric model.
Achilles' speech emphasises his love for Patroclus and the grief
that he feels, whereas Aeneas' emphasises his *pietas* and *fides*.

Aeneas' own grief at the death of Pallas is essentially transmitted via the narrative (*inlacrimans* 29, *lacrimis* 41, *deflevit* 59).
He sends one thousand men to Evander's Pallanteum out of
obligation to the father (60ff.). They prepare the bier for the
journey, then place the body on it (64ff.). He covers the body
with a robe made by Dido at Carthage,[2] and places also the spoils
which Pallas had won in battle. He now prepares to fulfil his
intention to sacrifice the Italian youths mentioned previously in
Book 10:

---

[1] See *Il.* 18,333ff.
[2] For the point of this reference to Dido, see Williams' note, ad 74.

1.                            Sulmone creatos
quattuor hic iuvenes, totidem quos educat Ufens,
viventis rapit, inferias quos immolet umbris
captivoque rogi perfundat sanguine flammas.

(10, 517–20)

2. vinxerat et post terga manus, quos mitteret umbris
inferias, caeso sparsurus sanguine flammas.

(11, 81–2)

Aeneas' sacrifice of the eight youths is modelled on that of twelve
youths by Achilles, an episode described in three different books:

1. "νῦν δ' ἐπεὶ οὖν, Πάτροκλε, σεῦ ὕστερος εἶμ' ὑπὸ γαῖαν,
οὔ σε πρὶν κτεριῶ, πρίν γ' Ἕκτορος ἐνθάδ' ἐνεῖκαι
τεύχεα καὶ κεφαλήν, μεγαθύμου σοῖο φονῆος·            335
δώδεκα δὲ προπάροιθε πυρῆς ἀποδειροτομήσω
Τρώων ἀγλαὰ τέκνα, σέθεν κταμένοιο χολωθείς."

(Il. 18, 333–7)

2.                            ὁ δ' ἐπεὶ κάμε χεῖρας ἐναίρων,
ζωοὺς ἐκ ποταμοῖο δυώδεκα λέξατο κούρους,
ποινὴν Πατρόκλοιο Μενοιτιάδαο θανόντος.
τοὺς ἐξῆγε θύραζε τεθηπότας ἠΰτε νεβρούς,
δῆσε δ' ὀπίσσω χεῖρας ἐϋτμήτοισιν ἱμᾶσι,             30
τοὺς αὐτοὶ φορέεσκον ἐπὶ στρεπτοῖσι χιτῶσι,
δῶκε δ' ἑταίροισιν κατάγειν κοίλας ἐπὶ νῆας.
αὐτὰρ ὁ ἂψ ἐπόρουσε δαϊζέμεναι μενεαίνων.

(Il. 21, 26–33)

3. "χαῖρέ μοι, ὦ Πάτροκλε, καὶ εἰν Ἀΐδαο δόμοισι·
πάντα γὰρ ἤδη τοι τελέω τὰ πάροιθεν ὑπέστην,         20
Ἕκτορα δεῦρ' ἐρύσας δώσειν κυσὶν ὠμὰ δάσασθαι,
δώδεκα δὲ προπάροιθε πυρῆς ἀποδειροτομήσειν
Τρώων ἀγλαὰ τέκνα, σέθεν κταμένοιο χολωθείς."

(Il. 23, 19–23)

4. δώδεκα δὲ Τρώων μεγαθύμων υἱέας ἐσθλοὺς           175
χαλκῷ δηϊόων· κακὰ δὲ φρεσὶ μήδετο ἔργα·
ἐν δὲ πυρὸς μένος ἧκε σιδήρεον, ὄφρα νέμοιτο.

ὤμωξέν τ' ἄρ' ἔπειτα, φίλον δ' ὀνόμηνεν ἑταῖρον·
"χαῖρέ μοι, ὦ Πάτροκλε, καὶ εἰν 'Αΐδαο δόμοισι·
πάντα γὰρ ἤδη τοι τελέω τὰ πάροιθεν ὑπέστην.          180
δώδεκα μὲν Τρώων μεγαθύμων υἱέας ἐσθλοὺς
τοὺς ἅμα σοὶ πάντας πῦρ ἐσθίει· Ἕκτορα δ' οὔ τι
δώσω Πριαμίδην πυρὶ δαπτέμεν, ἀλλὰ κύνεσσιν."

(Il. 23, 175–83)

Let us begin, not with why Vergil included Aeneas' human
sacrifice in the poem, but with how it is presented and how this
compares with the Homeric parallels.[1] Achilles' sacrifice of the
Trojan youths is straightforward. On hearing that Patroclus is
dead Achilles swears that no funeral rites will be performed until
he has killed Hector, and taken his head and armour. This done
he will cut the throats of twelve youths at Patroclus' pyre
(18,333ff.). In the battle itself he captures twelve youths for the
purpose, and has them bound and led away (21,26ff.). With
Hector killed Achilles slays the twelve youths and cries out aloud
to his former friend that he has fulfilled his promise (23,19ff.
and 175ff.). Vergil's presentation of Aeneas' sacrifice makes the
action less clear. After Pallas' death Aeneas erupts into a fury and
kills many men before taking alive eight youths with the
intention of sacrificing them (10,517ff.). Shortly afterwards
Aeneas' intention is restated: he had tied their hands behind their
backs in readiness for their sacrifice (11,81f.).

There are important differences in the presentation of the
episodes in the two poems, which seem to shed light on Vergil's
own attitude towards his hero's behaviour here. To begin with
the Homeric episode is longer and more detailed. Reference is
made to human sacrifice in three different books: whilst first
promised by Achilles in Book 18, it is not actually carried
through until five books later. It would seem a deliberate contrast to this presentation that Aeneas' plan for sacrifice is exceed-

[1] Aeneas' taking of the youths for sacrifice is also discussed above, p. 9f.

ingly brief and lacking in detail. It is mentioned in only two books and, more importantly, is described entirely in six lines of the poem. Significantly, Vergil compressed his own version of human sacrifice to approximately one-quarter the size of the Homeric model. The difference, however, between the two versions is not merely numerical. In the Homeric episode Achilles utters three speeches to complement his actions. In the first of these (18, 333–7), he declares his intention to perform sacrifice, and in the others (23, 19–23 and 179–83) declares that, as promised, he places in the fire twelve sons of the Trojans. The Homeric presentation is thus vivid and direct allowing no doubts as to the brutality and efficiency with which the act is carried through. Aeneas, by contrast, utters nothing. His actions are presented indirectly by means of the narrative alone. Rather than making the episode dramatically vivid, like Homer, Vergil merely refers obliquely to it. Thus, by using his indirect method of characterisation, Vergil clearly chooses not to underline the action of his hero here.[1] So brief and remote is the description of his planned sacrifice that it is possible to forget the reality of Aeneas' act. This could never happen in a reading of the *Iliad*, because Achilles' sacrifice is placed vividly and dramatically before our eyes.

Moreover, Vergil's language helps to cloud the reality of his actions. Homer describes clearly the fact that sacrifice takes place,[2] whereas Vergil presents Aeneas' intention to do so by means of a final subjunctive (*mitteret* 81) and a future participle (*sparsurus* 82). Thus it is never clear whether sacrifice actually takes place, although there is no evidence to the contrary.[3] Nor

---

[1] S. Farron, *Acta Classica* 20 (1977) 205, argues, implausibly it seems to me, that Vergil's description of the sacrifice is more vivid and brutal than that of Homer; see above, p. 9, n. 5. For another criticism of Aeneas' behaviour here, see G. Williams, 115f.

[2] χαλκῷ δηϊόων (23, 176).

[3] For an attempt to find such evidence by variant readings, see T. Crane, 'A note on Aeneas' "human sacrifice"', *Aeneid* 10, 517–20', *C. W.* 67 (1973–4) 176–7.

do we see Aeneas bind the hands of the youths behind their backs, for he had already done so (*vinxerat* 81). Vergil tells us what Aeneas had already done (tied their hands) and what he is about to do (sacrifice them, sprinkling the flames with blood); but he refrains from telling us the actions of the hero at the given moment. Thus he clouds the issue by referring to past and future but not to the reality of the act in the present. The indirect method is taken one stage further; for not only is there no dramatic role for Aeneas in this episode (as there is in Homer for Achilles) but the narrative description fails to state the reality of the sacrifice at all (as it is stated clearly in Homer).

Vergil's decision to describe the sacrifice by the indirect methods seems to tell us something about his own view of Aeneas' act. It has been seen[1] that Aeneas' brutality in the killing of Magus, Tarquitus and the other Latins is, for all its lack of *humanitas*, still within the scope of *pietas* because his actions are applied in the fated direction — bringing destiny closer to fulfilment. These same factors do not apply as Aeneas prepares for the sacrifice of the youths (81f.); for his act does not further the progress of fate. Thus Vergil clouds the reality of Aeneas' actions here by his indirect methods, because he views Aeneas' act as outside the scope of *pietas*. We see Vergil's familiar techniques of characterisation at work: the direct speeches underlining his *pietas*; and his *impietas* being conveyed by indirect methods.[2]

There may be another side to Vergil's technique here. Clearly, the episode is included (when it could easily have been omitted[3]) because Vergil wishes to show the extent of Aeneas' occasional brutality. In this sense it has the same kind of function as Aeneas'

---

[1] See above, p. 165ff.
[2] See above, p. 109ff.
[3] See Williams' note, ad 10, 519.

*aristeia* (10,510–605). In the later instance (11,81f.), however, the poet appears notably uncomfortable about the entire episode, as if conscious that his hero perpetrates an act that a Roman audience would find unsuitable for the legendary founder of the city. Vergil may particularly have been conscious of Augustus' reaction, who, it is said,[1] sacrificed 300 prisoners at Perusia in honour of Julius Caesar. Thus, whilst the Augustan connection may possibly explain the inclusion of the episode, it may also help to explain Vergil's reluctance to present it directly. The parallel may have been too close and the subject too contentious to present the episode in the same vivid manner as Homer.

At 85ff. Vergil concentrates on the effect that Pallas' death has on others: the aged Acoetes beats his breast and tears at his face with his nails, and the war-horse Aethon weeps profusely.[2] Aeneas now prepares to speak again:

> substitit Aeneas gemituque haec addidit alto:
> "nos alias hinc ad lacrimas eadem horrida belli
> fata vocant: salve aeternum mihi, maxime Palla,
> aeternumque vale."
>                                                      (95–8)

The Homeric model for this speech is that of Achilles to the dead Patroclus.[3] Vergil takes from Achilles' speech the part of it which, when adapted, will emphasise Aeneas' *pietas*.[4] Thus *salve ... maxime Palla* (97) resembles Achilles' χαῖρέ μοι, ὦ Πάτροκλε (*Il.* 23,179) as both heroes bid farewell to their dear comrades. Achilles' declaration, however, that he has fulfilled his promise and sacrificed twelve youths (*Il.* 23,181ff.) is deleted from the Vergilian version. Aeneas' speech, which again is uttered in a

---

[1] Suetonius, *Div. Aug.* 15. See Camps, 28f. and 142, who discusses Aeneas' act in its Roman context.

[2] Cf. *Il.* 17,426ff. in which Achilles' horses weep for Patroclus' death.

[3] Knauer, indices ad loc., compares *Il.* 23,179–183. For discussions of Vergil's adaptations of this Homeric passage, see above, p. 99f. and p. 183ff.

[4] Aeneas' utterance here also strongly resembles Catullus 101,10, where he laments his brother's death.

mood of lamentation (95), underlines his *pietas* both in his sombre concern for Pallas (97f.) and in his recognition and acceptance of the fact that the fates call them to other tears (96f.). Vergil is markedly selective in his modelling of Aeneas' words on those of Achilles. Here, as elsewhere, *pietas* is the criterion for selection.

To the Latin envoys, who arrive seeking a moratorium in the fighting to give funeral rites to their dead, Aeneas reacts as follows:

> quos bonus Aeneas haud aspernanda precantis
> prosequitur venia et verbis haec insuper addit:
> "quaenam vos tanto fortuna indigna, Latini,
> implicuit bello, qui nos fugiatis amicos?
> pacem me exanimis et Martis sorte peremptis        110
> oratis? equidem et vivis concedere vellem.
> nec veni, nisi fata locum sedemque dedissent,
> nec bellum cum gente gero; rex nostra reliquit
> hospitia et Turni potius se credidit armis.
> aequius huic Turnum fuerat se opponere morti.        115
> si bellum finire manu, si pellere Teucros
> apparat, his mecum decuit concurrere telis:
> vixet cui vitam deus aut sua dextra dedisset.
> nunc ite et miseris supponite civibus ignem."
>
> (106–119)[1]

The description of Aeneas as *bonus* (106) introduces the speech, yet, given the hero's response, Vergil could alternatively have described him as *pius*. The Latins' request could not be denied by Aeneas (106f.). He regards Trojans and Latins as friends who have been turned into enemies. Although they seek peace for the dead, he would like to grant it to the living (110f.). He stresses that in coming to Italy the Trojans follow a course laid down by

[1] Knauer, indices ad loc., cites no Homeric model for Aeneas' speech. This is hardly surprising given Aeneas' role here as a 'new kind of hero', with a strong commitment to peace and order for his people, as well as a desire to follow at all costs the will of heaven.

fate and asserts that it was Latinus who trusted in Turnus, and not he who broke the bonds of *hospitium*. It would have been more just, says Aeneas, if Turnus were now dead like those around them.[1] He now issues a challenge to Turnus (116ff.) to settle the issue by single combat, before telling the Latins to go and tend their dead (119).

This is Aeneas' last speech of Book 11, for Vergil switches his attention first to Pallanteum, and then to Laurentum, the Latin city. Fittingly, Aeneas' last speech in the book also underlines his *pietas* — his commitment to peace, his ready acceptance of a truce, his reiteration of the Trojans' fated role in Italy, and his willingness to decide the issue in accordance with the will of heaven and by his own right hand. Despite granting a truce to the Latins Aeneas is utterly determined to force the issue and fight Turnus, even before Evander's call for vengeance (11,176ff.). His recommencement of battle (445ff.) may be seen in the light of his own and Evander's desire to see the death of Turnus.

---

[1] See Williams, ad 115.

# BOOK 12

The opening of Book 12 (1–106) focuses almost entirely on Turnus who, in a state of wild *furor*, accepts that the time has come to fight Aeneas in single combat. Great care and attention are paid by Vergil to presenting emphatically the *furor* of Turnus in this section. On occasions this takes the form of abuse aimed at Aeneas himself. The attempts of Latinus (19ff.) and Amata (56ff.) to mollify Turnus' *furor* serve only to intensify it (45f., 70f.). The initial description of Aeneas in Book 12 is as follows:

> nec minus interea maternis saevus in armis
> Aeneas acuit Martem et se suscitat ira,
> oblato gaudens componi foedere bellum.
> tum socios maestique metum solatur Iuli        110
> fata docens, regique iubet responsa Latino
> certa referre viros et pacis dicere leges.

> (107–12)

Two aspects of this picture of Aeneas require comment. The first is his *furor* (107f.) and the second is his *pietas* (109ff.).[1] We shall see that throughout Book 12 Aeneas is characterised both by his *pietas* and by his *furor* — his *pius furor*. The characters described as *saevus* (107) in the poem are Hector 1,99; Achilles 2,29; Ulysses 3,273; Mars 7,608; Drances 11,220; and Jupiter 12,849.[2] *Saevus* conveys a natural fierceness most commonly seen in battle: significantly it is not used of Turnus in the entire poem. Aeneas' *furor*, unlike Turnus', is shown to rise naturally from within him in response to particular circumstances[3] — a

---

[1] Lyne, *C.Q.* 33 (1983) 196f., compares Turnus' Cacus-like *furor* at 101f. with Aeneas' desire for peace at 109. He argues, implausibly in my view, that Aeneas' anger at 107f. 'is not the passion that merits the term *furor*'. I prefer to make a distinction between Aeneas' *furor* and that of Turnus; see above, p. 162ff.

[2] M.N. Wetmore, *Index Verborum Vergilianus* (New Haven, 1930) s.v. The adjective is also used of female deities — Juno 1,4; 7,287 (etc.); Circe, 7,19; Allecto 7,511.

[3] See 10,270ff.; 10,813f. and discussion above, p. 162ff. and 174.

fact emphasised by the sharpening of 'his warlike spirit' and the rousing of his anger (108).[1] Both heroes are in a rage (Turnus 1–106; Aeneas 107–12) but each is in a different kind of rage.

The advantage that Aeneas holds is indicated by reference to his divinely made armour (*maternis* 107): 'it is almost as if Aeneas were fighting an unarmed man'.[2] He rejoices that the war is to be settled by means of a treaty (109). Moreover, he consoles his allies and his own son's fear, teaching them of fate (110f.), and commands them to give firm replies to Latinus and state the terms of peace (111f.). Thus *pietas* is shown in his concern for allies and son, in his determination to follow fate, and in his joyful acceptance of and respect for a treaty. *Furor* and *pietas* are shown in this passage to complement each other: Aeneas is motivated to sign a treaty, then to fight and kill Turnus. At this early stage of the book such a course looks almost certain to him; but Juno has not yet resigned herself to final defeat.

And so it is that when both sides gather to swear a formal treaty (113ff.) Juno encourages Iuturna to protect her brother and postpone his death (134ff.). As the gathering of both sides continues, Aeneas himself appears:

> hinc pater Aeneas, Romanae stirpis origo,
> sidereo flagrans clipeo et caelestibus armis
> et iuxta Ascanius, magnae spes altera Romae,
> procedunt castris.                                      (166–9)

The same kinds of things are stressed here as at 107ff. — Aeneas' paternal role, his foundation of the Roman race, the support given to him by Venus and Vulcan, and his devotion to Ascanius. Furthermore, Aeneas is ablaze (*flagrans* 167) in his celestial armour, reinforcing the foreboding picture of him seen on his

---

[1] Williams, ad loc.
[2] R. Beare, 'Invidious Success: some thoughts on *Aeneid* XII', *P.V.S.* 4 (1964–65) 22.

return from Pallanteum (10,270ff.). He proceeds to swear his oath as follows:

> tum pius Aeneas stricto sic ense precatur:                                         175
> "esto nunc Sol testis et haec mihi terra vocanti,
> quam propter tantos potui perferre labores,
> et pater omnipotens et tu Saturnia coniunx,
> (iam melior, iam, diva, precor), tuque inclute Mavors,
> cuncta tuo qui bella, pater, sub numine torques;                                   180
> fontisque fluviosque voco, quaeque aetheris alti
> religio et quae caeruleo sunt numina ponto:
> cesserit Ausonio si fors victoria Turno,
> convenit Euandri victos discedere ad urbem,
> cedet Iulus agris, nec post arma ulla rebelles                                     185
> Aeneadae referent ferrove haec regna lacessent.
> sin nostrum adnuerit nobis victoria Martem
> (ut potius reor et potius di numine firment),
> non ego nec Teucris Italos parere iubebo
> nec mihi regna peto: paribus se legibus ambae                                      190
> invictae gentes aeterna in foedera mittant.
> sacra deosque dabo; socer arma Latinus habeto,
> imperium sollemne socer; mihi moenia Teucri
> constituent urbique dabit Lavinia nomen."

>                                                                             (175–94)

The closest Homeric model[1] is the speech of Agamemnon prior to the single combat arranged between Menelaus and Paris:

> τοῖσιν δ᾽ Ἀτρεΐδης μεγάλ᾽ εὔχετο χεῖρας ἀνασχών·                              275
> "Ζεῦ πάτερ, Ἴδηθεν μεδέων, κύδιστε μέγιστε,
> Ἤέλιός θ᾽, ὃς πάντ᾽ ἐφορᾷς καὶ πάντ᾽ ἐπακούεις,
> καὶ ποταμοὶ καὶ γαῖα, καὶ οἳ ὑπένερθε καμόντας
> ἀνθρώπους τίνυσθον, ὅτις κ᾽ ἐπίορκον ὀμόσσῃ,
> ὑμεῖς μάρτυροι ἔστε, φυλάσσετε δ᾽ ὅρκια πιστά·                                280

---

[1] Knauer, indices ad loc., compares Agamemnon's oath at *Il.* 3,276–291 and that at *Il.* 19,258–265; in the latter of these Agamemnon swears that he did not lay a hand on Briseis. In situation, therefore, Agamemnon's earlier vow is a closer parallel, in that it precedes the single combat between Menelaus and Paris.

εἰ μέν κεν Μενέλαον Ἀλέξανδρος καταπέφνῃ,
αὐτὸς ἔπειθ᾽ Ἑλένην ἐχέτω καὶ κτήματα πάντα,
ἡμεῖς δ᾽ ἐν νήεσσι νεώμεθα ποντοπόροισιν·
εἰ δέ κ᾽ Ἀλέξανδρον κτείνῃ ξανθὸς Μενέλαος,
Τρῶας ἔπειθ᾽ Ἑλένην καὶ κτήματα πάντ᾽ ἀποδοῦναι,    285
τιμὴν δ᾽ Ἀργείοις ἀποτινέμεν ἥν τιν᾽ ἔοικεν,
ἥ τε καὶ ἐσσομένοισι μετ᾽ ἀνθρώποισι πέληται.
εἰ δ᾽ ἂν ἐμοὶ τιμὴν Πρίαμος Πριάμοιό τε παῖδες
τίνειν οὐκ ἐθέλωσιν Ἀλεξάνδροιο πεσόντος,
αὐτὰρ ἐγὼ καὶ ἔπειτα μαχήσομαι εἵνεκα ποινῆς    290
αὖθι μένων, ἧός κε τέλος πολέμοιο κιχείω."

(Il. 3,275–91)

Agamemnon prays to Zeus, the Sun, the rivers, the earth and
the gods of the underworld, who will punish him if his oath is
false. Aeneas prays to the Sun, the Earth, Jupiter, Juno, Mars,
fountains and rivers, and the 'sanctity of the high heavens and the
divinities in the blue sea'.[1] The introductory epithet *pius* (175) is
'used with full emphasis'[2] and is juxtaposed with that of *pater*
(166) where his fatherly proximity to Ascanius and his role as
*pater patriae* are stressed. Both Aeneas and Agamemnon call on
the gods to witness their vows,[3] yet the vows themselves differ
considerably. If Paris kills Menelaus the Greeks will simply
return to their own country leaving Helen at Troy. If Menelaus
kills Paris, however, the Trojans must return Helen and her
treasure and pay recompense to the Greeks: if no recompense is
forthcoming, then the war goes on. Agamemnon's oath to the
gods fulfils a pragmatic purpose: there is no attempt to present

[1] Williams, ad 181–2.
[2] Williams, ad loc.
[3] Cf. *esto nunc Sol testis* (176) and μάρτυροι ἔστε (280). Some detailed discussions of
Aeneas' oath have been provided by F.I. Zeitlin, 'An Analysis of *Aeneid* XII, 176–211.
The differences between the oaths of Aeneas and Latinus', *A.J.P.* 86 (1965) 337–62; J.E.
Fontenrose, 'The Gods Invoked in Epic Oaths: *Aeneid* XII, 175–215', *A.J.P.* 89 (1968)
20–38; G.K. Galinsky, 'Aeneas' Invocation of Sol (*Aeneid*, XII, 176)', *A.J.P.* 90 (1969)
453–8.

him as a pious hero. It is τιμή and κτήματα that motivate Agamemnon.

Aeneas states that, if Turnus defeats him, the Trojans will depart for Pallanteum and that they will never attack Latium in the future. If victory falls to Aeneas, he will not subject the Italians to Trojan rule, but both peoples will live unconquered under equal terms, entering into a treaty for all time. He will give sacred rites and gods; and furthermore Latinus, his father-in-law, will keep his *arma* and *imperium*. Aeneas will build his own city, which will take its name from that of Lavinia. Vergil conveys far more than Homer; for Aeneas does not see material possessions as his goal, like Agamemnon, but promises a range of things which he sees as assisting the future of the country. The emphasis is on giving rather than receiving, with his *pietas* strongly evident throughout. Moreover, unlike the Homeric parallel, Aeneas nowhere mentions his own death, should he be defeated, or that of Turnus, should he be victorious. Instead he talks periphrastically of victory.[1] There is little doubt that the loser will be killed,[2] but Vergil does not give dramatic emphasis to this probability. Aeneas talks in terms of victory or defeat rather than life or death. The reader is aware that Aeneas will prevail in the single combat:[3] Vergil, however, at this point, emphasises the positive results of Trojan victory rather than its human cost (in the person of Turnus).

The forthcoming combat, however, seems unequal to the Rutuli (216ff.), and Iuturna hastens to increase their doubts (222ff.). She produces an omen (244ff.) — an eagle snatching up

---

[1] Cf. *victoria* 183; *victoria* 187; καταπέφνῃ 281; κτείνῃ 284.

[2] Note 183ff., where it is Iulus who would organise the Trojans' departure to Pallanteum.

[3] Just as Aeneas himself is confident in battle because he helps to fulfil the fated will (cf. 8,532ff. and 12,109ff.). A further difference between the two speeches is Aeneas' reference to the will of the gods (187f.), which he sees as deciding the issue in his favour (*pietas*).

a swan — which the Rutulian augur Tolumnius interprets as the gods' approval for the renewal of hostilities (259ff.). He then dashes forward and casts his spear at the enemy (266ff.). The battle quickly re-commences with great ferocity on both sides. Aeneas' reaction is as follows:

> at pius Aeneas dextram tendebat inermem
> nudato capite atque suos clamore vocabat:
> "quo ruitis? quaeve ista repens discordia surgit?
> o cohibete iras! ictum iam foedus et omnes
> compositae leges. mihi ius concurrere soli;                  315
> me sinite atque auferte metus. ego foedera faxo
> firma manu; Turnum debent haec iam mihi sacra."
>
>                                                (311–17)

To begin with Aeneas asks where his men rush to and what is this sudden discord (313). He pleads with them to contain their wrath (314) and reminds them that the treaty has been struck and the terms (*leges* 315) agreed. Vergil stresses the *pietas* of his hero by means of the introductory epithet *pius* (311). As he speaks Aeneas stretches out his unarmed hand and is himself without a helmet on his head (311f.). We saw that there is no critical disagreement on the meaning of the first lines of this passage (311–315a), for Aeneas' *pietas* and *fides* are clear and unequivocal.[1] Aeneas' latter sentiments, however, are often ignored, that it is right for him alone to do battle (315) and that he should be allowed to do so. He will make the treaty true with his hand (316f.), and already the sacred rites promise (*debent* 317) Turnus to him.

The moral motivation for Aeneas' statement — that a treaty struck is a treaty to be honoured — is stressed forcefully by critics, but often at the expense of the more practical side of his purpose. His men must contain their anger and abide by the

---

[1] For a discussion of some of the critical approaches to this important episode, see above, p. 3ff.

treaty if he is to take his revenge and kill Turnus. Continued
hostilities will only delay his victory; his men must restrain their
anger (314) so that he can give vent to his. Thus *o cohibete iras*
(314) does not signal a simple appeal to the virtue of *ratio*[1] as a
desirable moral quality; it is the means whereby his faithful oath
(176ff.) will be kept (*pietas/fides*), and his great desire for vengeance (*furor*) sated. To call him 'humane'[2] merely confuses the
issue, for Vergil stresses that a desire to kill Turnus is a prime
motivating factor.

Aeneas' appeal fails to stop the fighting, and he receives his
reply with an arrow wound and is forced to withdraw from the
battlefield. Aided by Venus, Iapyx quickly tends the wound
(391ff.) and preparations are made for Aeneas' return to the
battlefield. Iapyx realises (425ff.) that some god assisted his
recovery and returns him to greater deeds. At this point, as he
prepares for battle, Aeneas turns to Ascanius:

> Ascanium fusis circum complectitur armis
> summaque per galeam delibans oscula fatur:
> "disce, puer, virtutem ex me verumque laborem,                435
> fortunam ex aliis. nunc te mea dextera bello
> defensum dabit et magna inter praemia ducet.
> tu facito, mox cum matura adoleverit aetas,
> sis memor et te animo repetentem exempla tuorum
> et pater Aeneas et avunculus excitet Hector."                 440
>
> (433–40)

The Homeric model[3] for the speech is Hector's address to
Astyanax in the sixth *Iliad*:

> αὐτὰρ ὅ γ' ὃν φίλον υἱὸν ἐπεὶ κύσε πῆλέ τε χερσίν,
> εἶπε δ' ἐπευξάμενος Διί τ' ἄλλοισίν τε θεοῖσι·                475
> "Ζεῦ ἄλλοι τε θεοί, δότε δὴ καὶ τόνδε γενέσθαι

---

[1] Similarly, *nec sat rationis in armis* (2, 314) is a simple statement on the nature of man in
war; see above, p. 48 and below, p. 211ff.

[2] *Sic* Warde Fowler, (op. cit. p. 3, n. 1).

[3] Knauer, indices ad loc.

παῖδ' ἐμόν, ὡς καὶ ἐγώ περ, ἀριπρεπέα Τρώεσσιν,
ὧδε βίην τ' ἀγαθόν, καὶ Ἰλίου ἶφι ἀνάσσειν·
καί ποτέ τις εἴποι 'πατρός γ' ὅδε πολλὸν ἀμείνων'
ἐκ πολέμου ἀνιόντα· φέροι δ' ἔναρα βροτόεντα        480
κτείνας δήϊον ἄνδρα, χαρείη δὲ φρένα μήτηρ."
                                                (Il. 6, 474–81)

Aeneas' love and concern for Ascanius demonstrates his *pietas*.
He stresses his own *virtus* and *labor* which Ascanius can learn from
him; but his son must learn of the role of chance from others. He
will defend Ascanius and lead him amongst great rewards. In the
future when Ascanius has reached adulthood he ought to remember the *exempla* of others, especially of Aeneas himself and those of
his uncle Hector. This is Aeneas' only speech to his son in the
entire poem,[1] a fact which makes the lack of a first person
singular usage all the more notable.[2] For all the warmth and love
shown towards his son in the narrative (433f.), the speech is
formal and impersonal.[3] Vergil does not attempt to convey the
same effect as Homer. Hector's speech is an imprecation to Zeus
and the other gods in the small boy's presence, whereas Aeneas
utters his speech to Ascanius himself.[4] Moreover, the reader
feels a deeper pathos for Hector and Astyanax than he does for
Aeneas and Ascanius. The reasons for this are to be seen in the
circumstances which surround the two episodes. Hector returns
to the city from the battlefield (237ff.) and urges the women and
old men to make prayer to the gods. In Priam's palace he meets
Hecuba (251ff.), whom he tells to lead the women to prayer at
Athena's temple in the hope that the goddess will take pity on
them and protect Troy and the Trojans from Diomedes' spear

[1] W. Clausen, 'An Interpretation of the *Aeneid*' in *Virgil*, ed. S. Commager (New Jer-
sey, 1966) 82.
[2] For Vergil's reluctance to use the first person singular in the speeches of Aeneas, see
above, p. 64ff.
[3] Contrast Perret's brief discussion on this speech, *Virgile* (Paris, 1965) 140.
[4] Astyanax is presented in the *Iliad* as a very small boy, about only two years old.

(264ff.). This Hecuba does, whilst Hector himself finds and rebukes Paris for shrinking from the war (326ff.). He then finds Andromache, who pleads with him (407ff.) to take pity on their son and on her, for the Achaeans will soon slay him (409ff.). She reminds Hector of the tragic history of her family — her father and seven brothers killed by Achilles and her mother killed by Artemis. Hector is mother, father, brother and husband to her, and he too will soon be killed. Hector himself knows that he will die and that Troy will fall, and he laments the probable fate of Andromache as the slave of a Greek (441–65). Hector then reaches out for his son who recoils in terror at the sight of his armour-clad father. This causes Andromache and Hector to laugh; the latter then utters his imprecation to Zeus and the other gods that his son may become a greater man than he.

The background to Aeneas' speech to Ascanius is totally different. The hero has just been wounded, has withdrawn from battle, and on being healed with the help of an immortal, prepares to re-enter the fray. There is no attempt on Vergil's part to elicit the same deep pathos from the reader for Aeneas and Ascanius as Homer does for Hector and his family. The assistance of Venus in healing Aeneas' wounds helps to convey the fact that his welfare is assured by the will of heaven.[1] Yet despite his role as the object of divine goodwill, Aeneas shows signs of melancholia and self-pity (435f.). Vergil does not allow us to sympathise with his hero's despondency by juxtaposing Aeneas' speech with an act of divine benevolence in his favour.[2] This is Vergil's significant departure from Homer's episode in which a tragic spirit prevails. Hector's meetings with Hecuba, Andromache and Astyanax are held at a time when he already anticipates his

[1] Vergil uses the same technique in Book 1, 407–14 and 437–40, where Venus' loving concern for her son, symbolised by the cloud in which she covers him, is contrasted with Aeneas' despondency at the sudden appearance and disappearance of his mother (1, 407ff.), and at the sight of Carthage (1, 437ff.). See above, p. 30ff.

[2] See 411ff. and esp. 427ff.

own death and the fall of Troy (447ff.). His imprecation to Zeus and the other gods (476ff.) is made more poignant by this foreshadowing of defeat and death. The reader anticipates that here is the last time that the family will be united. Moreover, Hector's sorrow is not for himself but for Andromache (450ff.) and for his son. Homer arouses our pity and fear for Hector and his family; but there is no sense of loss, no pity and fear aroused in Vergil's episode. Vergil places the emphasis on characteristic Roman virtues[1] and particularly on Aeneas' *pietas* — his love for Ascanius (433f.) and his dutiful behaviour in protecting and teaching him (435ff.).

Following his speech to Ascanius, Aeneas and the Trojans move forward into battle (441ff.). A cold tremor runs through the bones of Turnus and the Ausonians as they see the enemy coming. Iuturna herself flees in terror — a sign of the doom awaiting Turnus (448f.). Aeneas is like a storm (*nimbus* 451) moving over the sea towards the land, causing the farmers' hearts to tremble because it will bring down trees and crops and cause general ruin (451–7).[2] But Aeneas does not bother to kill those who flee from the Trojan attack or challenge those who come into his path: he seeks Turnus alone:

> solum densa in caligine Turnum
> vestigat lustrans, solum in certamina poscit.
>
> (466–7)

Aeneas' determined tracking of Turnus now begins as he systematically scans the battlefield for him. This passage has many

[1] During the course of discussion of this section, Professor Walsh pointed out to me Livy's similar contrast between *fortuna* and Roman virtues (esp. *ratio*) in the speech of Hannibal at Zama (30.30). Hannibal's speech, in which *fortuna* occurs on 11 occasions, might also be compared to that of Turnus at 11,378–444, in which *Fortuna* is referred to twice (cf. *fortunatus* 11,416).

[2] For a detailed analysis of this and the other similes in Book 12, see D. West, 'Virgilian Multiple-Correspondence Similes and their Antecedents', *Philologus* 114 (1970) 262–75.

echoes throughout the last three books of the poem.[1] The use of *solus ... solus* first conveyed Turnus' desire to kill Pallas (10,442f.) after which similar usages refer to Aeneas' desire to take revenge by single combat. His tracking of Turnus (*vestigare*) is reiterated on three further occasions in quick succession.[2] This imagery conveys the notion of the hunt, with Aeneas as the hunter and Turnus as the prey.[3]

Aeneas, however, has great difficulty in catching Turnus. Iuturna throws Metiscus, Turnus' charioteer, from the chariot, and in disguise takes his place, ensuring that they keep clear of Aeneas, who continues to track (*vestigat* 482) his man and call out aloud to him. Each time he traces Turnus, Iuturna causes him to lose him again. Aeneas reacts as follows:

> heu, quid agat? vario nequiquam fluctuat aestu,
> diversaeque vocant animum in contraria curae.

(486–7)

Aeneas' dilemma is expressed indirectly by free indirect speech (*style indirect libre*), perhaps indicative of the fact that the sentiments expressed do not emphasise his *pietas*. In Book 12, as elsewhere, the direct speeches of Aeneas essentially underline his *pietas*: the hero's *curae* here, as he attempts in vain to catch Turnus, do not so clearly fit into this category.[4]

During his pursuit of Turnus, Aeneas is attacked by Messapus (488ff.) and has his helmet-peak knocked off his head. He reacts as follows:

> tum vero adsurgunt irae, insidiisque subactus,
> diversos ubi sensit equos currumque referri,       495
> multa Iovem et laesi testatus foederis aras

[1] Cf. 11,220–1; 11,434; 11,442; 12,16; 12,315–7.

[2] See 482, 557, 588.

[3] On the imagery of the hunt, see Putnam, 171f. and J.R. Dunkle, 'The Hunter and Hunting in the *Aeneid* ', *Ramus* 2 (1973) 127–42.

[4] Cf. 4,283; 4,534; 10,675; 12,637; and discussion above, p. 79ff.

iam tandem invadit medios et Marte secundo
terribilis saevam nullo discrimine caedem
suscitat, irarumque omnis effundit habenas.

(494–9)

This passage too underlines Aeneas' *pius furor*.[1] He inflicts
*saevam nullo discrimine caedem* and breaks all the bounds of anger
(498f.). He does this having often called on Jupiter and the altars
of the broken treaty to bear him witness. His *pietas* is shown in
that 'for a long time Aeneas has been trying to observe the spirit
of the treaty for single combat by attacking only Turnus; but now
he yields to battle-fury and attacks indiscriminately'.[2] Again we
see that *pietas* and *furor* are clearly evident in the person of Aeneas.
His rage erupts as at 10,510ff.; and as in the earlier case it is
shown to be *pius furor* —rage indiscriminate and brutal, yet
applied in such a direction that the progress of fate is advanced.[3]

Both Aeneas and Turnus kill many of the enemy and are
described as follows sweeping through the battlefield:

ac velut immissi diversis partibus ignes
arentem in silvam et virgulta sonantia lauro,
aut ubi decursu rapido de montibus altis
dant sonitum spumosi amnes et in aequora currunt
quisque suum populatus iter: non segnius ambo                525
Aeneas Turnusque ruunt per proelia; nunc, nunc
fluctuat ira intus, rumpuntur nescia vinci
pectora, nunc totis in vulnera viribus itur.

(521–8)

The effect that they have on the battle is devastating: they are like
fires moving through a dry forest or thickets rustling with laurel

---

[1] As did the first description of Aeneas in the twelfth book — 107ff.

[2] Williams, ad 497.

[3] Putnam, 173, describes Aeneas' rage here as 'purposeless', referring presumably to
*nullo discrimine* (498). Aeneas' slaughter is indiscriminate but it has purpose in the sense
that it helps to bring the issue to a head, to force Turnus to face Aeneas, and, therefore, to
further the progress of fate. In this sense it has the same purpose as his *aristeia*
(10,510–605).

and like foaming rivers coming from the mountain-tops and rushing towards the sea. The emphasis is on the *furor* (*ignes*; *spumosi*; *fluctuat ira intus*) of *both* men (*ambo Aeneas Turnusque*), and on the destruction which they leave in their path (*quisque suum populatus iter*). They have far greater prowess in battle than the ordinary men (*arentem in silvam et virgulta sonantia lauro*). Turnus may be inferior in stature to Aeneas (12, 216ff.), yet he is still great and powerful, and his effect in battle here is the same. They are both motivated by *furor*. Aeneas is in a state of *pius furor* because, in seeking out Turnus to kill him, he helps to advance the progress of fate and also fulfils his duty to Evander. Turnus' *furor*, originally implanted by Allecto, is *impius*, because it opposes the course of fate. Yet whilst there are differences in the natures of their *furor*, Vergil, on this occasion, heightens the heroes' similarity in battle. This is a new technique, for more generally Vergil presents the two men individually and refrains from inclusive descriptions, content to highlight the particular qualities which characterise them. As the single combat finally approaches, he draws the two heroes together by equating their battle-exploits. Thus the reader is being prepared for the single combat which, although never an even match, has at least a semblance of equality,[1] in that, compared with the ordinary warrior, Aeneas and Turnus are both great.

As the battle continues Venus proceeds to inspire Aeneas with the thought of attacking the city (554ff.). Whilst he is tracking Turnus (*vestigans* 557), he catches sight of the undisturbed city and is fired towards a greater battle (557ff.). He addresses his captains as follows:

---

[1] Turnus was greater in stature than Pallas (10, 445ff.) yet the build-up to their single combat (10, 362ff.) presented the latter as a great hero in his own right. Turnus is likened to a lion (10, 454) and Pallas to a bull (10, 455). It is not an even match but Pallas has the aggression of a bull in battle and is capable of defending himself.

"ne qua meis esto dictis mora, Iuppiter hac stat,                        565
neu quis ob inceptum subitum mihi segnior ito.
urbem hodie, causam belli, regna ipsa Latini,
ni frenum accipere et victi parere fatentur,
eruam et aequa solo fumantia culmina ponam.
scilicet exspectem libeat dum proelia Turno                              570
nostra pati rursusque velit concurrere victus?
hoc caput, o cives, haec belli summa nefandi.
ferte faces propere foedusque reposcite flammis."

(565–73)

The speech underlines Aeneas' *pius furor*. He has no doubts that
Jupiter supports his course (*pietas*).[1] Similarly, he feels that he
has acted rightly and that the Rutuli are the cause of the war
(567). The enemy must, therefore, as a result of their defeat,
agree to receive the yoke (*frenum* 568) and to obey Trojan will. If
they do not Aeneas will raze the city. He sees no reason why he
should await Turnus' pleasure for single combat, especially after
the Rutulian has already been defeated (*victus* 571) in battle.[2]
Aeneas regards the war as heinous (*nefandi* 572) but his action
here will bring it to a head. He calls on his men to bring *faces* to
reimpose the treaty.[3]

Aeneas' *pietas* centres on his awareness that he follows a course
ordained by Jupiter and that he seeks to reimpose the treaty by
which he abided all along and over which he swore a sacred oath.
He believes, in short, that his course of action is just and right.
His *furor* complements his *pietas* and can be seen in his determination, unless the enemy submit, to show no mercy to the city

---

[1] Cf. 8,532ff. and 12,109ff. Of course, Aeneas is right in his belief in Jupiter's support; see 12,793ff. and the role of the *Dira* in Turnus' defeat, esp. 914.

[2] See Williams, ad 571: 'Aeneas interprets Turnus' avoidance of single combat as a defeat'.

[3] Knauer, indices ad loc., compares Aeneas' speech with *Il.* 8,489–542, in which Hector is prevented by nightfall from attacking and destroying the ships but will try again in
the morning. As a parallel it is closer to Turnus' address to his men at 9,128–58.

but to raze it to the ground. His intention here is in contrast to his stated vow (12,187ff.), but Aeneas' point (573) is that the Rutuli broke the treaty,[1] and therefore he is entitled to make them pay a heavy price for doing so. Aeneas' use of fire here parallels that of Turnus at 9,69ff. and 535ff., and helps to convey his *furor*: Vergil externalises the fire that lies within Aeneas himself.

They begin the attack on the city and Vergil again concentrates on Aeneas:

> ipse inter primos dextram sub moenia tendit
> Aeneas, magnaque incusat voce Latinum
> testaturque deos iterum se ad proelia cogi,
> bis iam Italos hostis, haec altera foedera rumpi.
>
> (579–82)

Here again Vergil stresses Aeneas' *pietas* as he calls the gods to witness that again he is compelled to battle, that for a second time the Italians are his enemy and that another treaty has been broken. Essentially, these points reiterate indirectly those made in the speech (565ff.): that he acts out of awareness of his duty to gods and men to reimpose the treaty, and thereafter to fight and kill Turnus. The Latins attempt to defend their city and rush to and fro in terror of those outside (584–92).

Vergil now concentrates on the fortune of the Italians (593ff.). Amata commits suicide (595ff.), thinking that Turnus is dead. The doleful sounds from the city reach Turnus' ears (617ff.) and he decides to return there and face Aeneas (632ff.), although

---

[1] This, of course, is true, but they do so as a pious response to the portent of Iuturna who purposely dupes them. The great difference is in the reactions of Aeneas (311ff.) and Turnus (324ff.) to the breaking of the treaty. The former had felt certain of victory in single combat (12,107–12), whereas the latter seemed to anticipate defeat (12,74 and 216–21). Vergil is careful to show that Turnus does not break the treaty in the first place, although he profits by it in that he sees possible escape from imminent death. Aeneas as he is presented would never break a treaty (*fides, pietas*), but his options are uncomplicated by any anticipation of defeat or death.

encouraged otherwise by Iuturna (625ff.). A messenger arrives confirming the news of the queen's death (653ff.), making Turnus all the more determined to face Aeneas (676ff.). He returns to the scene and tells his men to lay down their weapons (693ff.). Aeneas hears Turnus' name and reacts as follows:

> at pater Aeneas audito nomine Turni
> deserit et muros et summas deserit arces
> praecipitatque moras omnis, opera omnia rumpit
> laetitia exsultans horrendumque intonat armis:            700
> quantus Athos aut quantus Eryx aut ipse coruscis
> cum fremit ilicibus quantus gaudetque nivali
> vertice se attollens pater Appenninus ad auras.

(697–703)

The simile conveys the great stature of Aeneas (701ff.) like that of Athos, Eryx or Appenninus. Aeneas is joyful[1] (like the rejoicing Appenninus 'as he towers high'[2]), because he sees at last that he will face Turnus and fulfil his fate. Aeneas' joy has been contrasted with the terror of Turnus at the prospect of single combat.[3] Furthermore, the thundering of Appenninus resembles that of Aeneas as he thunders terribly (*intonat*).[4] The connection between the two is reinforced by repetition of *pater* at 697 and 703.

All eyes now turn on Aeneas and Turnus. Latinus himself is amazed at the sight of these two huge men (*ingentis* 708) meeting each other and deciding the issue with the sword (707ff.). When the field is clear they commence battle (710ff.): the earth gives a groan as they fight like two bulls fighting for the command of the herds (713ff.). The combat here is pictured as an even contest,

---

[1] For Aeneas' joy as he prepares for a kill in battle, cf. 10,787; 10,874; 12,109.

[2] Williams, ad 701f.

[3] Cf. 12,107ff. (Aeneas' confidence), and 12,74 and 216–21 (Turnus' anticipation of defeat).

[4] F. Cairns, 'Geography and nationalism in the *Aeneid*', L.C.M. 2 (1977) 109ff., argues that reference to *pater Appenninus* (703) expresses the Italianisation of Aeneas.

although reference to Jupiter's scales (725ff.)[1] induces us to anticipate a quick conclusion. Turnus springs forward (728ff.), but his sword snaps and he is forced to flee from Aeneas. The contest is now far from even:

> insequitur trepidique pedem pede fervidus urget:
> inclusum veluti si quando flumine nactus
> cervum aut puniceae saeptum formidine pennae          750
> venator cursu canis et latratibus instat;
> ille autem insidiis et ripa territus alta
> mille fugit refugitque vias, at vividus Umber
> haeret hians, iam iamque tenet similisque tenenti
> increpuit malis morsuque elusus inani est.          755
>
> (748–55)

The simile of the hunting-dog is modelled on *Il*. 22, 188ff. in which Achilles is likened to a hunting-dog and Hector to the fawn that is chased.[2] The hunting simile is particularly appropriate in Vergil's episode in that it furthers the hunting motif seen throughout Book 12. Aeneas' *furor* here is conveyed by his description as *fervidus* (748).[3] The hero is in complete control as Turnus runs for his life[4] like a terrified stag. The Rutulian calls for his sword as he runs but Aeneas continues to press him:

> Aeneas mortem contra praesensque minatur
> exitium, si quisquam adeat, terretque trementis
> excisurum urbem minitans et saucius instat.
>
> (760–2)

---

[1] Cf. *Il*. 22,209ff.; see D. West, 'The Deaths of Hector and Turnus', *G. &R.* 21 (1974) 21ff., who compares the deaths of Hector and Turnus and highlights some interesting differences. Reference to Jupiter at 725 complements that at 791ff., 829ff. and 843ff., when through the *Dira* he helps to defeat Turnus. Zeus performs no such action in the *Iliad*.

[2] For Vergil's adaptation and enlargement of the Homeric simile, see West, *Philologus* 114 (1970) 267ff. and Williams, ad 749f.

[3] For other instances of Aeneas as *fervidus*, see 10,788; 12,951; cf. Turnus at 9,72; 12,325.

[4] As Hector runs for his life when he sees Achilles at *Il*. 22,136ff.

Aeneas not only threatens (*minatur* 760) instant death to anyone who helps Turnus by giving him his sword, but also threatens (*minitans* 762) to destroy the city. The indirect presentation of these threats helps to retain the tempo of the narrative.[1] Homer uses the same kind of technique at *Il.* 22,205ff. where Achilles nods his head to his own men as a signal to them not to throw any weapons at Hector in case he himself should be robbed of μέγα κῦδος. Aeneas' threat to destroy the city can be coupled with that at 12,569. In each case his *furor* is in evidence.

Aeneas attempts to pull his spear from the root of the olive tree sacred to Faunus (772ff.).[2] Turnus prays to Faunus (777ff.) to hold the spear, which he proceeds to do until Venus releases it (786f.). Iuturna in the meantime has given Turnus back his sword (783ff.). Jupiter now questions Juno on her reasons for opposing Aeneas even though he is fated to triumph in Italy (793ff.). He appeals to her to cease her actions and bend to his entreaties. He ends by forbidding her to make further attempts to block Aeneas' path (*ulterius temptare veto* 806).[3] Juno agrees (808ff.) to accede to her husband's appeal but asks that the Latins not be forced to change their name nor to become Trojans.[4] She seeks that the Italian element be strong in future Roman stock. Jupiter gives his assent to these requests (830ff.). A new people will arise sprung from Italians and Trojans; the Latin language will be spoken. Moreover, the new race will excel all others in *pietas*. This new design leaves Juno happy, and she joyfully changes her purpose.

[1] See discussion above, p. 10f.

[2] Note the reference (766–71) to the indiscriminate desecration of the sacred tree by the Trojans so that combat may proceed. For contrasting views on the significance of the reference, see West, *G. & R.* 21 (1974) 27 and Boyle, *Ramus* 1 (1972) 70f.

[3] Cf. Turnus' plea *ulterius ne tende odiis* (938). Juno, in response to Jupiter's command, changes her purpose (808ff.), but Aeneas does not (941ff.). The victory of Jupiter is seen in both episodes.

[4] Buchheit, 133–43, analyses in detail the reconciliation between Jupiter and Juno.

The victory of Jupiter/Fate over Juno/anti-Fate is seen in the goddess' decision to alter her purpose to his wishes. It is further shown in Jupiter's decision to send one of the *Dirae* to the scene of single combat (843ff.). The task of the *Dira* is to come upon Iuturna as a signal of Turnus' imminent death (854) but she also weakens Turnus himself (867, 914). She is both a symbol of his imminent death and an assistant in it. She flits about Turnus' face in the shape of a black bird and, as a result, a *novus torpor* loosens his limbs with fear (867). Iuturna sees the *Dira* and recognises the significance of her work. She pities her brother and her own lot — forced by her immortality to mourn him forever (872–84).

Aeneas now proceeds to move in for the kill:

> Aeneas instat contra telumque coruscat
> ingens arboreum, et saevo sic pectore fatur:
> "quae nunc deinde mora est? aut quid iam, Turne, retractas?
> non cursu, saevis certandum est comminus armis.          890
> verte omnis tete in facies et contrahe quidquid
> sive animis sive arte vales; opta ardua pennis
> astra sequi clausumque cava te condere terra."

> (887–93)

This is the only occasion in the poem when Aeneas addresses Turnus face-to-face by name. His *furor* is underlined by the savage manner (*saevo ... pectore* 888)[1] in which the speech is uttered. It is a speech which has all the qualities to be expected from Homer's heroes in the *Iliad*.[2] He taunts his man — what is the delay now, and why does he draw back (889)? The battle must be fought hand to hand (890). Even if Turnus were to change his shape, like Proteus, he would not escape Aeneas' clutches. Turnus, in reply (894f.), realises that Jupiter is his

---

[1] Cf. 9,736 and 740, where, prior to their combat, Pandarus speaks *fervidus ira* and Turnus replies *sedato pectore*.

[2] Knauer, indices ad loc., compares *Il.* 22, 261–72 where Achilles abuses Hector prior to hurling a spear.

enemy and this is his only fear.[1] After saying this the Rutulian attempts to lift a huge stone but is unable to do so (896ff.). The *Dira* denies any successful course (913f.). Aeneas casts the fateful spear (919ff.) which wounds Turnus in the thigh (926) and forces him to sink to the ground. The whole hill reverberates with the shouts of those watching (928f.). Turnus now appeals to the victor as follows:

> ille humilis supplex oculos dextramque precantem                930
> protendens "equidem merui nec deprecor" inquit;
> "utere sorte tua. miseri te si qua parentis
> tangere cura potest, oro (fuit et tibi talis
> Anchises genitor) Dauni miserere senectae
> et me, seu corpus spoliatum lumine mavis,                        935
> redde meis. vicisti et victum tendere palmas
> Ausonii videre; tua est Lavinia coniunx,
> ulterius ne tende odiis."                                       (930–8)

This appeal moves Aeneas to show mercy — the speech has its effect on the hero (938ff.). He then catches sight of the baldric which Turnus took[2] from Pallas' body (941ff.). The poem ends as follows:

> ille, oculis postquam saevi monimenta doloris                    945
> exuviasque hausit, furiis accensus et ira
> terribilis: "tune hinc spoliis indute meorum
> eripiare mihi? Pallas te hoc vulnere, Pallas
> immolat et poenam scelerato ex sanguine sumit."
> hoc dicens ferrum adverso sub pectore condit                     950
> fervidus; ast illi solvuntur frigore membra
> vitaque cum gemitu fugit indignata sub umbras.
>                                                                 (945–52)

---

[1] The tragedy of Turnus is anchored on his delusion that Jupiter actually supports him in the war against the Trojans; see 9, 16ff.; 9, 128ff.; 10, 668ff.

[2] 10, 495ff. Note the important verbal parallel *Pallas ... Pallas* at 10, 442 and 12, 948. The parallel helps to link the deaths of Pallas and Turnus.

In Book 10, Magus as *supplex* (523) clasps Aeneas by the knees and prays by Anchises' spirit and the hope of growing Iulus that Aeneas will spare his life for his own father and son (524ff.). Aeneas replies (531ff.) that the killing of Pallas makes such mercy impossible. Turnus too is *supplex* (12,930) and holds out his hand in a plea for mercy. Like Magus, Turnus thinks of his own father. Moreover, in the hope of gaining mercy, Turnus, like Magus, urges Aeneas to think of his own father Anchises. The sight of Turnus humiliated and begging for his life is made more pitiful by our knowledge that before his death he lives out his greatest fear.[1] On the brink of death he thinks of his father, concedes Lavinia to Aeneas, and urges the victor not to carry his hatred further. Our pity rests with the tragic figure of Turnus largely because Vergil narrates the story from 'the point of view of the defeated'.[2] The reader is aware that Turnus is fated to die[3] but nonetheless hopes that somehow his death may be avoided. One of the paradoxes at the end of the poem is that we regret the progress of fate and seek to see Turnus survive against all the odds. In this sense we follow what might be called a Junonian course.

Turnus' plea, unlike that of Magus, has an effect on the hero. Aeneas holds back the blow (938ff.) and, for the first time since the killing of Pallas, he has second thoughts about killing Turnus. It is a momentary hesitation, but an important one dramatically, in that it marks the climax of the Iliadic *Aeneid*. The reason for Aeneas' hesitation is not made completely clear by Vergil. It is stated that more and more (*iam iamque* 940) Turnus' speech began to deflect him from his intended course. Given the general portrayal of Aeneas in the poem as a man who has deep

[1] "*ille mihi ante alios fortunatusque laborum
egregiusque animi, qui, ne quid tale videret,
procubuit moriens et humum semel ore momordit.*"    (11,416–8).
[2] Beare, *P.V.S.* 4 (1964–5) 18ff.
[3] 10,467ff.; 10,606ff.; 12,793ff.; 12,843ff.

filial and paternal love, it is reasonable to infer that his motivation for restraining his hand is the thought of his father
Anchises.[1] Turnus in his speech (933f.) plays upon the victor's
love of his father (*pietas*). *Clementia* might well have been expected
of Aeneas by a Roman audience and, for a moment at least, it is
considered.

Yet just when it seems possible that mercy might be shown,
Aeneas catches sight of the baldric of Pallas now being worn by
Turnus. He becomes fired with anger (*furiis accensus et ira terribilis*
946f.). He makes it clear that Turnus will not be snatched from
him wearing the spoils of his people (947f.). He emphasises the
point that it is Pallas who immolates him and takes vengeance
(948f.). In his rage (*fervidus* 951), he buries his sword in
Turnus' breast. The latter's life with a groan passes complaining
to the shades below (951f.).

Before analysing the end of the poem and critical reaction to it,
let us return briefly to some earlier episodes. We saw[2] that on the
night of Troy's collapse Aeneas sees Helen lurking close to Vesta's
shrine and decides to kill her (2,567ff.). On the prompting of
Venus, however, he leaves Helen and continues on his way. We
saw that it is a mistake to see the episode as the beginning of
'Aeneas's acquisition of true rational courage'.[3] In this context it
was argued that Aeneas' statement at Carthage (*arma amens capio*;
*nec sat rationis in armis* 2,314) is not the utterance of a man who
has learnt to be rational in battle, but is a basic truth about man's
nature in war. As a statement of Aeneas' nature it is as true at the
end of the poem as it was at the beginning; for there are clear
similarities in the Helen episode and the killing of Turnus. In
each case Aeneas' consideration to preserve life (his family

[1] We might compare Aeneas' response to the visage of the dying Lausus at 10,821ff.
Servius, ad 940, argues that Aeneas is *pius* both in his consideration of mercy and in his
killing of Turnus.

[2] See above, p. 52ff.

[3] R. Bond, *Prudentia* 6 (1974) 76.

2,559ff.; Turnus 12,938ff.) is forgotten or overturned as he catches sight of somebody (Helen) and something (the baldric) which causes his fury to erupt. Thus, in the context of Aeneas' behaviour in a war situation, the *balteus* and Helen perform a similar function. In each case the sight suddenly attracts his attention and drives him into *furor*; he speaks of what Helen (2,577ff.) and Turnus (12,947ff.) have done to his own people.[1]

The fact that Aeneas does not kill Helen is testimony, not to any newly acquired sense of *ratio*, but to Venus' admonition that what he attempts to do is without purpose.[2] Aeneas is *impius* in the Helen episode, not because in his *furor* he decides to kill her, but because the direction of that proposed act is contrary to the interests of his family and in opposition to the will of fate. Venus interferes for this reason: because Aeneas must be shown that it is a futile act and that his future lies elsewhere. The same kind of divine admonition is given to him at Carthage, because there too his actions hinder the progress of fate. The intervention of Venus (2,589ff.) and those of Mercury (4,265ff. and 560ff.)[3] are designed to ensure that Aeneas continues in the right or fated direction. When Aeneas flies into a terrible rage after Pallas' death (10,510–605) the same factors do not apply. He is in a state of *pius furor*[4] because his actions align themselves with fate. No benevolent deity interferes there because in his slaughter of the enemy he furthers the progress of fate.[5] The immortals are no more interested in the savagery of his actions[6] than was Venus in the Helen episode: it is the *direction* of these actions that concerns

[1] Pallas, of course, is not a Trojan, although we may include him as one on the strength of Aeneas' use of *meorum* at 12,947.

[2] See esp. 2,594f. and above, p. 54ff.

[3] Note too Jupiter's speech, 4,223ff. That Aeneas fights against Jupiter at Troy is shown by the reference at 2,617f.

[4] Note *pius* 10,591, discussed above, p. 170ff.

[5] The conversation between Jupiter and Juno (10,606ff.), which follows the slaughter, helps to make this clear. Jupiter has a similar function at 12,791ff.

[6] Contrast Warde Fowler's view, *The Death of Turnus* (Oxford, 1919) 150 n.1.

them. Thus *pietas* can be divorced from the brutality of actions.

The *pietas* of Aeneas in killing Turnus in the final scene of the poem is clearer still. The same factors exist as in the *aristeia* of Book 10: Aeneas not only fulfils an obligation to Evander, but also, in defeating and killing Turnus, helps to further the progress of fate. This fact is shown by the assistance rendered to Aeneas by the *Dira* acting as the agent of Jupiter. She is not only an omen of Turnus' forthcoming death, but is also an active helper in bringing that death about (867, 914). Her role emphasises the *pietas* of Aeneas' course as much as the roles of Venus (2,589ff.) and Mercury (4,265ff. and 560ff.) had stressed the *impietas* of his behaviour at Troy and Carthage. In killing Turnus, Aeneas brings to fruition both the Rutulian's fate and his own.

Let us, therefore, before concluding, test this interpretation against the views of two influential critics of recent times.[1] The first of these, M.C.J. Putnam, argues that Aeneas takes on the mantle of Turnus and becomes the epitome of *impius furor*: 'Aeneas becomes himself *impius furor*, as rage wins the day over moderation, disintegration defeats order'.[2] His argument is that 'Aeneas, by bringing death to Turnus, becomes a victim of that very unreason which hitherto he had done his best to shun'.[3] There are two main problems with this view. The first is that nowhere, to my knowledge, in the poem does Aeneas attempt to restrain himself from violence in the war situation.[4] On the contrary, the reverse applies as he displays consistent traits of irrational violence.[5] Some of his acts rank amongst the most inhumane in the poem.[6] Against this background the killing of

---

[1] For some other views on the killing of Turnus, see Jackson Knight, 142; A.H.F. Thornton, 'The Last Scene of the *Aeneid* ', *G. &R.* 22 (1953) 82–4; Binder, 146.

[2] Putnam, 193f.

[3] *Ibid.*, 162.

[4] See above, p. 55 n. 3.

[5] In saying this, I think specifically of his role in war — Books 2, 10, 11 and 12.

[6] 10,510–605; 11,81f.

Turnus should be seen as standard treatment for the conquered in battle — particularly after the death of Pallas. On the one occasion that Aeneas does call on his men to contain their anger,[1] it is made perfectly clear that this is done so that he can retain his opportunity to kill Turnus. His men must restrain their anger so that Aeneas can give vent to his. After Pallas' death there is never any doubt that Aeneas will kill Turnus. The momentary consideration of mercy (12,938ff.) conflicts with the reader's understanding of Aeneas' intentions[2] as they are presented throughout the last three books.[3] Given Aeneas' nature and his determination to kill Turnus, the death blow is neither out of character nor a surprise. The second problem with Putnam's interpretation is his assumption that *furor* is necessarily *impius*. As we have seen, there is nothing in the text to support this view. The complicity of Jupiter in the defeat of Turnus emphasises the *pietas* of Aeneas' *furor*. The text leaves us in no doubt whatever that at the end of the poem Aeneas exhibits irrational violence (*furor*)[4] but there is no justification at all for the view that he is *impius* because of it.

The same two misconceptions lie at the heart of a contrasting, yet no less influential, interpretation. Brooks Otis[5] argues that 'Aeneas thus stands for a new idea in history, the idea that *violentia* and *superbia* can be controlled, that a just *imperium* can be established, that universal peace can be a fact as well as an ideal'. This view of Aeneas as the moral champion of *pietas* against *furor*, of right against wrong, is even more difficult to

[1] 12,311ff.

[2] 11,116ff.; 12,107ff.; 12,317; 12,466f. etc.

[3] Contrast Williams, ad 887f.: 'But the fact remains that the reader expects Aeneas to show mercy and is profoundly disquieted when he does not'.

[4] Note the emphasis at the beginning of alternate lines, 945ff.: *ille* (945) ... *terribilis* (947) ... *immolat* (949) ... *fervidus* (951); see also 946f. The emphasis that Vergil places on Aeneas' *furor* here should not be underestimated.

[5] Otis, 382.

justify from the text. Otis supports his interpretation by concentrating on detail which suits his thesis at the expense of that which does not. No mention is made of Aeneas' *furor* (945ff.), although Vergil gives emphasis to it. Otis' embarrassment in response to the end of the *Aeneid* results from the assumption that *furor* is necessarily *impius* and therefore unsuitable for *pius Aeneas*. It is for this reason that he scrupulously avoids reference to Aeneas' *furor* at 945ff.: 'it is really the *Dira*, not Aeneas, that defeats Turnus'.[1] But it is not the *Dira* that *kills* him.

Whilst actively assisting in the defeat of Turnus, the *Dira* also symbolises the will of Jupiter/*Fata*. The decision to kill him, however, belongs to Aeneas. It is a decision made in alignment with, though independent of, the fated will. It is presented notably as a human decision, with the emphasis on natural violent rage rather than noble aspirations for the future. We should not question the justice of Aeneas' act: Turnus killed Pallas and thus Aeneas has every right in his own terms to kill Turnus. Such is the law of the battlefield — the defeated have no right to mercy. We accept this law, often without question, throughout the poem, but in Turnus' case Vergil makes us feel a strong sense of loss, which in turn has led many to question the morality and significance of Aeneas' act. The poem could have been ended with Turnus being spared by an act of mercy from Aeneas, but such a conclusion would have conflicted seriously with the concept of fate (as it is expressed throughout the poem) and with the hero's nature in war (*nec sat rationis in armis*). We learnt at the beginning that Aeneas was a man distinguished by his *pietas* (*insignem pietate virum* 1,10) and at the end this is also true, although to the exclusion of *ratio*, *clementia* and *humanitas*. The point at the end of the *Aeneid* is that only by killing Turnus and denying him mercy and humanity can Aeneas, by furthering the progress of fate, be described as *pius*.

[1] *Ibid.*, 380.

# CONCLUSION

Vergil uses complex and deliberate methods of characterisation which differ enormously from those of Homer in the *Iliad* and *Odyssey*. This work has sought to identify, against the Homeric background, some of the main techniques used by Vergil. Clearly, one of the most significant differences is Vergil's use of two methods — direct and indirect — to present Aeneas in different ways at particular points in the poem. It is all the more interesting that, as we have seen, Vergil seems to follow specific criteria for his choice of method. This is true too in the case of Turnus.[1] Vergil is in something of a dilemma, for he desires that the Rutulian be a prime mover in the war against the Trojans as well as the poem's final tragic hero. If Turnus, after his infection by Allecto, had been characterised from Book 7 to Book 12 as a violent savage, then the reader would respond to the Rutulian's death with positive relief rather than a sense of regret. The last thing that Vergil wants is to blacken the character of Turnus, who must therefore be given noble qualities like those of Homer's Hector, whilst also being depicted as one consumed with demonic fury. Vergil circumvents his dilemma by conveying the more rational, more noble side of Turnus' character by his direct method, and at the same time presenting indirectly his demonic *furor*.[2] In Turnus' case there are two concurrent strands of characterisation which convey a composite picture of the hero's nature. Not until Book 12 (note 1–106), by which time Turnus' heroic

[1] For a full discussion, see my thesis *Speech and Narrative: Characterisation Techniques in the 'Aeneid '*, University of Glasgow, 1984, 20ff.

[2] It is noteworthy, for example, that Turnus' words in Book 7 after the demonic infection are conveyed indirectly (7,467–70; 578–9). In his only direct speech in Book 7 Turnus is sane and unresponsive to 'Calybe's' war-cry (7,436–444). Similarly, in Book 9 Turnus' *pietas* (e.g. 18–22) and *virtus* (e.g. 51–2) are presented directly whereas his un-Homeric demonic fury is presented indirectly (e.g. 67f.; 563ff.; 691ff.; 728ff.). There is a dramatic alteration in Vergil's technique at 12, 1–106.

stature has been firmly established, does Vergil focus to the full extent, in both speech and narrative, on the Rutulian's irrational rage.

The decisions of Aeneas to leave Dido (Book 4) and to kill Turnus (Book 12) signify not only the victory of *pietas* over *impius furor* but also that of *pietas* over *humanitas*.[1] In theory at least Aeneas could have preserved both lives by staying with Dido and by sparing Turnus; but in so doing he would have forfeited his *pietas* — the fundamental Roman ideal that characterises him throughout. The conflict in the *Aeneid* between *pietas* and *humanitas* is a central motif which has received comparatively little attention in the critical works. At Carthage Aeneas' *pietas*, although severely tested, prevails over his *humanitas* but, as we saw,[2] the reverse applies in his dream-experience of Book 6. At the end of the poem the competing claim of mercy and humanity is briefly considered by Aeneas, but again his *pietas* comes to the fore and he kills Turnus.

One effect of this conflict between *pietas* and *humanitas* has been to polarise critical interpretations of the poem. It might be argued that religious men have on the whole found Aeneas a far more appealing figure and the *Aeneid* a far more satisfying poem than have the humanists. Aeneas' killing of Turnus, however, has caused almost universal anguish. The difficulty for the modern reader, who tends to associate piety and humanity closely together, is to grasp the fact that *pietas* in the *Aeneid* can result from such an inhuman act as the slaying of Turnus. To some degree Vergil's methods of characterising his main heroes lead us towards a subjective response. Homer ensures that, at the end of the *Iliad*, our sympathy rests with both Achilles and Priam. The conclusion of the *Iliad* is that the lot of man is a tragic, sorrowful

---

[1] By *humanitas* I mean specifically the care and concern of a person for another human being *not of the same race*; see above, pp. 34; 37, n. 3; 43, n. 1; 134; 167; 186; 215.

[2] See above, p. 130.

one. Yet there is a mood of reconciliation at the end of both Homeric poems in which the gods, who act with human interests at heart, have a significant role.[1] The ending of the *Aeneid* is markedly different. Vergil denies the reader a close rapport with Aeneas throughout much of the poem by underlining only one dimension of his character. The purpose of Vergil's judicious use of two methods to characterise Aeneas is not only to project the hero forcefully as an *exemplum* of *pietas*, an ideal Roman, but also to some extent to dehumanise him in the process. Conversely, Vergil scrupulously ensures that the reader has great sympathy for the tragic victims in the poem. The poet plays the one against the other. Unlike the Homeric poems the *Aeneid* contains no mood of reconciliation on the human level at the end because Vergil's gods commit an act which the reader has cause to regret. By mobilising our sympathy for the victim against the victor, and by showing us with full horror the gods' part in the final workings of fate, Vergil causes us to confront the inhumanity of the universe in which the *Aeneid* takes place.

[1] *Il.* 24, 329ff. (etc.); *Od.*, 24, 526ff.

# APPENDIX

*Numerical analysis of the speeches*

Comparative numerical analysis of the speeches in the *Iliad*, *Odyssey* and *Aeneid*,[1] and particularly those of the protagonists in them, showed the following results:

*Iliad*
| | |
|---|---|
| Total no. of lines | 15,693 |
| Total no. of speeches | 677 |
| Total no. of lines of speeches | 7,054 (45%) |

*Odyssey*[2]
| | |
|---|---|
| Total no. of lines | 12,110 |
| Total no. of speeches | 639 |
| Total no. of lines of speeches | 6,833 (56%) |

*Aeneid*[2]
| | |
|---|---|
| Total no. of lines | 9,883 |
| Total no. of speeches | 333 |
| Total no. of lines of speeches | 3,667 (37%) |

These figures show that Homer places far greater reliance on the direct speech in his poems than does Vergil in his. Accordingly, Homer's heroes are projected more prominently into the dramatic spotlight than is Vergil's hero. Recorded below are the numbers of lines of direct speech uttered by each hero as a percentage of the total number of lines of the books in which they appear.

Achilles (*Iliad*)

962 lines out of 7,410 (Achilles does not appear in Books 2, 3, 4, 5, 6, 7, 8, 10, 12, 13, 14, 15 and 17): 13%

---

[1] Figures for the *Iliad* and *Odyssey* are my own, whereas those for the *Aeneid* are from Highet, 302f.

[2] The long narrations of Odysseus (*Od.* 9, 10, 11, 12) and Aeneas (*Aen.* 2, 3) are not counted above as direct speeches, whereas those speeches within them are included.

Odysseus (*Odyssey*)[1]

1,732 lines out of 9,588 (Odysseus does not appear in Books 1, 2, 3, 4, 15 (1–300)): 18%

Aeneas (*Aeneid*)[1]

527 lines out of 9,018 (Aeneas does not appear in Book 9): 6%

These figures show that for every line of direct speech that Aeneas utters, Achilles utters two lines and Odysseus three.[2] Vergil's preference for using indirect methods to characterise Aeneas is reflected clearly in these figures. In my view this comparative taciturnity on Aeneas' part is one of the major reasons for the long held view that he is a shadow of Homer's Achilles and Odysseus.[3]

[1] Excluding their respective long narrations but including their speeches within them. It is a notable difference in these long narrations that Odysseus makes many more autobiographical references than does Aeneas; see above, p. 61ff.

[2] It is worth noting that as Odysseus is more verbose in the *Odyssey* than is Achilles in the *Iliad*, so Aeneas is more verbose in the Odyssean *Aeneid* than in the Iliadic half of the poem.

[3] See above, p. 8, n. 3.

# BIBLIOGRAPHY OF WORKS CITED

*1. Editions, Commentaries and Translations*

| | |
|---|---|
| Austin, R. G. | *P. Vergili Maronis Aeneidos Liber Quartus* (Oxford, 1955). |
| —— | *P. Vergili Maronis Aeneidos Liber Secundus* (Oxford, 1964). |
| —— | *P. Vergili Maronis Aeneidos Liber Primus* (Oxford, 1971). |
| —— | *P. Vergili Maronis Aeneidos Liber Sextus* (Oxford, 1977). |
| Conington, J. and Nettleship, H. | *The Works of Virgil* Vols. 2 and 3 (London, 1883, 1884). |
| Day Lewis, C. | *The Aeneid of Virgil* (London, 1952). |
| Fordyce, C. J. | *P. Vergili Maronis Aeneidos Libri VII–VIII* (Oxford, 1977). |
| Gransden, K. W. | *Virgil: Aeneid Book VIII* (Cambridge, 1976). |
| Knight, W. F. J. | *Virgil: The Aeneid* (Harmondsworth, 1956). |
| Mackail, J. W. | *The Aeneid* (Oxford, 1930). |
| Mynors, R. A. B. | *P. Vergili Maronis Opera* (Oxford, 1969). |
| Norden, E. | *P. Vergilius Maro Aeneis Buch VI* (Stuttgart, 1957). |
| Page, T. E. | *The Aeneid of Virgil I–VI* (London, 1894). |
| Pease, A. S. | *P. Vergili Maronis Aeneidos Liber Quartus* (Harvard, 1935). |
| Servius. | *Servii Grammatici qui feruntur in Vergilii carmina commentarii*, ed. G. Thilo and H. Hagen, Vols. 1–3 (Leipzig, 1881–1887). |
| Williams, R. D. | *P. Vergili Maronis Aeneidos Liber Quintus* (Oxford, 1960). |
| —— | *P. Vergili Maronis Aeneidos Liber Tertius* (Oxford, 1962). |
| —— | *The Aeneid of Virgil: Books 1–6* (London, 1972). |
| —— | *The Aeneid of Virgil: Books 7–12* (London, 1973). |

## 2. Secondary Works

Allain, R.   'Une "nuit spirituelle" d'Énée', *R.E.L.* 24 (1946) 189–98.

Anderson, W. B.   '*Sum pius Aeneas*', *C.R.* 44 (1930) 3–4.

Austin, R. G.   'Virgil *Aeneid* 2. 567–88', *C.Q.* 11 (1961) 185–98.

——   '*Aeneid* VI. 384–476', *P.V.S.* 8 (1968–1969) 51–60.

Bacon, J. R.   'Aeneas in Wonderland: A Study of *Aeneid* VIII', *C.R.* 53 (1939) 97–104.

Beare, R.   'Invidious Success: some thoughts on *Aeneid* XII', *P.V.S.* 4 (1964–1965) 18–30.

Becker, C.   'Der Schild des Aeneas', *W.S.* 77 (1964) 111–27.

Bellessort, A.   *Virgile: son œuvre et son temps* (Paris, 1920).

Berres, T.   *Die Entstehung der Aeneis* (Wiesbaden, 1982).

Binder, G.   *Aeneas und Augustus: Interpretationen zum 8. Buch der Aeneis* (Meisenheim am Glan, 1971).

Bömer, F.   'Studien zum VIII. Buche der Aeneis', *Rh.M.* 92 (1944) 319–69.

Bond, R. P.   'Aeneas and the Cardinal Virtues', *Prudentia* 6 (1974) 67–91.

Bowra, C. M.   'Aeneas and the Stoic Ideal', *G. & R.* 3 (1933–4) 8–21.

——   *From Virgil to Milton* (London, 1945).

Boyancé, P.   *La Religion de Virgile* (Paris, 1963).

Boyle, A. J.   'The Meaning of the *Aeneid*: A Critical Inquiry', *Ramus* 1 (1972) 63–90 and 113–51.

Bray, J. J.   'The Ivory Gate' in *For Service to Classical Studies: Essays in Honour of Francis Letters* (Melbourne, 1966) 55–69.

Brisson, J. P.   'Le "pieux Énée"!', *Latomus* 31 (1972) 379–412.

Buchheit, V.   *Vergil über die Sendung Roms: Untersuchungen zum Bellum Poenicum und zur Aeneis* (Heidelberg, 1963).

| | |
|---|---|
| Büchner, K. | *P. Vergilius Maro: der Dichter der Römer.* Reprinted from *R.E.* 8A (Stuttgart, 1955). |
| Cairns, F. | 'Geography and nationalism in the *Aeneid*', *L.C.M.* 2 (1977) 109–16. |
| Camps, W. A. | *An Introduction to Virgil's 'Aeneid'* (Oxford, 1969). |
| Carlsson, G. | 'The Hero and Fate in Virgil's *Aeneid*', *Eranos* 43 (1945) 111–35. |
| Clausen, W. | 'An Interpretation of the *Aeneid*' *H.S.C.P.* 68 (1964) 139–47. |
| Coleman, R. | 'The Gods in the *Aeneid*', *G. & R.* 29 (1982) 143–68. |
| Constans, L. A. | *L'Énéide de Virgile* (Paris, 1938). |
| Conway, R. S. | 'Vergil's Creative Art', *P.B.A.* 17 (1931) 17–38. |
| Crane, T. | 'A note on Aeneas' "human sacrifice", *Aeneid* 10, 517–20", *C.W.* 67 (1973) 176–7. |
| Crump, M. | *The Growth of the 'Aeneid'* (Oxford, 1920). |
| Di Cesare, M. A. | *The Altar and the City: A Reading of Vergil's 'Aeneid'* (New York, 1974). |
| Drew, D. | *The Allegory of the 'Aeneid'* (Oxford, 1927). |
| Dryden, J. | *The Works of Virgil, Translated into English Verse*, ed. J. Carey, Vol. 1 (London, 1819). |
| Dudley, D. R. | *Virgil*, ed. D. R. Dudley (London, 1969). |
| Dunkle, J. R. | 'The Hunter and Hunting in the *Aeneid*' *Ramus* 2 (1973) 127–42. |
| Eden, P. T. | Review of Binder's *Aeneas und Augustus*, *J.R.S.* 62 (1972) 221–3. |
| Eichholz, D. E. | 'The Shield of Aeneas: some elementary notions', *P.V.S.* 6 (1966–7) 45–9. |
| —— | 'Symbol and Contrast in the *Aeneid*', *G. & R.* 15 (1968) 105–112. |
| Farron, S. | 'The *Furor* and *Violentia* of Aeneas', *Acta Classica* 20 (1977) 204–8. |
| —— | 'The Aeneas-Dido Episode as an attack on |

|  | Aeneas' mission and Rome', *G. & R.* 27 (1980) 34–47. |
| Fenik, B. | 'Parallelism of Theme and Imagery in *Aeneid* II and IV', *A.J.P.* 80 (1959) 1–24. |
| Fitzgerald, W. | 'Aeneas, Daedalus and the Labyrinth', *Arethusa* 17 (1984) 51–65. |
| Fontenrose, J. E. | 'The Gods Invoked in Epic Oaths: *Aeneid* XII, 175–215', *A.J.P.* 89 (1968) 20–38. |
| Fowler, W. W. | *Religious Experience of the Roman People* (London, 1911). |
| —— | *Aeneas at the Site of Rome* (Oxford, 1918). |
| —— | *The Death of Turnus* (Oxford, 1919). |
| Galinsky, G. K. | 'The Hercules-Cacus Episode in *Aeneid* VIII', *A.J.P.* 87 (1966) 18–51. |
| —— | '*Aeneid* V and the *Aeneid*', *A.J.P.* 89 (1968) 157–85. |
| —— | 'Aeneas' Invocation of Sol (*Aeneid*, XII, 176)', *A.J.P.* 90 (1969) 453–8. |
| Glazewski, J. | 'The Function of Vergil's Funeral Games', *C.W.* 66 (1972) 85–96. |
| Glover, T. R. | *Virgil* (London, 1930). |
| Goold, G. P. | 'Servius and the Helen Episode', *H.S.C.P.* 74 (1970) 101–68. |
| Gossage, A. J. | 'Aeneas at Sea', *Phoenix* 17 (1963) 131–6. |
| Griffin, J. | '*Haec super arvorum cultu*', *C.R.* 31 (1981) 23–37. |
| Hahn, E. A. | 'Note on Vergil's Use of *Anchisiades*', *C.W.* 14 (1920–21) 3–4. |
| Harris, H. A. | 'The Games in *Aeneid* V', *P.V.S.* 8 (1968–9) 14–26. |
| Harrison, E. L. | 'Divine Action in *Aeneid* Book Two', *Phoenix* 24 (1970) 320–32. |
| Heinze, R. | *Virgils epische Technik* (Leipzig, 1903). |
| Henry, J. | *Aeneidea*, Vols. 1–3 (London-Dublin, 1873–1889). |

Highet, G.                *The Speeches in Vergil's 'Aeneid'* (Princeton, 1972).

Hudson-Williams, A.       '*Lacrimae Illae Inanes*', *G. & R.* 25 (1978) 16–23.

Jacob, P.                 'L'Épisode de Palinure', *Ét. Cl.* 20 (1952) 163–7.

Johnson, W. R.            'Aeneas and the Ironies of *Pietas*', *C.J.* 60 (1965) 359–64.

————                      *Darkness Visible* (Berkeley, 1976).

Klingner, F.              *Virgil: 'Bucolica', 'Georgica', 'Aeneis'* (Zurich, 1967).

Knauer, G. N.             *Die Aeneis und Homer* (Göttingen, 1964).

Knight, W. F. J.          *Roman Vergil* (London, 1944).

Knox, B. M. W.            'The Serpent and the Flame', *A.J.P.* 71 (1950) 379–400.

Kopff, E. C. & N. M.      'Aeneas: False Dream or Messenger of the *Manes* (*Aeneid* 6, 893ff.)', *Philologus* 120 (1976) 246–50.

Körte, A.                 'Zum zweiten Buch von Vergils *Aeneis*', *Hermes* 51 (1916) 145–50.

Kraggerud, E.             *Aeneisstudien, Symbolae Osloenses* Supp. 22 (Oslo, 1968).

Lee, M. O.                *Fathers and sons in the Aeneid: tum genitor natum* (Albany, 1979).

Little, D. A.             'The Death of Turnus and the Pessimism of the *Aeneid*', *A.U.M.L.A.* 33 (1970) 67–76.

Lloyd, R. B.              '*Aeneid* III: A new approach', *A.J.P.* 78 (1957) 133–51.

————                      'The Character of Anchises in the *Aeneid*', *T.A.Ph.A.* 88 (1957) 44–55.

Lossau, M.                'Elpenor und Palinurus', *W.S.* 14 (1980) 102–24.

Lyne, R. O. A. M.         'Vergil and the Politics of War', *C.Q.* 33 (1983) 188–203.

Mackie, C. J.             *Speech and Narrative: Characterisation Tech-*

*niques in the 'Aeneid'*, Ph.D. Thesis (University of Glasgow, 1984).

McGushin, P.    'Virgil and the Spirit of Endurance', *A.J.P.* 85 (1964) 225–53.

Mehl, E.    'Die Leichenspiele in der Äneis als turngeschichtliche Quelle', *R.E.* 8A 2 (1958) 1487–93.

Michels, A. K.    'The *Insomnium* of Aeneas', *C.Q.* 31 (1981) 140–6.

Miniconi, P.    'La joie dans l'*Énéide*', *Latomus* 21 (1962) 563–71.

Monti, R. C.    *The Dido Episode and the 'Aeneid'* (Leiden, 1981).

Otis, B.    'Three Problems of Aeneid 6', *T.A.Ph.A.* 90 (1959) 165–79.

——    *Virgil: A Study in Civilized Poetry* (Oxford, 1963).

——    'The Originality of the *Aeneid*', in *Virgil* ed. D. R. Dudley (London, 1969) 27–66.

Parry, A.    'The Two Voices of Virgil's *Aeneid*', *Arion* 2 (1963) 66–80; and in *Virgil*, ed. Commager (Englewood Cliffs, 1966) 107–23.

Pascal, R.    *The Dual Voice* (Manchester, 1977).

Perrett, J.    *Virgile, l'homme et l'œuvre* (Paris, 1965).

Poe, J. P.    'Success and Failure in the Mission of Aeneas', *T.A.Ph.A.* 96 (1965) 321–36.

Pöschl, V.    *Die Dichtkunst Virgils* (Innsbruck-Wien, 1950); trans. by G. Seligson as *The Art of Vergil: Image and Symbol in the Aeneid* (Ann Arbor, 1962).

Prescott, H. W.    *The Development of Virgil's Art* (2d. ed. New York, 1963).

Putnam, M. C. J.    *The Poetry of the 'Aeneid'* (Cambridge Mass., 1965).

Quinn, K.    *Latin Explorations: Critical Studies in Roman Literature* (London, 1963).

——                      *Virgil's 'Aeneid': A Critical Description*
                        (London, 1968).

Rand, E. K.            *The Magical Art of Virgil* (Cambridge Mass.,
                        1931).

Reed, N.               'The Gates of Sleep in *Aeneid* 6', *C.Q.* 23
                        (1973) 311–5.

Richardson, L. J. D.   *'Facilis iactura sepulcri*. With a Note on the
                        Character of Anchises in the *Aeneid*', *Proc.
                        Roy. Irish Acad.* 46 (1940) 85–101.

Ridley, M. R.          *Studies in Three Literatures* (London, 1962).

Rowell, H. T.          'The Scholium on Naevius in *Parisinus Latinus*
                        7930', *A.J.P.* 78 (1957) 1–22.

Rudd, N.               *Lines of Enquiry: Studies in Latin Poetry* (Cam-
                        bridge, 1976).

Rutledge, H. C.        'Vergil's Daedalus', *C.J.* 62 (1967) 309–11.

——                      'The Opening of *Aeneid* 6', *C.J.* 67 (1971–2)
                        110–15.

Sainte-Beuve, C. A.    *Étude sur Virgile* (Paris, 1857).

Sanderlin, G.          'Vergil's Protection of Aeneas in *Aeneid* II',
                        *C.W.* 66 (1972–3) 82–4.

Seel, O.               'Um einen Vergilvers (*Aeneis*, VI, 468)' in
                        *Hommages à M. Renard* 1 (Collection Latomus
                        Vol. 101, Brussels, 1969) 677–88.

Segal, C. P.           *'Aeternum per Saecula Nomen*, The Golden
                        Bough and the Tragedy of History: Part 1',
                        *Arion* 4 (1965) 617–57.

Sellar, W. Y.          *The Roman Poets of the Augustan Age: Virgil*
                        (Oxford, 1877).

Semple, W. H.          'War and Peace in Virgil's *Aeneid*', *B.R.L.* 36
                        (1953–4) 211–27.

Stanford, W. B.        *The Ulysses Theme. A Study in the Adaptability of
                        a Traditional Hero* (Oxford, 1954).

Steiner, H. R.         *Der Traum in der Aeneis* (Berne, 1952).

Thaniel, G.            *'Ecce…Palinurus'*, *Acta Classica* 15 (1972)
                        149–52.

Thornton, A. H. F.    'The Last Scene of the *Aeneid*', *G. & R.* 22 (1953) 82–4.

Ullmann, S.          *Style in the French Novel* (Cambridge, 1957).

van Ooteghem, J.     '*Somni Portae*', *Ét. Cl.* 16 (1948) 386–90.

Verstraete, B. C.    'The Implication of the Epicurean and Lucretian Theory of Dreams for *Falsa Insomnia* in *Aeneid* 6, 896', *C.W.* 74 (1980–1) 7–10.

West, D.             'Multiple-Correspondence Similes in the *Aeneid*', *J.R.S.* 59 (1969) 40–49.

——                   'Virgilian Multiple-Correspondence Similes and their Antecedents', *Philologus* 114 (1970) 262–75.

——                   'The Deaths of Hector and Turnus', *G. & R.* 21 (1974) 21–31.

Wetmore, M. N.       *Index Verborum Vergilianus* (New Haven, 1930).

Wigodsky, M.         'The Arming of Aeneas', *C. & M.* 26 (1965) 192–221.

Williams, G.         *Technique and Ideas in the 'Aeneid'* (New Haven and London, 1983).

Williams, R. D.      'The Pictures on Dido's Temple (*Aeneid* 1.450–93)', *C.Q.* 10 (1960) 145–51.

——                   'The Sixth Book of the *Aeneid*', *G. & R.* 11 (1964) 48–63.

——                   *Virgil. Greece and Rome*, New Surveys in the Classics, No. 1 (Oxford, 1967).

——                   'Changing Attitudes to Virgil: a Study in the history of taste from Dryden to Tennyson', in *Virgil*, ed. D. R. Dudley (London, 1969) 119–38.

Willis, W. H.        'Athletic Contests in the Epic', *T.A.Ph.A.* 72 (1941) 392–417.

Zarker, J. W.        'Aeneas and Theseus in *Aeneid* 6', *C.J.* 62 (1967) 220–6.

Zeitlin, F. I.        'An Analysis of *Aeneid* XII, 176–211. The differences between the oaths of Aeneas and Latinus', *A.J.P.* 86 (1965) 337–62.

# GENERAL INDEX

# INDEX OF PASSAGES CITED